Anonymous

General School Laws of the State of New York in Force July 1st, 1893

Vol. 3

Anonymous

General School Laws of the State of New York in Force July 1st, 1893
Vol. 3

ISBN/EAN: 9783337779467

Printed in Europe, USA, Canada, Australia, Japan

Cover: Foto ©Suzi / pixelio.de

More available books at **www.hansebooks.com**

GENERAL

SCHOOL LAWS

OF THE

STATE OF NEW YORK,

IN FORCE JULY 1st, 1893 ;

TOGETHER WITH THE

Rules of Practice Governing Appeals to the Department of Public Instruction.

PREPARED UNDER THE SUPERVISION OF
JAMES F. CROOKER,
State Superintendent of Public Instruction.

ALBANY:
THE ARGUS COMPANY, PRINTERS.
1893.

TABLE OF CONTENTS.

CONSOLIDATED SCHOOL ACT—CHAP. 555, LAWS OF 1864.

		PAGE.
TITLE	I. Election of State Superintendent, his term of office, powers and duties..	5
TITLE	II. Election of School Commissioners, term of office, powers and duties.	11
TITLE	III. State school moneys, their apportionment and distribution...	17
TITLE	IV. Supervisors of towns, powers and duties relative to the disbursement of school moneys...	29
TITLE	V. Town clerks, and their duties, to preserve records, etc.	31
TITLE	VI. Formation, dissolution and alteration of school districts.	33
TITLE	VII. FIRST ARTICLE—School district meetings, power and duties of,	36
	SECOND ARTICLE — School-houses and sites.	42
	THIRD ARTICLE — School district officers, selection of.	44
	FOURTH ARTICLE — School district clerk and librarian, powers and duties of.	46
	FIFTH ARTICLE — Pupils and teachers.	48
	SIXTH ARTICLE — Trustees, powers and duties of.	49
	SEVENTH ARTICLE — School district taxes, collection of; powers, duties and liability of collectors..	57
TITLE	VIII. Common school and public libraries.	66
TITLE	IX. Union free schools, their formation and government; powers of boards of education in; officers of.	68
TITLE	X. Schools for colored children.	81
TITLE	XI. Teachers' institutes..	82
TITLE	XII. Appeals to State Superintendent.	85
TITLE	XIII. Miscellaneous provisions.	86

GENERAL STATUTES.

AMERICAN MUSEUM OF NATURAL HISTORY.	91
ARBOR DAY.	94
COMPULSORY EDUCATION.	95
HOLIDAYS.	99
SCHOOLS:	
Colored, in New York city.	100
Cornell University.	100
Indian.	103
Nautical.	104
Normal.	105
Orphan.	114
Teachers' Training Classes.	115

SCHOOLS — (Continued) ;   PAGE
   Industrial training.. 117
   Industrial Drawing, Evening Schools 118
   Industrial or Free Hand Drawing....................................... 120
   Free Kindergarten Schools... 118
   Instruction in vocal music in certain schools......................... 119
SCHOOL COMMISSIONERS:
   Salaries, how payable... 120
   To describe definitely district lines................................. 121
SCHOOL COMMISSIONER DISTRICTS:
   Cities not to be included in.. 121
   Division of certain districts... 122
SCHOOL DISTRICTS:
   Acquisition of sites.. 122
   Elections in certain districts.. 129
   Plans for school buildings.. 132
   Requiring fire escapes in connection with certain school buildings.... 132
   Trustees may contract for instruction of children in adjoining districts, 133
   Tuition of non-residents, deduction................................... 134
   Teachers, employment and pay of....................................... 134
   Health and decency.. 135
   Vaccination of children... 136
   Dissolution of Union Free School Districts............................ 137
SCHOOL OFFICERS:
   Not to become individually interested in official contracts........... 139
TAXATION:
   Rate bills abolished.. 139
   Banks and bankers... 140
   Delaware and Hudson Canal Company, apportionment of valuation of
      property of... 143
   Forest Preserve... 145
   Railroads, telegraph, telephone and pipe line companies, apportion-
      ment of valuation of property of.................................. 146
   Railroads, collection of taxes of..................................... 147
TEXT BOOKS:
   Adoption and change of.. 149
   Physiology and Hygiene.. 150
WOMEN:
   May vote at school meetings and hold office........................... 150
   Determining those who have right to vote for School Commissioners .. 150
CODE:
   Custody of.. 152
REPORTS OF DEPARTMENT:
   To be printed for distribution.. 153
APPEALS:
   Rules of practice... 154
INDEX... 160

CONSOLIDATED SCHOOL ACT.

CHAP. 555.

AN ACT to revise and consolidate the General Acts relating to Public Instruction.

PASSED May 2, 1864; three-fifths being present.

The People of the State of New York, represented in Senate and Assembly, do enact as follows:

TITLE I.

OF THE STATE SUPERINTENDENT OF PUBLIC INSTRUCTION, HIS ELECTION AND GENERAL POWERS AND DUTIES.

*SECTION 1. The office of state superintendent of public instruction is continued and the term of said office shall be three years, commencing hereafter on the seventh day of April. Such superintendent shall be elected by joint ballot of the senate and assembly on the second Wednesday of February next preceding the expiration of the term of the then incumbent of said office, and on the second Wednesday of February next after the occurrence of any vacancy in the office. _{State superintendent; his election and term of office.}

†§ 2. He shall appoint a deputy, who shall receive an annual salary of four thousand dollars; and in case of a vacancy in the office of superintendent the deputy may perform all the duties of the office until the day hereinbefore fixed for the commencement of the term of said office. In case the office of both superintendent and deputy shall be vacant, the governor shall appoint some person to perform the duties of the office until the superintendent shall be elected and his term of office commence as hereinbefore provided. _{Deputy superintendent; salary. Vacancy.}

§ 3. The superintendent's office shall continue to be in the state hall, and maintained at the expense of the state. _{Office of.}

---
*As amended by sec. 1, chap. 75, Laws of 1883; and by sec. 1, chap. 591, Laws of 1886.
† As amended by sec. 2, chap. 75, Laws of 1883; and by chap. 533, Laws of 1898.

CONSOLIDATED SCHOOL ACT OF 1864.

TITLE 1.
Salary.

*§ 4. His salary shall be five thousand dollars a year, payable quarterly, by the treasurer, on the warrant of the comptroller.

Clerk hire.

†§ 5. He may appoint as many clerks as he may deem necessary, but the compensation of such clerks shall not exceed in the aggregate the sum of nine thousand dollars in any one year, and shall be payable monthly by the treasurer, on the warrant of the comptroller, and the certificate of the superintendent. ‡

Seal.

§ 6. The seal of the superintendent, of which a description and impression are now on file in the office of the secretary of state, shall continue to be his official seal, and when necessary, may be renewed from time to time. Copies of all papers deposited or filed in the superintendent's office, and of all acts, orders and decisions made by him, and of the drafts or machine copies of his official letters, may be authenticated under the said seal, and when so authenticated, shall be evidence equally with and in like manner as the orignal.

Copies of papers on file under seal to be evidence.

Superintendent's ex officio duties.

|§ 7. The superintendent shall be ex officio a trustee of Cornell University and of the New York State Asylum for Idiots, and a regent of the University of the State of New York. He shall also have general supervision over the state normal schools at Brockport, Buffalo, Cortland, Fredonia, Geneseo, Oswego and Potsdam, and over any other state normal schools, which may hereafter be established; and he shall provide for the education of the Indian children of the state, as required by chapter seventy-one of the laws of eighteen hundred and fifty-six.¶

Superintendent's general supervision.

Institution for deaf and dumb, blind.

§ 8. The institution for the instruction of the deaf and dumb, the New York institution for the blind, and all other similar institutions, incorporated, or that may be hereafter incorporated, shall be subject to the visitation of the superintendent of public instruction, and it shall be his duty : (a)

---

* As amended by sec. 1, chap. 567, Laws of 1875.
† As amended by sec. 2, chap. 567, Laws of 1875.
‡ Appropriation for fiscal year ending September 30, 1894, $16,000.
| As amended by sec. 3, chap. 567, Laws of 1875.
¶ See Law, page 103.

(a) DEAF AND DUMB INSTITUTIONS.

The institutions for deaf and dumb, authorized by law to receive persons appointed as state pupils therein by the superintendent of public instruction under the provisions of section 9, title 1, chap. 555, Laws of 1864, and the special acts relating to the same are :
New York Institution for the Instruction of the Deaf and Dumb. (Incorporated by chap. 264, Laws of 1817.)
Institution for the Improved Instruction of Deaf-Mutes, New York city. (Chap. 180, Laws of 1870.)
Central New York Institution for Deaf-Mutes, at Rome, N. Y. (Chap. 13, Laws of 1876, and chap. 355, Laws of 1880.)

(Continued on page 7.)

OF SUPERINTENDENT OF PUBLIC INSTRUCTION.   7

1. To inquire, from time to time, into the expenditures of each institution, and the systems of instruction pursued therein, respectively. TITLE 1.
Superintendent's duties.

2. To visit and inspect the schools belonging thereto, and the lodgings and accommodations of the pupils.

3. To ascertain, by a comparison with other similar institutions, whether any improvements in instruction and discipline can be made; and for that purpose to appoint, from time to time, suitable persons to visit the schools.

4. To suggest to the directors of such institutions and to the legislature such improvements as he shall judge expedient.

5. To make an annual report to the legislature on all the matters before enumerated, and particularly as to the condition of the schools, the improvement of the pupils, and their treatment in respect to board and lodging. Superintendent to report annually.

* § 9. All deaf and dumb persons resident in this state and upwards of twelve years of age, who shall have been resident in this state for three years immediately preceding the application, or, if a minor, whose parent or parents or, if an orphan, whose nearest friend shall have been resi- Terms of admission.

Western New York Institution for Deaf-Mutes at Rochester. (Chap. 331, Laws of 1876.)
St. Joseph's Institute for the Improved Instruction of Deaf-Mutes, at Fordham. (Chap. 378, Laws of 1877.)
Le Couteulx St. Mary's Institution for the Improved Instruction of Deaf-Mutes, at Buffalo. (Chap. 670, Laws of 1872.)
Northern New York Institution for Deaf-Mutes, at Malone. (Chap. 275, Laws of 1884.)

HIGH CLASS IN.

In addition to the term of appointment of state pupils, provided for in section 10, title 1, of the General School Act, the superintendent is authorized to appoint pupils to the high class in the New York Institution. (Chap. 272, Laws of 1854, as amended by chap. 58, Laws of 1885.)
Western New York Institution. (Chap. 331, Laws of 1876.)
Central New York Institution. (Chap. 355, Laws of 1880.)

INSTITUTION FOR THE BLIND.

The only institution to which the state superintendent of public instruction is authorized by law to send indigent blind persons, as state pupils, is the New York Institution for the Blind. (Incorporated by chap. 214, Laws of 1831.)
To that institution, he can appoint only residents of the counties of New York, Kings, Queens, Suffolk and Richmond. (Chap. 555, Laws of 1864, as amended by chap. 615, Laws of 1886.)
To be eligible, the applicant, by the provisions of one act, must be between the ages of eight and twenty-five years; by another, of suitable age.
The term of such appointments shall not exceed five years, but may be extended from time to time by the superintendent of public instruction on the recommendation of the board of managers.
The supervisors of each of the counties of New York, Kings, Queens and Suffolk are required to raise and appropriate each year, while such pupils are in said institution, fifty dollars for each of said pupils whose parents or guardians shall, in the opinion of the superintendent of public instruction, be unable to clothe them to be applied to the furnishing such pupils with a suitable clothing. (Chap. 166, Laws of 1870, as amended by chapter 166, Laws of 1871.)
* As amended by sec. 4, chap. 567, Laws of 1875, and by sec. 1, chap. 615, Laws of 1886.
NOTE.— See chap. 166, Laws of 1870; chap. 180, Laws of 1870, and chap. 166, Laws of 1871.
NOTE.— Section 9 does not apply to, or affect the New York State Institution for the Blind located at Batavia, N. Y. Sec. 2, chap. 615, Laws of 1886.

dent in this state for three years immediately preceding the application, shall be eligible to appointment as state pupils in one of the deaf and dumb institutions of this State, authorized by law to receive such pupils; and all blind persons of suitable age and similar qualifications shall be eligible to appointment to the institutions for the blind in the city of New York or in the village of Batavia, as follows: All such as are residents of the counties of New York, Kings, Queens, Suffolk and Richmond shall be sent to the institution for the blind in the city of New York; those who reside in other counties of the state shall be sent to the institution for the blind in the village of Batavia.

Appointments to. All such appointments, with the exception of those to the institution for the blind in the village of Batavia, shall be made by the superintendent of public instruction upon application, and in those cases in which, in his opinion, the parents or guardians of the applicants are able to bear a portion of the expense, he may impose conditions whereby some proportionate share of expense of educating and clothing such pupils shall be paid by their parents, guardians or friends, in such manner and at such times as the superintendent shall designate, which conditions he may modify from time to time, if he shall deem it expedient to do so.

State pupils; accommodation, compensation, etc. * § 10. Each pupil so received into either of the institutions aforesaid shall be provided with board, lodging and tuition; and the directors of the institution shall receive for each pupil so provided for, the sum of   dollars per annum, in quarterly payments, to be paid by the treasurer of the state, on the warrant of the comptroller, to the treasurer of said institution, on his presenting a bill showing the actual time and number of such pupils attending the institution, and which bill shall be signed by the president and secretary of the institution, and verified by their oaths. *Term of instruction.* The regular term of instruction for such pupils shall be five years; but the superintendent of public instruction may, in his discretion, extend the term of any pupil for a period not exceeding three years. The pupils provided for in this and the preceding section of this title shall be designated state pupils; and all the existing provisions of law applicable to state pupils now in said institutions shall apply to pupils herein provided for.

Time of admission. § 11. The superintendent of public instruction may make such regulations and give such directions to parents

---

* See chap. 180. Laws of 1870.

OF SUPERINTENDENT OF PUBLIC INSTRUCTION.

TITLE 1.

and guardians, in relation to the admission of pupils into either of the above-named institutions, as will prevent pupils entering the same at irregular periods.

§ 12. The superintendent may, in his discretion, appoint persons to visit and examine all or any of the common schools in the county wherein such persons reside, and to report to him all such matters respecting their condition and management, and the means of improving them, as he shall prescribe; but no allowance or compensation shall be made to such visitors for their services or expenses. *School visitor.*

§ 13. So often as he can, consistently with his other duties, he shall visit such of the common schools of the state as he shall see fit, and inquire into their course of instruction, management and discipline, and advise and encourage the pupils, teachers and officers thereof. *Superintendent to visit schools.*

*§ 14. He shall submit to the legislature an annual report containing: *Annual report.*
1. A statement of the condition of the common schools of the state, and of all other schools and institutions under his supervision, and subject to his visitation as superintendent.
2. Estimates and accounts of expenditures of the school moneys, and a statement of the apportionment of school moneys made by him.
3. All such matters relating to his office, and all such plans and suggestions for the improvement of the schools and the advancement of public instruction in the state, as he shall deem expedient.

† § 15. He may grant under his hand and seal of office, a certificate of qualification to teach, and may revoke the same. While unrevoked, such certificate shall be conclusive evidence that the person to whom it was granted is qualified by moral character, learning and ability, to teach any common school in the state. Such certificate may be granted by him only upon examination. He shall determine the manner in which such examination shall be conducted, and may designate proper persons to conduct the same, and report the result to him. He may also appoint times and places for holding such examinations, at least once in each year, and cause due notice thereof to be given. He may also, in his discretion, issue a certificate, without examination, to any graduate of a college or *State certificate.* *Examination for state certificate.* *College graduate's certificate.*

---
* NOTE.— Sec. 10 of chap. 588, Laws of 1886, provides that the annual report shall be presented to the legislature on or before February first, and shall be placed with the printer by December fifteenth preceding, and transmitted to the legislature printed.
† As amended by sec. 5, chap. 567, Laws of 1875, and by sec. 1, chap. 331, Laws of 1888. See chap. 353, Laws of 1875.

CONSOLIDATED SCHOOL ACT OF 1864.

TITLE 1.

Normal diplomas and state certificates from other states.

university who has had three years' experience as a teacher. Such last-mentioned certificate shall be known as the "college graduate's certificate," and may be revoked at any time for cause. He may also, in his discretion, indorse a diploma issued by a state normal school or a certificate issued by a state superintendent or state board of education in any other state, which indorsement shall confer upon the holder thereof the same privileges conferred by law upon the holders of diplomas or certificates issued by state normal schools or by the state superintendent in this state. He may also issue temporary licenses to teach, limited to any school commissioner district or school district, and for a period not exceeding six months, whenever, in his judgment, it may be necessary or expedient for him to do so.

Temporary licenses.

May annul certificates.

§ 16. Upon cause shown to his satisfaction, he may annul any certificate of qualification granted to a teacher by a school commissioner, or declare any diploma issued by the state normal school ineffective and null as a qualification to teach a common school within this state, and he may reconsider and reverse his action in any such matter.

Lists of persons holding state certificates and normal school diplomas.

§ 17. He shall prepare and keep in his office alphabetical lists of all persons who have received, or shall receive, certificates of qualification from himself, or diplomas of the state normal school, with the dates thereof, and shall note thereon all annulments and reversals of such certificates and diplomas, with the date and causes thereof, together with such other particulars as he may deem expedient.

Superintendent may remove school commissioners or other school officers.

May withhold share of public money from district willfully disobeying order, etc.

* § 18. Whenever it shall be proven to his satisfaction that any school commissioner or other school officer has been guilty of any willful violation or neglect of duty under this act, or any other act pertaining to common schools, or wilfully disobeying any decision, order or regulation of the superintendent, the superintendent may, by an order under his hand and seal, which order shall be recorded in his office, remove such school commissioner or other school officer from his office. *Said superintendent may also withhold any share of the public money of the state from any district for willfully disobying any decision, order or regulation as aforesaid.*

Shall prepare registers, blanks, etc.

§ 19. He shall prepare suitable registers, blanks, forms and regulations for making all reports and conducting all necessary business under this act, and shall cause the

---

* As amended by sec. 1, chap. 500 of Laws of 1893.

OF SCHOOL COMMISSIONERS. 11

same, with such information and instructions as he shall deem conducive to the proper organization and government of the common schools and the due execution of their duties by school officers, to be transmitted to the officers and persons intrusted with the execution of the same.

TITLE 2.

* § 20. The superintendent may administer oaths and take affidavits concerning any matter relating to the schools.

May administer oaths.

TITLE II.

OF THE SCHOOL COMMISSIONERS, THEIR ELECTION, POWERS AND DUTIES.

SECTION 1. The office of school commissioner is continued, and the present incumbents shall continue in office in their respective districts, for the residue of the terms for which they were elected or appointed.

School commissioners.

† § 2. The districts as organized under existing laws and as recognized in the election of school commissioners at the annual election in eighteen hundred and sixty-three, shall continue to be held and regarded as the school commissioner districts in this state, except as the same shall be altered or modified by the legislature. ‡

School commissioner districts.

‖ § 3. The school commissioner for each school commissioner district shall be elected by the electors thereof, by separate ballot, at the general election in the year one thousand eight hundred and sixty-six, and tri-ennially thereafter, and the ballots shall be indorsed "School Commissioner." The laws regulating the election of and canvassing the votes for county officers shall apply to such elections. And it shall further be the duty of county clerks, and they are hereby required, as soon as they shall have official notice of the election or appointment of a school commissioner, for any district in their county, to forward to the superintendent of public instruction a duplicate certificate of such election or appointment attested by their signature and the seal of the county.

How elected.

County clerk to certify to superintendent the election or appointment of commissioner.

· § 4. The term of office of such commissioner shall commence on the first day of January next after his election,

Term of office.

---

* Added by section 2, chapter 331, Laws of 1898.
† NOTE.—Cities electing superintendents, etc., are not included in commissioner districts. See chapter 179, Laws of 1856, as amended by section 1, chapter 414, Laws of 1883, page 121, *post.*
‡ Boards of supervisors may erect new commissioner district when commissioner district contains more than 200 school districts. See chap. 686, Laws of 1892, article 11, sub. 9 of section 12, page 122, *post.*
‖ As amended by section 1, chapter 406, Laws of 1867. See also chap. 214, Laws of 1892, determining who have a right to vote for school commissioners, page 150, *post.*

TITLE 2.
Oath of office.

and shall be for three years, and until his successor qualifies. Every person elected to the office, or appointed to fill a vacancy, must take the oath of office prescribed by the constitution, before the county clerk, or a judge of a court of record, and file it with the county clerk, within ten days after the commencement of the term or after notice of his appointment; and if he omit so to do, the office shall be deemed vacant.

Commissioner may resign.
Vacates office.

§ 5. A commissioner may at any time vacate his office, by filing his resignation with the county clerk. His removal from the county, or his acceptance of the office of supervisor, town clerk or trustee of a school district, shall vacate his office.

How vacancy in office of school commissioner filled.

* § 6. The county clerk, so soon as he has official or other notice of the existence of a vacancy in the office of commissioner, shall give notice thereof to the county judge, or, if that office be vacant, to the superintendent of public instruction. In case of a vacancy, the county judge, or, if there be no county judge, then the superintendent shall appoint a commissioner, who shall hold his office until the first of January succeeding the next general election, and until his successor, who shall be chosen at such general election, shall have qualified. A person elected to fill a vacancy shall hold the office only for the unexpired term.

Commissioner elected to fill vacancy to hold only for the unexpired term.

Salary of school commissioner $1,000; payable from free school fund.

† § 7. After the first day of October, eighteen hundred and eighty-five, every school commissioner shall receive an annual salary of one thousand dollars, payable quarterly out of the free school fund appropriated for this purpose, or to the support of common schools.

Supervisors to increase salary of commissioner.

‡ § 8. Whenever a majority of the supervisors from all the towns composing a school commissioner district shall adopt a resolution to increase the salary of their school commissioner beyond the one thousand dollars, payable to him from the free school fund, it shall be the duty of the board of supervisors of the county to give effect to such resolution, and they shall assess the increase stated therein upon the towns composing such commissioner district, ratably, according to the corrected valuations of the real and personal estate of such towns.

How assessed.
Commissioner's expenses $200.

∥ § 9. The board of supervisors shall annually audit and allow to each commissioner within the county the fixed

---

* As amended by sec. 1, chap. 647, Laws of 1865.
† As amended by sec. 2, chap. 84, Laws of 1867, and sec. 3, chap. 1, Laws of 1881, and by sec. 5, chap. 340, Laws of 1885.
‡ As amended by sec. 6, chap. 567, Laws of 1875, and sec. 6, chap. 340, Laws of 1885.
∥ As amended by sec. 2, chap. 84, Laws of 1867.

OF SCHOOL COMMISSIONERS.

sum of two hundred dollars for his expenses, and shall assess and levy that amount annually, by tax upon the towns composing his district. _{TITLE 2.}

§ 10. Whenever the superintendent of public instruction is satisfied that a school commissioner has persistently neglected to perform his duties, he may withhold his order for the payment of the whole or any part of such commissioner's salary as it shall become due, and the salary so withholden shall be forfeited; but the superintendent may remit the forfeiture, in whole or in part, upon the commissioner disproving or excusing such neglect. *Superintendent may withhold commissioner's salary.*

§ 11. A commissioner, upon the written request of the commissioner of an adjoining district, may perform any of his duties for him, and upon requirement of the state superintendent of public instruction must perform the same. *Commissioner to serve for another.*

* § 12. No school commissioner shall act as agent for any author, publisher or bookseller, nor directly or indirectly receive any gift, emolument, reward or promise of reward, for his influence in recommending or procuring the use of any book, or school apparatus, or furniture of any kind whatever, in any common school, or the purchase of any book for a district library. Any one who shall procure or solicit a violation of this provision, or of any part thereof, shall be guilty of a misdemeanor; and any such violation shall subject the guilty commissioner to removal from his office by the superintendent of public instruction. *Not to act as agent for author or publisher, etc.*

§ 13. Every commissioner shall have power, and it shall be his duty: *Duties of school commissioner.*

† 1. From time to time to inquire and ascertain whether the boundaries of the school districts within his district are definitely and plainly described in the records of the proper town clerks; and in case the record of the boundaries of any school district shall be found defective or indefinite, or if the same shall be in dispute, then to cause the same to be amended, or an amended record of the boundaries to be made. All necessary expenses incurred in establishing such amended records shall be a charge upon the district or districts affected, to be audited and allowed by the trustee or trustees thereof, upon the certificate of the school commissioner. *To define district boundaries.* *Expense of defining boundaries.*

2. To visit and examine all the schools and school dis- *To visit and examine schools.*

---
* NOTE.—See sec. 473 of the Penal Code, page 139, *post.*
† As amended by sec. 7. chap. 567, Laws of 1875.

14 CONSOLIDATED SCHOOL ACT OF 1864.

TITLE 2.

tricts within his district as often in each year as shall be practicable; to inquire into all matters relating to the management, the course of study and mode of instruction, and the text-books and discipline of such schools, and the condition of the school-houses, sites, out-buildings and appendages, and of the district generally; to examine the district libraries; to advise with and counsel the trustees and other officers of the district in relation to their duties, and particularly in respect to the construction, warming and ventilation of school-houses, and the improving and adorning of the school grounds connected therewith; and to recommend to the trustees and teachers the proper studies, discipline and management of the schools, and the course of instruction to be pursued.

Libraries, school-houses, etc.

Studies.

To direct trustees to make repairs.

* 3. Upon such examination, to direct the trustees to make any alteration or repair on the school-house or outbuildings which shall, in his opinion, be necessary for the health or comfort of the pupils, but the expense of making such alterations or repairs shall, in no case, exceed the sum of two hundred dollars, unless an additional sum shall be voted by the district. He may also direct the trustee to make any alterations or, repairs to school furniture, or when in his opinion any furniture is unfit for use and not worth repairing, or when sufficient furniture is not provided, he may direct that new furniture shall be provided as he may deem necessary, provided that the expense of such alterations, repairs or additions to furniture shall not, in any one year exceed the sum of one hundred dollars. He may also direct the trustees to abate any nuisance in or upon the premises, provided the same can be done at an expense not exceeding twenty-five dollars.

May direct repairs and additions to school furniture.

May direct abatement of nuisance.

To condemn unfit school-houses.

† 4. By an order under his hand, reciting the reason or reasons, to condemn a school-house, if he deems it wholly unfit for use and not worth repairing, and to deliver the order to the trustees, or one of them, and transmit a copy to the superintendent of public instruction. Such order, if no time for its taking effect be stated in it, shall take effect immediately. He shall also state what sum, not exceeding eight hundred dollars, will, in his opinion, be necessary to erect a school-house capable of accommodating the children of the district. Immediately upon the receipt of said order, the trustee or trustees of such dis-

To estimate sum necessary to build school-house.

Trustee to call special meeting.

---

* As amended by sec. 2, chap. 406, Laws of 1867, and by sec. 3, chap. 331, Laws of 1888.
† As amended by sec. 2, chap. 406, Laws of 1867, and by chap. 592, Laws of 1887.

trict shall call a special meeting of the inhabitants of said district, for the purpose of considering the question of building a school-house therein. Such meeting shall have power to determine the size of said school-house, the material to be used in its erection, and to vote a tax to build the same; but such meeting shall have no power to reduce the estimate made by the commissioner aforesaid by more than twenty-five per centum of such estimate. And where no tax for building such house shall have been voted by such district within thirty days from the time of holding the first meeting to consider the question, then it shall be the duty of the trustee or trustees of such district to contract for the building of a school-house capable of accommodating the children of the district, and to levy a tax to pay for the same, which tax shall not exceed the sum estimated as necessary by the commissioner aforesaid, and which shall not be less than such estimated sum by more than twenty-five per centum thereof. But such estimated sum may be increased by a vote of the inhabitants at any school meeting subsequently called and held according to law. *Trustees to build school-house and levy tax for same, if district neglect.*

* 5. To examine persons proposing to teach common schools within his district, and not possessing the superintendent's certificate of qualification or a diploma of the state normal school, and to inquire into their moral fitness and capacity, and, if he find them qualified, to grant them certificates of qualification, in the forms which are or may be prescribed by the superintendent. *To examine and license teachers.*

6. To re-examine any teacher holding his or her predecessor's certificate, and if he find him deficient in learning or ability, to annul the certificate. *Re-examine.*

7. To examine any charge affecting the moral character of any teacher within his district, first giving such teacher reasonable notice of the charge, and an opportunity to defend himself therefrom; and if he find the charge sustained, to annul the teacher's certificate, by whomsoever granted, and to declare him unfit to teach; and if the teacher held a certificate of the superintendent, or a diploma of the state normal school, to notify the superintendent forthwith of such annulment and declaration. *To examine charges against teachers. Annul certificates.*

8. And, generally, to use his utmost influence and most strenuous exertions to promote sound education, elevate the character and qualifications of teachers, improve the means of instruction and advance the interest of the schools under his supervision.

---
* For additional duties, see chap. 318, Laws of 1882; and chap. 30, Laws of 1884.

TITLE 2.

Commissioners to take affidavits.

* § 14. Every school commissioner shall have power to take affidavits and administer oaths in all matters pertaining to common schools, but without charge or fee; and, under the direction of the superintendent of public instruction, to take and report to him the testimony in any case of appeal.

May issue subpœnas.

When so directed by the superintendent, said commissioner shall have power to issue subpœnas to compel the attendance of witnesses. Service of said subpœnas shall be made a reasonable time before the time therein named for the hearing, by exhibiting the same to the person so served, with the signature of the commissioner attached, and by leaving with such person a copy thereof. The person so served shall be entitled to receive from the person or officer at whose instance he is subpœnaed, at the time of service, the same fees as are

Penalty.

provided by law for witnesses in courts of record. Disobedience of such subpœna shall subject the delinquent to a penalty of twenty-five dollars, which shall, unless sufficient excuse is shown, upon the certificate of the commissioner showing such facts, be imposed by the county judge of the county in which such commissioner resides, and shall be paid forthwith to the county treasurer for the benefit of the poor of the county, or, in case such penalty shall not be paid, such delinquent shall stand committed to the county jail of the county for the period of twenty-five days, unless sooner paid.

School commissioners, how subject to certain rules.

† § 15. The commissioners shall be subject to such rules and regulations as the superintendent of public instruction shall, from time to time, prescribe, and appeals from their acts and decisions may be made to him, as hereinafter provided.

Reports to state superintendent.

They shall, whenever thereto required by the superintendent, report to him as to any particular matter or act, and shall severally make to him annually, to the twenty fifth day of July in each year, a report in such form and containing all such particulars as he shall prescribe and call for; and, for that purpose, shall procure

Annual report, from returns of school trustees.

the reports of the trustees of the school districts from the town clerks' offices, and, after abstracting the necessary contents thereof, shall arrange and indorse them properly and deposit them, with a copy of his own abstract thereof, in the office of the county clerk, and the clerk shall safely keep them.

---

* As amended by sec. 5, chap. 331, Laws of 1889.
† As amended by sec. 1, chap. 413, Laws of 1883, and by sec. 1, chap. 245, Laws of 1889.

TITLE III.

OF THE STATE AND OTHER SCHOOL MONEYS, THEIR APPORTIONMENT AND DISTRIBUTION, AND OF TRUSTS AND GIFTS FOR THE BENEFIT OF COMMON SCHOOLS.

FIRST ARTICLE.

Of the state school moneys and their apportionment by the superintendent of public instruction, and payment to the county and city treasurers.

* SECTION 1. There shall be raised by tax, in the present and each succeeding year, upon the real and personal estate of each county within the State, one mill and one-fourth of a mill upon each and every dollar of the equalized valuation of such estate, for the support of common schools in the state; and the proceeds of such tax shall be apportioned and distributed as herein provided. [State tax for the support of schools.]

§ 2. No clerk of any board of supervisors, or other person who shall make out the tax list or assessment-roll of any town, shall omit to include and apportion among the moneys to be raised thereby the amount hereby required to be raised for the support of schools, by reason of the omission of the board of supervisors to pass a resolution for that purpose. [Clerk of board of supervisors shall not omit to include the state school tax.]

† § 3. The moneys so raised shall be paid into the state treasury, and the treasurer may transfer them from one depository to another, by his draft, countersigned and entered by the superintendent of public instruction. On the first working day of each month the treasurer shall make to the superintendent of public instruction a written statement of the condition of the free school fund, showing the amount received and paid during the preceding month, and the balance remaining on hand. The bank in which such moneys are deposited shall furnish the superintendent of public instruction a book, in which the officers of such banks shall make entries of all sums deposited therein by the treasurer, from time to time, to the credit of said free school fund. No such money shall be paid out of the treasury except upon such warrant of the superintendent, countersigned by the comptroller, referring to the law under which it is drawn. The superintendent shall countersign and enter all checks drawn [Money, how to be deposited. Treasurer to report. Bank book. Warrants and receipts; how drawn and entered.]

---
* As amended by chap. 406, Laws of 1867. NOTE.— Sec. 1 is not followed, as the legislature of each year fixes the rate.
† As amended by sec. 8, chap. 567, Laws of 1875.

CONSOLIDATED SCHOOL ACT OF 1864.

TITLE 3.

by the treasurer in payment of his warrants, and all receipts of the treasurer for such money paid to the treasurer, and no such receipt shall be evidence of payment unless it be so countersigned.

Comptroller may withhold moneys from counties.

* § 4. The comptroller may withhold the payment of any moneys, to which any county may be entitled, from the appropriation of the incomes of the school fund and the United States deposit fund for the support of common schools, until satisfactory evidence shall be furnished to him that all moneys required by law to be raised by taxation upon such county, for the support of schools throughout the State have been collected and paid, or accounted for to the state treasurer; and whenever, after the first day of March in any year, in consequence of the failure of any county to pay such moneys on or before that day, there shall be a deficiency of moneys in the treasury applicable to the payment of school moneys, to which any other county may be entitled, the treasurer and superintendent of public instruction are hereby authorized to make a temporary loan of the amount so deficient, and such loan, and the interest thereon at the rate of twelve per cent per annum, until payment shall be made to the treasury, shall be a charge upon the county in default, and shall be added to the amount of state tax, and levied upon such county by the board of supervisors thereof at the next ensuing assessment, and shall be paid into the treasury in the same manner as other taxes.

Treasurer and superintendent may borrow moneys.

State school moneys.

§ 5. The moneys raised by the state tax or borrowed as aforesaid to supply a deficiency thereof, and such portion of the income of the United States deposit fund as shall be appropriated, and the income of the common school fund, when the same are appropriated to the support of common schools, constitute the state school moneys, and shall be divided and apportioned by the superintendent of public instruction, on or before the twentieth day of January in each year as follows: and all moneys so apportioned, except the library moneys, shall be applied exclusively to the payment of teachers' wages.

Apportionment by superintendent

Applied to teachers' wages.

From free school fund.

† § 6. He shall apportion and set apart from the free school fund appropriated therefor the amounts required

---

* As amended by sec. 4, chap 406, Laws of 1867.
† As amended by chap. 374, Laws of 1876, and by sec. 1, chap. 340, Laws of 1885. This section was changed by sec. 3, chap. 1, Laws of 1881, which reads as follows:
§ 3. In making the annual apportionment of school moneys, the superintendent of public instruction shall hereafter set apart a sum sufficient to pay the salaries of the several school commissioners from the free school fund, instead of from the United States deposit fund as heretofore. Also amended by sec. 1, chap. 333, Laws of 1889. Also amended by sec. 1 of chap 534, Laws of 1890.

OF STATE AND OTHER SCHOOL MONEYS. 19

TITLE 3.

to pay the annual salaries of the school commissioners elected or elective under this act, to be drawn out of the treasury and paid to the several commissioners as hereinbefore provided; and he shall also apportion to each of the cities of the state, and to each of the incorporated villages of the state having a population of five thousand and upwards, and to each union free school district having a like population, which employs a superintendent of common schools, out of the income of the said fund, and if insufficient, the deficiency out of the free school fund so appropriated, the sum of eight hundred dollars; and in case any city is entitled to more than one member of assembly, according to the unit of representation adopted by the legislature, five hundred dollars for each additional member of assembly, to be expended according to law for the support of the common schools of the city. But said superintendent shall make no allotment to any city or district for the expenses of a superintendent unless satisfied that such city, village or district, employs a competent person as superintendent whose time is exclusively devoted to the general supervision of the schools of said city, village or district; nor shall he make any allotment to any district in the first instance without first causing an enumeration of the inhabitants thereof to be made which shall show the population thereof to be at least five thousand, the expense of which enumeration, as certified by said state superintendent, shall be paid by the district in whose interest it is made. He shall then set apart, from the income of the United States deposit fund, for and as library moneys, such sums as the legislature shall appropriate for that purpose. He shall also set apart from the free school fund a sum, not exceeding four thousand dollars, for a contingent fund. He shall then set apart and apportion, for and on account of the Indian schools under his supervision, a sum which will be equitably equivalent to their proportion of the state school money, upon the basis of distribution established by this act, such sum to be wholly payable out of the proceeds of the state tax for the support of common schools. After deducting the said amounts he shall divide the remainder of the state school moneys into two parts, and shall apportion them as hereinafter specified.

Apportionment for salaries to school commissioners and to cities and villages employing a superintendent of schools.

Library moneys.

Indian schools.

To divide remainder into two equal parts.

* § 7. He shall apportion such remainder equally among the school districts and cities from which reports shall

One-half apportionment.

---

* As amended by sec. 2, chap. 340, Laws of 1885; and by sec. 1, chap. 328, Laws of 1889; and by sec. 2, chap. 534, Laws of 1890; and by sec. 2, chap. 500, Laws of 1893.

CONSOLIDATED SCHOOL ACT OF 1864.

TITLE 3.

What districts to receive district quota. have been received in accordance with law, as follows: Making the distributive portion or each district quota one hundred dollars. To entitle a district to a distributive portion or district quota, a qualified teacher, or successive qualified teachers, must have actually taught the common school of the district for at least the term of time hereinafter mentioned, during the last preceding school year.

One quota for each qualified teacher. For every additional qualified teacher and his successors who shall have actually taught in said school during the whole of said term, the district shall be entitled to another distributive quota; but pupils employed as monitors, or otherwise, shall not be deemed teachers.

Term of school. The aforementioned term *during the current school year* shall be thirty-two weeks of five school days each, inclusive of legal holidays, and any other day which shall be by law declared a holiday, which shall occur during the term, *and thereafter said term, during every school year, shall be one hundred and sixty days of school, inclusive of legal holidays that may occur during the term of said schools, and exclusive of Saturday. No Saturday shall be counted as part of said one hundred and sixty days of school, and no school shall be in session on a legal holiday.*

Teacher's attendance at institute. A deficiency not exceeding three weeks during the current year, or in any subsequent year, caused by a teacher's attendance upon a teachers' institute within the county, shall be excused by the superintendent of public instruction.

The remaining half to be apportioned. * § 8. Having so apportioned and distributed the said district quotas as specified in section 7 of this act, the superintendent shall apportion the remainder of said state school moneys, and also the library moneys separately, among the counties of the state, according to their respective population, excluding Indians residing on their reservations, as the same shall appear from the last preceding state or United States census; but as to counties in which are situated cities having special school acts, he shall apportion to each city the part to which it shall so appear entitled, and to the residue of the county the part to which it shall appear to be so entitled. If the census according to which the apportionment shall be made does not show the sum of the population of any county or city, the superintendent shall, by the best evidence he can procure, ascertain and determine the population of such

Apportionment and payment to cities.

---
* As amended by sec. 3, chap. 340, Laws of 1885, and by sec. 3, chap. 534, Laws of 1890.
For days declared by law to be holidays, see chap. 677, Laws of 1892, sec. 24, vol. 2, page 99, *post*.

OF STATE AND OTHER SCHOOL MONEYS.

TITLE 3.

county or city at the time the census was taken, and make his apportionment accordingly.

§ 9. The superintendent shall apportion to each separate neighborhood which shall have duly reported such fixed sum as will, in his opinion, be equitably equivalent to its portion of all the state school moneys upon the basis of distribution established by this act; such sum to be payable out of the contingent fund hereinbefore established. *Separate neighborhoods.*

* § 10. Whenever any school district or separate neighborhood shall have been excluded from participation in any apportionment made by the superintendent, or by the school commissioners, by reason of its having omitted to make any report required by law, or to comply with any other provision of law, or with any rule or regulation made by the superintendent under the authority of law, and it shall be shown to the superintendent that such omission was accidental or excusable, he may, upon the application of such district or neighborhood, make to it an equitable allowance; and if the apportionment was made by himself, cause it to be paid out of the contingent fund; and, if the apportionment was made by the commissioners, direct them to apportion such allowance to it, at their next annual apportionment, in addition to any apportionment to which it may then be entitled. And the superintendent may, in his discretion, upon the recommendation of the school commissioner having jurisdiction over the district in default, direct that the money so equitably apportioned shall be paid in satisfaction of teachers wages earned by a teacher not qualified in accordance with the provisions of the law as hereinafter set forth. *When districts have been excluded from the apportionment; superintendent may make an equitable allowance. From contingent fund. When made by the commissioners. May direct the payment of teachers' quota, when teacher was not a duly qualified teacher.*

§ 11. If money to which it is not entitled, or a larger sum than it is entitled to, shall be apportioned to any county, or part of a county, or school district, and it shall not have been so distributed or apportioned among the districts, or expended, as to make it impracticable so to do, the superintendent may reclaim such money or excess, by directing any officer in whose hands it may be to pay it into the state treasury, to the credit of the free school fund; and the state treasurer's receipt, countersigned by the superintendent, shall be his only voucher; but if it be impracticable so to reclaim such money or excess, then the superintendent shall deduct it from the portions of such county, part of a county or district, in his next annual *Moneys apportioned in excess may be reclaimed by the superintendent. When impracticable to reclaim moneys.*

---
* As amended by section 1, chapter 27, Laws of 1880.
NOTE.—By section 2 of chapter 27, Laws of 1880, all acts and parts of acts inconsistent with this act are thereby repealed.

TITLE 3.

apportionment, and distribute the sum thus deducted equitably among the counties and parts of counties, or among the school districts in the state entitled to participate in such apportionment, according to the basis of apportionment in which such excess occurred.

Deficiencies to be supplied by supplemental apportionment.

§ 12. If a less sum than it is entitled to shall have been apportioned by the superintendent to any county, part of a county or school district, the superintendent may make a supplementary apportionment to it, of such a sum as shall make up the deficiency, and the same shall be paid out of the contingent fund, if sufficient, and if not, then the superintendent shall make up such deficiency in his next annual apportionment.

To certify to county clerk, treasurer, commissioner, etc.

§ 13. As soon as possible after the making of any annual or general apportionment, the superintendent shall certify it to the county clerk, county treasurer, school commissioners and city treasurer or chamberlain, in every county in the state; and if it be a supplemental apportionment, then to the county clerk, county treasurer and school commissioners of the county in which the neighborhood or the school-house of the district concerned is situate.

Moneys annually apportioned payable on the first day of April.

*§ 14. The moneys so annually apportioned by the superintendent shall be payable on the first day of April next after the apportionment, to the treasurers of the several counties and the chamberlain of the city of New York, respectively; and the said treasurers and the chamberlain shall apply for and receive the same as soon as payable.

SECOND ARTICLE.

Of trusts for the benefit of common schools, and of town school funds, fines, penalties and other moneys held or given for their benefit.

Real and personal estate given in trust for the benefit of common schools.

§ 15. Real and personal estate may be granted, conveyed, devised, bequeathed and given in trust and in perpetuity or otherwise, to the state, or to the superintendent of public instruction, for the support or benefit of the common schools within the state, or within any part or portion of it, or of any particular common school or schools within it; and to any county, or the school commissioner or commissioners of any county, or to any city or any board or officers thereof, or to any school commissioner district or its commissioner, or to any town or supervisor of a town, or to any school district or its

---

* As amended by sec. 10, chap. 567, Laws of 1875.

OF STATE AND OTHER SCHOOL MONEYS; TRUSTS, ETC.

trustee or trustees, for the support and benefit of common schools within such county, city school commissioner district, town or school district, or within any part or portion thereof respectively, or for the support and benefit of any particular common school or schools therein.

§ 16. No such grant, conveyance, devise or bequest shall be held void for the want of a named or competent trustee or donee, but where no trustee or donee, or an incompetent one is named, the title and trust shall vest in the people of the state, subject to its acceptance by the legislature, but such acceptance shall be presumed. Trust not invalid for want of trustee or donee.

§ 17. The legislature may control and regulate the execution of all such trusts; and the superintendent of public instruction shall supervise and advise the trustees, and hold them to a regular accounting for the trust property and its income and interest, at such times, in such forms, and with such authentications, as he shall from time to time prescribe. Legislature to control and regulate trusts. Superintendent to require trustees to account.

§ 18. The common council of every city, the board of supervisors of every county, the trustees of every village, the supervisor of every town, the trustee or trustees of every school district, and every other officer or person who shall be thereto required by the superintendent of public instruction, shall on or before the thirtieth day of September next, report to him whether any, and if any, what trusts are held by them respectively, or by any other body, officer or person, to their information or belief for school purposes, and shall transmit therewith an authenticated copy of every will, conveyance instrument or paper embodying or creating the trust; and shall, in like manner, forthwith report to him the creation and terms of every such trust subsequently created. Certain officers and boards to report trusts, etc., to superintendent.

§ 19. Every supervisor of a town shall, by the thirtieth day of September next, report to the superintendent whether there be, within the town, any gospel or school lot, and, if any, shall describe the same, and state to what use, if any, it is put by the town; and whether it be leased, and if so, to whom, for what term and upon what rents; and whether the town holds or is entitled to any land, moneys or securities arising from any sale of such gospel or school lot, and the investment of the proceeds thereof, or of the rents and income of such lots and investments, and shall report a full statement and account of such lands, moneys and securities. Gospel and school lots.

§ 20. Every supervisor of a town shall in like manner, by the thirtieth day of September next, report to the Moneys in the hands of overseers of the poor.

TITLE 3.

superintendent whether the town has a common school fund orginated under the "Act relative to moneys in the hands of overseers of the poor" passed April 27, 1829, and, if it have, the full particulars thereof, and of its investment, income and application, in such form as the superintendent may prescribe.

Superintendent to report to the legislature.

§ 21. In respect to the property and funds in the two last sections mentioned, the superintendent shall, at the next session of the legislature, and annually thereafter, include in his annual report a statement and account thereof. And, to these ends, he is authorized, at any time and from time to time, to require from the supervisor, board of town auditors, or any officer of a town, a report as to any fact, or any information or account, he may deem necessary or desirable.

Superintendent can require report from supervisor or other town officer.

Penalties and fines, how paid and apportioned.

§ 22. Whenever, by any statute, a penalty or fine is imposed for the benefit of common schools, and not expressly of the common schools of a town or school district, it shall be taken to be for the benefit of the common schools of the county within which the conviction is had; and the fine or penalty, when paid or collected, shall be paid forthwith into the county treasury, and the treasurer shall credit the same as school moneys of the county, unless the county comprise a city having a special school act, in which case he shall report it to the superintendent, who shall apportion it upon the basis of population by the last census, between the city and the residue of the county, and the portion belonging to the city shall be paid into its treasury.

District attorney to report fines and penalties to supervisors.

§ 23. Every district attorney shall report, annually, to the board of supervisors, all such fines and penalties imposed in any prosecution conducted by him during the previous year; and all moneys collected or received by him or by the sheriff, or any other officer, for or on account of such fines or penalties, shall be immediately paid into the county treasury, and the receipt of the county treasurer shall be a sufficient and the only voucher for such money.

Fines and penalties, to whom paid.

§ 24. Whenever a fine or penalty is inflicted or imposed for the benefit of the common schools of a town or school district, the magistrate, constable or other officer collecting or receiving the same shall forthwith pay the same to the county treasurer of the county in which the school-house is located, who shall credit the same to the town or district for whose benefit it is collected. If the fine or penalty be inflicted or imposed for the benefit of the common schools of a city having a special school act, or of any part or district of a city, it shall be paid into the city treasury.

§ 25. Whenever, by this or any other act, a penalty or fine is imposed upon any school district officer for a violation or omission of official duty, or upon any person for any act or omission within a school district, or touching property or the peace and good order of the district, and such penalty or fine is declared to be for, or for the use or benefit of the common schools of the town or of the county, and such school district lies in two or more towns or counties, the town or county intended by the act shall be taken to be the one in which the school-house, or the school-house longest owned or held by the district, is at the time of such violation, act or omission. *Penalties in joint districts.*

§ 26. (Repealed by chap. 593, Laws of 1886, § 1, ¶ 39; the following provisions of the Penal Code applying in such cases:)

Sec. 470. Misappropriation, etc., and falsification of accounts by public officers:
A public officer, or a deputy or clerk of any such officer, and any other person receiving money on behalf of, or for account of, the people of this state, or of any department of the government of this state, or of any bureau or fund created by law, and in which the people of this state are directly or indirectly interested, or for or on account of any city, county, village or town, who
1. Appropriates to his own use, or to the use of any person not entitled thereto, without authority of law, any money so received by him as such officer, clerk or deputy, or otherwise; or
2. Knowingly keeps any false account, or makes any false entry or erasure in any account of, or relating to, any money so received by him; or,
3. Fraudulently alters, falsifies, conceals, destroys or obliterates any such account; or.
4. Willfully omits or refuses to pay over to the people of this State, or their officer or agent authorized by law to receive the same, or to such city, village, county or town, or the proper officer or authority empowered to demand and receive the same, any money received by him as such officer, when it is his duty imposed by law to pay over or account for the same, is guilty of felony.
Sec. 471. Other violations of law:
An officer or other person mentioned in the last section, who willfully disobeys any provision of law regulating his official conduct, in cases other than those specified in that section, is guilty of a misdemeanor, punishable by a fine not exceeding one thousand dollars, or imprisonment not exceeding two years, or both.
Sec. 473. A public officer or school officer, who is authorized to sell or lease any property, or to make any contract in his official capacity, or to take part in making any such sale, lease or contract, who voluntarily becomes interested individually in such sale, lease or contract, directly or indirectly, except in cases where such sale, lease or contract, or payment under the same, is subject to audit or approval by the superintendent of public instruction, is guilty of a misdemeanor.
See, also, secs. 114 and 515 of Penal Code.

THIRD ARTICLE.

Of the apportionment of the state school moneys, and of other school moneys by the school commissioners, and their payment to the supervisors.

§ 27. The school commissioner, or commissioners of each county, shall proceed, at the county seat, on the third Tuesday of March in each year, to ascertain, apportion and divide the state and other school moneys as follows: *Apportionment of school moneys by commissioners.*

TITLE 3.

Library moneys. 1. They shall set apart any library moneys apportioned by the superintendent.

Shall set apart moneys especially apportioned by the superintendent. 2. From the other moneys apportioned to the county, they shall set apart and credit to each separate neighborhood and school district the amount apportioned to it by the state superintendent, and to every district which did not participate in the apportionment of the previous year, and which the superintendent shall have excused, such equitable sum as he shall have allowed to it.

Return of unexpended moneys by supervisors. 3. They shall procure from the treasurer of the county a transcript of the returns of the supervisors hereinafter required, showing the unexpended moneys in their hands applicable to the payment of teachers' wages and to library purposes, and shall add the whole sum of such moneys to the balance of the state moneys to be apportioned for teachers' wages. The amounts in each supervisor's hands shall be charged as a partial payment of the sums apportioned to the town for library moneys and teachers' wages, respectively.

Returns from treasurer of fines and penalties. 4. They shall procure from the county treasurer a full list and statements of all payments to him of moneys for or on account of fines and penalties, or accruing from any other source, for the benefit of schools and of the town or towns, district or districts for whose benefit the same were received. Such of said moneys as belong to a particular district, they shall set apart and credit to it; and such as belong to the schools of a town, they shall set apart and credit to the schools in that town, and shall apportion them together with such as belong to the schools of the county as hereinafter provided for the payment of teachers' wages.

How apportioned.

Apportionment of library moneys according to aggregate attendance of children. *5. They shall apportion library moneys to the school districts, and parts of school districts, joint with parts in any city or in any adjoining county, which shall be entitled to participate therein as hereinafter specified, in proportion to the aggregate number of days of attendance of children in each between the ages of five and twenty-one years, as the same shall appear from the reports of the trustees for the last preceding school year.

Remaining moneys. 6. They shall apportion in like manner and upon the same basis, until the apportionment of the year eighteen hundred and sixty-six, the remaining unapportioned moneys upon such school districts and parts of school districts.

---

* As amended by chap. 602, Laws of 1887.

OF APPORTIONMENT BY SCHOOL COMMISSIONERS.

*7. In the apportionment of eighteen hundred and eighty-nine, and in every subsequent apportionment, they shall apportion all of such remaining unapportioned moneys, in the like manner and upon the same basis among such school districts and parts of districts in proportion to the aggregate number of days of attendance of the pupils resident therein, between the ages of five and twenty-one years, at their respective schools during the last preceding school year. The aggregate number of days in attendance of the pupils is to be ascertained from the records thereof kept by the teachers, as hereinafter prescribed, by adding together the whole number of days attendance of each and every such pupil in the district, or part of a district. *(TITLE 3. New basis in 1889. According to aggregate number of days of attendance.)*

8. They shall then set apart to each town the moneys so set apart and apportioned to each separate neighborhood; to each district, the school-house of which is therein; and to each part of a joint district therein the school-house of which is located in a city or in a town in an adjoining county. *(Separate neighborhoods.)*

9. They shall sign, in duplicate, a certificate, showing the amounts apportioned and set apart to each separate neighborhood, school district and part of a district, and the towns in which they were situated, and shall designate therein the source from which each item of the aggregate to each district and town was derived; and shall forthwith deliver one of said duplicates to the treasurer of the county and transmit the other to the superintendent of public instruction. *(Certificates of apportionment.)*

10. They shall certify to the supervisor of each town the amount of school moneys so apportioned to his town, and the portions thereof to be paid by him for library purposes and for teachers' wages, to each such distinct separate neighborhood, district and part of a district. *(Certify to the supervisor.)*

§ 28. If in their apportionment, through any error of the commissioners, any district shall have apportioned to it a larger or a less share of the moneys than it is entitled to, the commissioners may in their next annual apportionment, with the approbation of the superintendent, correct the error by an equitable deduction from or augmentation of the share of such district. *(Erroneous apportionment, how remedied.)*

§ 29. No district or part of a district shall be entitled to any portion of such school moneys on such apportionment unless the report of the trustees for the preceding *(What district entitled to public moneys.)*

---

* As amended by sec. 1, chap. 492, Laws of 1881, and sec. 4, chap. 310, Laws of 1885, and chap. 602, Laws of 1887.

CONSOLIDATED SCHOOL ACT OF 1864.

TITLE 3.

school year shall show that a common school was supported in the district and taught by a qualified teacher for such a term of time as would, under section seven of this title, entitle it to a distributive share under the apportionment of the superintendent.

Supervisor to make apportionment and file the original.

§ 30. On receiving the certificate of the commissioners, each supervisor shall forthwith make a copy thereof for his own use, and deposit the original in the office of the clerk of his town; and the moneys so apportioned to his town shall be paid to him immediately on his compliance with the requirements of the next section, and not before.

Supervisor to give bonds.

* § 31. Immediately on receiving the commissioners' certificate of apportionment, the county treasurer shall require of each supervisor, and each supervisor shall give to the treasurer, in behalf of the town, his bond, with two or more sufficient sureties, approved by the treasurer, in the penalty of at least double the amount of the school moneys set apart or apportioned to the town, and of any such moneys unaccounted for by his predecessors, conditioned for the faithful disbursement, safe-keeping and accounting for such moneys, and of all other school moneys, that may come into his hands from any other source. If the condition shall be broken, the county treasurer shall sue the bond in his own name, in behalf of the town, and the money recovered shall be paid over to the successor of the supervisor in default, such successor

In case of vacancy in office of supervisor.

having first given security as aforesaid. Whenever the office of a supervisor shall become vacant, by reason of the expiration of his term of service or otherwise, the county treasurer shall require the person elected or appointed to fill such vacancy to execute a bond, with two or more sureties, to be approved by the treasurer, in the penalty of at least double the sum of the school moneys remaining in the hands of the old supervisor, when the office became vacant, conditioned for the faithful disbursement, safe-keeping and accounting for such moneys. But the execution of this bond shalt not relieve the supervisor from the duty of executing the bond first above mentioned.

Refusal to give security a misdemeanor.

§ 32. The refusal of a supervisor to give such security shall be a misdemeanor, and any fine imposed on his conviction thereof shall be for the benefit of the common schools of the town. Upon such refusal, the moneys so set apart and apportioned to the town shall be paid to and

---

* As amended by sec. 11, chap. 567, Laws of 1875.

DISBURSEMENT OF MONEYS BY SUPERVISORS.   29

disbursed by some other officer or person to be designated by the county judge, under such regulations and with such safeguards as he may prescribe, and the reasonable compensation of such officer or person, to be adjusted by the board of supervisors, shall be a town charge.

TITLE 4. County judge may appoint person to whom the moneys set apart and apportioned to the town shall be paid.

TITLE IV.

OF THE DISBURSEMENT OF THE SCHOOL MONEYS BY THE SUPERVISORS, AND OF SOME OF THEIR SPECIAL POWERS, DUTIES AND LIABILITIES UNDER THIS ACT.

SECTION 1. The several supervisors continue vested with the powers and charged with the duties formerly vested in and charged upon the trustees of the gospel and school lots, and transferred to and imposed upon town superintendents of common schools by chapter one hundred and eighty-six of the laws of one thousand eight hundred and forty-six. *Supervisors to be trustees of gospel and school lots.*

§ 2. The several supervisors continue vested with the powers and charged with the duties conferred and imposed upon the commissioners of common schools by the act of eighteen hundred and twenty-nine (chap. 287), entitled "An act relative to moneys in the hands of overseers of the poor." *Powers under former acts.*

§ 3. (Relating to the embezzlement of moneys by supervisors, repealed by sec. 1, subdivision 39 of chap. 593, Laws of 1886.) Sections 470 and 471 of the Penal Code are applicable to such cases, and are printed page 25, *ante*. *Repealed.*

§ 4. On the first Tuesday of March in each year, each supervisor shall make a return in writing to the county treasurer for the use of the school commissioners, showing the amounts of school moneys in his hands not paid out on the orders of trustees for teachers' wages, nor drawn by them for library purposes, and the districts to which they stand accredited (and if no such money remain in his hands, he shall report that fact); and thereafter he shall not pay out any of said moneys until he shall have received the certificate of the next apportionment; and the moneys so returned by him shall be reapportioned as hereinbefore directed. *To make a return of moneys in their hands.*

§ 5. (Providing a penalty for neglect of duty by a supervisor, repealed by section 1, subdivision 39 of chapter 593, Laws of 1886.) Sections 470 and 471 of the Penal Code are applicable. See page 25, *ante*. *Repealed.*

TITLE 4.

Supervisors' duties.

§ 6. It is the duty of every supervisor:

How to disburse the school moneys for teachers' wages.

*1. To disburse the school moneys in his hands applicable to the payment of teachers' wages, upon and only upon the written orders of a sole trustee or a majority of the trustees, in favor of qualified teachers, or upon the order of a trustee of a separate neighborhood in favor of any teacher of a school in an adjoining state, recognized by him and patronized by the inhabitants of such neighborhood. Such teacher shall be deemed a qualified teacher. But whenever the collector in any school district shall have given bonds for the due and faithful performance of the duties of his office as such disbursing agent, as required by section eighty-three of title seven of this act, the said supervisor shall pay over to such collector all moneys in his hands applicable to the payment of teachers' wages in such district, and the said collector shall disburse such moneys so received by him upon such orders as are specified above, to the teachers entitled to the same.

Payment thereof to collector.

Library money.

† 2. To disburse the library moneys upon, and only upon the written orders of a sole trustee, or of a majority of the trustees.

To pay to the treasurer of a union free school district.

3. In the case of a union free school district, to pay over all the school money apportioned thereto, whether for the payment of teachers' wages, or as library moneys, to the treasurer of such district, upon the order of its board of education.

To keep an account of all school moneys received and disbursements.

4. To keep a just and true account of all the school moneys received and disbursed by him during each year, and to lay the same, with proper vouchers, before the board of town auditors at each annual meeting thereof.

To enter on blank book receipts and disbursements.

5. To have a bound blank book (the cost of which shall be a town charge), and to enter therein all his receipts and disbursements of school moneys, specifying from whom and for what purposes they were received, and to whom and for what purposes they were paid out; and to deliver the book to his successor in office.

To file account with the town clerk and notify his successor thereof.

6. Within fifteen days after the termination of his office, to make out a just and true account of all school moneys theretofore received by him and of all disbursements thereof, and to deliver the same to the town clerk, to be filed and recorded, and to notify his successor in office of such rendition and filing

---

* As amended by section 12, chapter 567, Laws of 1875, and section 1, chapter 175 Laws of 1890.
† As amended by section 13, chapter 567, Laws of 1875.

OF THE DUTIES OF THE TOWN CLERK. 31

7. So soon as the bond to the county treasurer, by the third article of the third title of this act required, shall have been given by him and approved by the treasurer, to deliver to his predecessor the treasurer's certificate of these facts, to procure from the town clerk a copy of his predecessor's account, and to demand and receive from him any and all school moneys remaining in his hands. TITLE 5. To procure predecessor's account, and demand and receive moneys.

8. Upon receiving such a certificate from his successor, and not before, to pay to him all school moneys remaining in his hands, and to forthwith file the certificate in the town clerk's office. When to pay to successor moneys remaining in his hands.

9. By his name of office, when the duty is not elsewhere imposed by law, to sue for and recover penalties and forfeitures imposed for violations of this act, and for any default or omission of any town officer or school district board or officer under this act; and after deducting his costs and expenses to report the balances to the school commissioner. To sue for and recover penalties and forfeitures. To report balance to commissioner.

10. To act, when thereto legally required, in the erection or alteration of a school district, as in the sixth title of this act provided, and to perform any other duty which may be devolved upon him by this act, or any other act relating to common schools. Erection or alteration of a school district.

TITLE V.

OF THE DUTIES OF THE TOWN CLERK UNDER THIS ACT.

SECTION 1. It shall be the duty of the town clerk of each town : Duties of town clerk

1. Carefully to keep all books, maps, papers and records of his office touching common schools, and forthwith to report to the supervisor any loss of or injury to any of them which may happen.

2. To receive from the supervisors the certificates of apportionment of school moneys to the town, and to record them in a book to be kept for that purpose.

3. Forthwith to notify the trustees of the several school districts and separate neighborhoods of the filing of each such certificate.

*4. To see that the trustees of the school districts and separate neighborhoods make and deposit with him their annual reports within the time prescribed by law, and to deliver them to the school commissioner on demand; and to furnish the school commissioner of the school commissioner district in which his town is situated the names Town clerk to report names of district officers to commissioners.

---
* As amended by sec. 5, chap. 647, Laws of 1865.

CONSOLIDATED SCHOOL ACT OF 1864.

TITLE 5.

and post-office address of the school district officers reported to him by the district clerks.

To distribute blanks, books and circulars from superintendent of public instruction.

*5. To distribute to the trustees of the school districts and separate neighborhoods all books, blanks and circulars which shall be delivered or forwarded to him by the state superintendent or school commissioner for that purpose.

Account to be kept by.

6. To receive from the supervisor, and record in a book kept for that purpose, the annual account of the receipts and disbursements of school moneys required to be submitted to the town auditors, together with the action of the town auditors thereon, and to send a copy of the account and of the action thereon, by mail, to the superintendent of public instruction, whenever required by him, and to file and preserve the vouchers accompanying the account.

7. To receive and to record, in the same book, the supervisor's final account of the school moneys received and disbursed by him, and deliver a copy thereof to such supervisor's successor in office.

8. To receive from the outgoing supervisor, and file and record in the same book, the county treasurer's certificate, that his successor's bond has been given and approved.

To record description of school district.

9. To receive, file and record the descriptions of the school districts and neighborhoods, and all papers and proceedings delivered to him by the school commissioner pursuant to the next title of this act.

10. To act, when thereto legally required, in the erection or alteration of a school district, as in the next title of this act provided.

To preserve records of dissolved district.

†11. To receive and preserve the books, papers and records of any dissolved school district, which shall be ordered, as hereinafter provided, to be deposited in his office.

12. To perform any other duty which may be devolved upon him by this act, or by any other act touching common schools.

Clerk's charges and expenses.

§ 2. The necessary expenses and disbursements of the town clerk in the performance of his said duties, are a town charge, and shall be audited and paid as such.

---

* As amended by sec. 6, chap. 331, Laws of 1888.
† Original subdivision 11 stricken out by sec. 18, chap. 647, Laws of 1865, and subdivisions 12 and 13, numbered 11 and 12, respectively.

FORMATION AND ALTERATION OF SCHOOL DISTRICTS. 33

TITLE 6.

TITLE VI.

OF THE FORMATION, DISSOLUTION AND ALTERATION OF SCHOOL DISTRICTS AND SEPARATE NEIGHBORHOODS.

SECTION 1. It shall be the duty of each school commissioner, in respect to the territory within his district: *Commissioner's duties in respect to school districts.*

1. To divide it, so far as practicable, into a convenient number of school districts, and alter the same as herein provided;

2. In conjunction with the commissioner or commissioners of an adjoining school commissioner district or districts, to set off joint districts, composed of adjoining parts of their respective districts; *To set off joint districts.*

3. To set off by itself any neighborhood adjoining any other state of the Union, where it shall be found most convenient for the inhabitants to send their children to a school in such adjoining state; *To set off neighborhood.*

4. To describe and number the school districts, and joint districts, and to deliver, in writing, to the town clerk, the description and number of each district lying in whole or in part in his town, together with all notices, consents and proceedings relating to the formation or alteration thereof, immediately after such formation or alteration. Every joint district shall bear the same number in every school commissioner district of whose territory it is in part composed. *To number and describe districts.*

5. To deliver to the town clerk of the town in which it lies, in whole or in part, a description of each such separate neighborhood. *To deliver description of separate neighborhood.*

* § 2. With the written consent of the trustees of all the districts to be affected thereby, he may, by order, alter any school district within his jurisdiction, and fix, by said order, a day when the alteration shall take effect. *May alter districts with consent of trustees.*

† § 3. If the trustees of any such district refuse to consent, he may make and file with the town clerk his order making the alteration, but reciting the refusal, and directing that the order shall not take effect, as to the dissenting district or districts, until a day therein to be named, and not less than three months after the notice in the next section mentioned. *When trustees refuse to give consent.*

‡ § 4. Within ten days after making and filing such order he shall give at least a week's notice in writing to one or more of the assenting and dissenting trustees of any dis- *Procedure on the refusal of trustees to the alteration of a school district.*

---

* As amended by sec. 5, chap. 406, Laws of 1867.
† As amended by sec. 6, chap. 406, Laws of 1867.
‡ As amended by sec. 6, chap. 647, Laws of 1865.

3

trict or districts to be affected by the proposed alterations, that at a specified time, and at a named place within the town in which either of the districts to be affected lies, he will hear the objections to the alteration. The trustees of any district to be affected by such order may request the supervisor and town clerk of the town or towns within which such district or districts shall wholly or partly lie, to be associated with the commissioner. At the time and place mentioned in the notice the commissioner or commissioners, with the supervisors and town clerks, if they shall attend and act, shall hear and decide the matter; and the decision shall be final unless duly appealed from. Such decision must either confirm or vacate the order of the commissioner, and must be filed with and recorded by the town clerk of the town or towns in which the district or districts to be affected shall lie.

Fees of supervisor and town clerk.

§ 5. The supervisor and town clerk shall be entitled each, to one dollar and fifty cents a day, for each day's service in any such matter, to be levied and paid as a charge upon their town.

Formation of joint districts.

§ 6. Whenever it may become necessary or convenient to form a school district out of parcels of two or more school commissioner districts, the commissioners of such districts, or a majority of them, may form such district; and the commissioners within whose districts any such school district lies, or a majority of them, may alter or dissolve it.

Alteration or dissolution of a joint district.

§ 7. If a school commissioner, by notice in writing, shall require the attendance of the other commissioner or commissioners, at a joint meeting for the purpose of altering or dissolving such a joint district, and a majority of all the commissioners shall refuse or neglect to attend, the commissioner or commissioners attending, or any one of them, may call a special meeting of such school district for the purpose of deciding whether or no such district shall be dissolved; and its decision of that question shall be as valid as though made by the commissioners.

Consolidation of districts.

§ 8. When two or more districts shall be consolidated into one, the new district shall succeed to all the rights of property possessed by the annulled districts.

Supervisor to sell property of annulled districts.

* § 9. When a district is parted into portions, which are annexed to other districts, its property shall be sold by the supervisor of the town within which its school-house is situate, at public auction, after at least five days' notice,

---

*. As amended by sec. 14. chap. 567, Laws of 1875.

FORMATION AND ALTERATION OF SCHOOL DISTRICTS.

TITLE 6.

by notices posted in three or more public places of the town in which the school-house is, one of which shall be posted in the district so dissolved. The supervisor, after deducting the expenses of the sale, shall apply its proceeds to the payment of the debts of the district, and apportion the residue, if any, among the owners or possessors of taxable property in the district, in the ratio of their several assessments on the last corrected assessment-roll or rolls of the town or towns, and pay it over accordingly.

§ 10. The supervisor of the town within which the school-house of the dissolved district was situate may demand, sue for, and collect, in his name of office, any money of the district outstanding in the hands of any of its former officers, or any other person; and, after deducting his costs and expenses, shall report the balance to the school commissioner who shall apportion the same equitably among the districts to which the parts of the dissolved districts were annexed, to be by them applied as their district meetings shall determine. *Supervisor to sue for outstanding moneys.*

§ 11. Though a district be dissolved, it shall continue to exist in law, for the purpose of providing for and paying all its just debts; and to that end the trustees and other officers shall continue in office, and the inhabitants may hold special meetings, elect officers to supply vacancies, and vote taxes; and all other acts necessary to raise money and pay such debts shall be done by the inhabitants and officers of the district. *Dissolved district to exist in law for settlement of its affairs.*

§ 12. The commissioner, or a majority of the commissioners in whose district or districts a dissolved school district was, shall by his or their order in writing, delivered to the clerk of the district, or to any person in whose possession the books, papers and records of the district, or any of them, may be, direct such clerk or other person to deposit the same in the clerk's office in a town in the order named. Such clerk or other person, by neglect or refusal to obey the order, shall forfeit fifty dollars, to be applied to the benefit of common schools of said town. The commissioner or commissioners shall file a duplicate of the order with such clerk. *Records, etc., to be deposited with town clerk. Penalty for refusal to obey commissioner's order.*

TITLE VII.

OF SCHOOL DISTRICT AND NEIGHBORHOOD MEETINGS, AND OF THE CHOICE, DUTIES AND POWERS OF SCHOOL DISTRICT AND NEIGHBORHOOD OFFICERS.

FIRST ARTICLE.

Of school district and neighborhood meetings, the voters and their powers generally.

Commissioner to describe new district; and appoint a time for first meeting.

SECTION 1. Whenever any school district or separate neighborhood shall be formed, the commissioner or any one or more of the commissioners, within whose district or districts it may be, shall prepare a notice describing such district or neighborhood, and appointing a time and place for the first district or neighborhood meeting, and deliver such notice to a taxable inhabitant of the district or neighborhood.

Notice of such meeting.

§ 2. It shall be the duty of such inhabitant to notify every other inhabitant of the district or neighborhood, qualified to vote at the meeting, by reading the notice in his hearing, or in case of his absence from home, by leaving a copy thereof, or so much thereof as relates to the time, place and object of the meeting, at the place of his abode at least six days before the time of the meeting.

Notice of such meeting.

§ 3. In case such meeting shall not be held, and in the opinion of the commissioner it shall be necessary to hold such meeting before the time herein fixed for the first annual meeting, he shall deliver another such notice to a taxable inhabitant of the district or neighborhood, who shall serve it as hereinbefore provided.

When commissioner may call meeting.

§ 4. When the clerk and all the trustees of a school district shall have removed from the district, or their office shall be vacant, so that a special meeting cannot be called, as hereinafter provided, the commissioner may in like manner give notice of and call a special district meeting.

Penalty for refusal to give notice.

§ 5. Every taxable inhabitant to whom a notice of any district meeting shall be delivered for service, pursuant to any provision of this article, who shall refuse or neglect to serve the same, as hereinbefore prescribed, shall forfeit five dollars for the benefit of the district.

Special meetings.

* § 6. A special district meeting shall be held whenever called by the trustees. The notice thereof shall state the purposes for which it is called, and no business shall be transacted at such special meeting, except that

---

* As amended by sec. 15, chap. 567, **Laws of 1875.**

which is specified in the notice; and the district clerk, or if the office be vacant, or he be sick or absent, or shall refuse to act, a trustee or some taxable inhabitant, by order of the trustees, shall serve the notice upon each inhabitant of the district qualified to vote at district meetings, at least five days before the day of the meeting, in the manner prescribed in the second section of this title. But the inhabitants of any district may, at any annual meeting, adopt a resolution prescribing some other mode of giving notice of special meetings, which resolution and the mode prescribed thereby shall continue in force until rescinded or modified at some subsequent annual meeting. *Annual meeting may prescribe manner of giving notice for special meetings.*

§ 7. The proceedings of no neighborhood or district meeting, annual or special, shall be held illegal for want of a due notice to all the persons qualified to vote thereat, unless it shall appear that the omission to give such notice was willful and fraudulent. *Proceedings legal, except in case of fraudulent neglect.*

* § 8. The annual meeting of each neighborhood shall be held on the *fourth* Tuesday of August in each year, at the hour and place fixed by the last previous neighborhood meeting, or, if such hour and place have not been so fixed, then the same shall be held in the school-house at seven thirty o'clock in the evening. If a neighborhood possesses more than one school-house, it shall be held in the one usually used for that purpose, unless the trustees designate in the notice another. If there is no school building, or if the school-house shall be no longer accessible, then at such other place as the trustees, or, if there be no trustees, the clerk shall in the notice designate. *Annual neighborhood school meetings, when and where held.*

† § 9. The annual meeting of each school district shall be held the *fourth* Tuesday of August in each year, and unless the hour and place thereof shall have been fixed by a vote of a previous district meeting, the same shall be held in the school-house at seven-thirty o'clock in the evening. If a district possesses more than one school-house, it shall be held in the one usually employed for that purpose, unless the trustees designate another. If the district possesses no school-house, or if the school-house shall be no longer accessible, then the annual meeting shall be held at such place as the trustees, or, if there be no trustee, the clerk shall designate in the notice. *Annual school district meetings, when and where held.*

§ 10. Whenever the time for holding the annual meeting in school districts, shall pass without such meeting *Procedure when the annual meeting has not*

---

* As amended by sec. 7, chap. 647, Laws of 1865, and by sec. 2, chap. 413, Laws of 1883, and by sec. 2 of chap. 245, Laws of 1889, and by sec. 3, chap. 500, Laws of 1893.
† As amended by sec. 16, chap. 567, Laws of 1875, and by sec. 3, chap. 413, Laws of 1883, and by sec. 3, of chap. 245, Laws of 1889, and by sec. 4, chap. 500, Laws of 1893.

being held in any district, a special meeting shall thereafter be called by the trustees or by the clerk of such district for the purpose of transacting the business of the annual meeting; and if no such meeting be called by the trustees or the clerk within twenty days after such time shall have passed, the supervisor or the superintendent of public instruction may order any inhabitant of such district to give notice of such meeting in the manner provided in the second section of this title, and the officers of the district shall make to such meeting the reports required to be made at the annual meeting, subject to the same penalty in case of neglect; and the officers elected at such meeting shall hold their respective offices only until the next annual meeting and until their successors are elected and shall have qualified as in this act provided.

Duty of inhabitants when meeting is called. § 11. Whenever any district or neighborhood meeting shall be duly called, it shall be the duty of the inhabitants qualified to vote thereat, to assemble at the time and place fixed for the meeting.

Voters; their qualifications. * § 12. Every person of full age residing in any neighborhood or school district, and entitled to hold lands in this state, who owns or hires real property in such neighborhood or school district liable to taxation for school purposes, and every resident of such neighborhood or district who is a citizen of the United States above the age of twenty-one years, and who is the parent of a child or children of school age, some one or more of whom shall have attended the district school for a period of at least eight weeks within one year preceding, and every such person not being the parent who shall have permanently residing with him or her such child or children, and every such resident and citizen as aforesaid, who owns any personal property assessed on the last preceding assessment-roll of the town, exceeding fifty dollars in value, exclusive of such as is exempt from execution, and no other, shall be entitled to vote at any school meeting held in such neighborhood or district.

Unqualified voters. Challenge. § 13. If any person offering to vote at any neighborhood or school district meeting shall be challenged as unqualified, by any legal voter in such neighborhood or district, the chairman presiding at such meeting shall require the person so offering, to make the following declaration: "I do declare and affirm that I am an actual resident of this school district (or separate neighborhood), and that I am qualified to vote at this meeting." And

---

* As amended by sec. 7, chap. 406, Laws of 1867, and by sec. 2, chap. 492, Laws of 1881, and by sec. 1, chap. 655, Laws of 1886.

OF SCHOOL DISTRICTS, MEETINGS, ETC.

every person making such declaration shall be permitted to vote on all questions proposed at such meeting; but if any person shall refuse to make such declaration, his vote shall be rejected.

TITLE 7. Declarations.

* § 14. Any person who, upon being so challenged, shall willfully make a false declaration of his right to vote at any such meeting, shall be deemed guilty of a misdemeanor, and punished by imprisonment in the county jail for not less than six months nor more than one year. And any person not qualified to vote at any such meeting, who shall vote thereat, shall thereby forfeit five dollars, to be sued for by the supervisor for the benefit of the common schools of the town.

Illegal voting, etc.

§ 15. The inhabitants of any neighborhood entitled to vote, when assembled in any annual meeting or any other neighborhood meeting duly called by the commissioner, pursuant to the first or third sections of this title, shall have power by a majority of the votes of those present:

Powers of neighborhood meeting.

1. To appoint a chairman for the time being.
2. To choose a neighborhood clerk and one trustee, and to fill vacancies in office.

§ 16. The inhabitants so entitled to vote, when duly assembled in any district meeting, shall have power, by a majority of the votes of those present:

Powers of district meeting.

1. To appoint a chairman for the time being.
2. If the district clerk be absent to appoint a clerk for the time.
3. To adjourn from time to time as occasion may require.
¶†4. To choose one or three trustees as hereinafter provided, a district clerk, a district collector, a librarian, at their first meeting, and so often as such offices or any of them become vacated, except as hereinafter provided. *Said district officers shall be elected by ballot. The persons having the majority of votes, respectively, for the several offices, shall be elected, except in school districts in which the election of officers is made under and pursuant to the provisions of chapter two hundred and forty-eight of the Laws of eighteen hundred and seventy-eight, and the acts amendatory thereof.*
5. To fix the amount in which the collector shall give bail for the due and faithful performance of the duties of his office.

Amount of collector's bail.

---

* NOTE.— See chap. 692, Laws of 1893, to take effect Oct. 1, 1893, amending Penal Code. § 41k, subdivision.18, willfully makes a false declaration of his right to vote at a neighborhood or school district meeting, after his right to vote thereat challenged, is guilty of a misdemeanor.
¶ As amended by sec. 5, chap. 500, Laws of 1893.
† NOTE.— In relation to election of trustees in districts having over 300 children of school age, see chap. 248, Laws of 1878, page 129, *post*.

TITLE 7.
Sites.

*6. To designate a site for a school-house, or, with the consent of the commissioner or commissioners within whose district or districts the school district lies, to designate sites for two or more school-houses for the district.

Tax for sites, etc.

†7. To vote a tax upon the taxable property of the district, to purchase, lease or improve such site or sites, and to hire, build or purchase such school-houses, and to keep in repair and furnish the same with necessary fuel and appendages.

Tax for apparatus and text-books.

8. To vote a tax, not exceeding twenty-five dollars in any one year, for the purchase of maps, globes, blackboards and other school apparatus, and for the purchase of text-books and other school necessaries for the use of poor scholars of the district.

Tax for district library.

‡9. To vote a tax, not exceeding ten dollars in any one year, for the purchase of such books as they shall direct for the district library, and such further sum as they may deem necessary for the purchase of a book-case.

For deficiency.

10. To vote a tax to supply a deficiency in any former tax arising from such tax, being, in whole or in part, uncollectible.

Insurance on school-house.

11. To authorize the trustees to cause the school-house or school-houses, and their furniture, appendages and school apparatus to be insured by any insurance company created by or under the laws of this state.

12. To alter, repeal and modify their proceedings from time to time, as occasion may require.

13. To vote a tax for the purchase of a book for the purpose of recording their proceedings.

To replace moneys embezzled; and to pay costs of suits and appeals.

14. To vote a tax to replace moneys of the district, lost or embezzled by district officers; and to pay the reasonable expenses incurred by district officers in defending suits or appeals brought against them for their official acts, or in prosecuting suits or appeals by direction of the district against other parties.

Tax for contingencies.

15. To vote a tax, not exceeding twenty-five dollars in each year, for anticipated deficiencies or contingencies, or to pay the wages of teachers in anticipation of the ordinary collections for that purpose, to be replaced by such collections when made.

Tax for teachers' wages.

∥16. To vote a tax to pay whatever deficiency there may be in teachers' wages after the public money appor-

---

* NOTE.—To acquire title to sites, see chap. 800, Laws of 1866, as amended, on page 122, *post*.
† As amended by sec. 7, chap. 567, Laws of 1875.
‡ See title 8, as adopted by chap. 573, Laws of 1892, relative to libraries.
∥ This subdivision added by sec. 8, chap. 406, Laws of 1867.

tioned to the district shall have been applied thereto; but if the inhabitants shall neglect or refuse to vote a tax for this purpose, or if they shall vote a tax which shall prove insufficient to cover such deficiency, then the trustees are authorized, and it is hereby made their duty, to raise by district tax, any reasonable sum that may be necessary to pay the balance of teachers' wages remaining unpaid, the same as if such tax had been authorized by a vote of the inhabitants.

* 17. To vote a tax to pay and satisfy of record any judgment or judgments of a competent court which may have been or shall hereafter be obtained in an action against the trustees of the district for unpaid teachers' wages, against the trustees of the district where the time to appeal from said judgment or judgments shall have lapsed, or there shall be no intent to appeal on the part of such district, or the said judgment or judgments is or are or shall be of the court of highest resort; but if the inhabitants shall neglect or refuse to vote a tax for this purpose or if they vote a tax which shall prove insufficient to fully satisfy said judgment or judgments, then the trustees are authorized and it is hereby made their duty to raise by district tax the amount of said judgment or judgments or the deficiency which may exist in any tax voted by said inhabitants to pay said judgment or judgments, the same as if such tax had been authorized by a vote of the inhabitants, and the trustees are hereby authorized and it is hereby made their duty forthwith, after the expiration of thirty days from notice of any judgment or judgments having been entered against the district or the trustees thereof for unpaid teachers' wages, to call a meeting of the inhabitants of said district, who shall have power as aforesaid to vote a tax to pay said judgment or judgments, and in case they refuse or neglect to do so, the trustees are authorized, and it is hereby made their duty, unless said judgment or judgments are appealed from, to raise by district tax the amount of said judgment or judgments as hereinbefore provided.

¶ 18. *In all propositions arising at said district meetings involving the expenditure of money, or authorizing the levy of a tax or taxes, the vote thereon shall be by ballot, or ascertained by taking and recording the ayes and noes of such qualified voters attending and voting at such district meetings.*

---
* This subdivision added by sec. 1, chap. 632, Laws of 1881.
¶ Added to section 16 by sec. 6, chap. 500, Laws of 1893.

Second Article.
Of district school-houses and sites.

School-house, location of.
§ 17. No school-house shall be built so as to stand, in whole or in part, upon the division line of any two towns.

Cannot levy tax for building school-house exceeding $500 without approval of school commissioner.

Plans to be approved.

*§ 18. No tax voted by a district meeting for building, hiring or purchasing a school-house, exceeding the sum of five hundred dollars, shall be levied by the trustees unless the commissioner in whose district the school-house of said district is situated shall certify, in writing, his approval of such larger sum. And no school-house shall be built in any school district of this State until the plan of such school-house, so far as ventilation, heat and lighting is concerned, shall be approved in writing by said school commissioner. But nothing herein contained shall invalidate any tax that shall or may be hereafter levied for building or repairing school-houses which in other respects comply with existing statutes. †

Tax may be levied in installments.

‡ § 19. Whenever a majority of all the inhabitants of any school district entitled to vote, to be ascertained by taking and recording the ayes and noes of such inhabitants attending at any annual, special or adjourned school district meeting, legally called or held, shall determine that the sum proposed and provided for in the next preceding section shall be raised by installments, it shall be the duty of the trustees of such district, and they are hereby authorized to cause the same to be raised, levied and collected in equal installments in the same manner and with the like authority that other school taxes are raised, levied and collected, and to make out their tax list and warrant for the collection of such installments, with interest thereon, as they become payable, according to the vote of the said inhabitants; but the payment or collection of the last installment shall not be extended beyond ten years from the time such vote was taken; and no vote to levy any such tax shall be reconsidered except at an adjourned, general or special meeting to be held within thirty days thereafter, and the same majority shall be required for reconsideration that was had to impose such tax.

Trustees may borrow.

For the purpose of giving effect to these provisions, trustees are hereby authorized, whenever a tax shall have been voted to be collected in installments for the purpose

---

* As amended by sec. 9, chap. 406, Laws of 1867, and by sec. 1, chap. 528, Laws of 1881, and by sec. 1, chap. 294, Laws of 1883.
† Plans for school buildings will be furnished. See chap. 675, Laws of 1887, on page 132, *post.*
‡ As amended by sec. 19, chap. 567, Laws of 1875, and by sec. 2, chap. 528, Laws of 1881.

OF DISTRICT SCHOOL-HOUSES AND SITES. 43

of building a new school-house, to borrow so much of the sum voted as may be necessary, at a rate of interest not exceeding six per cent, and to issue bonds or other evidences of indebtedness therefor which shall be a charge upon the district, and be paid at maturity and which shall not be sold below par; due notice of the time and place of the sale of such bonds shall be given at least ten days prior thereto. *(May issue bonds.)*

* § 20. So long as a district shall remain unaltered, the site of a school-house owned by it, upon which there is a school-house erected or in process of erection, shall not be changed, nor such school-house be removed, unless by the consent, in writing, of the school commissioner having jurisdiction; nor with such consent, unless a majority of all the legal voters of said district present and voting, to be ascertained by taking and recording the ayes and noes, at a special meeting called for that purpose, shall be in favor of such new site. *(Provisions in regard to change of school-house site.)*

§ 21. Whenever the site of a school-house shall have been changed, as herein provided, the inhabitants of a district entitled to vote, lawfully assembled at any district meeting, shall have power, by a majority of the votes of those present, to direct the sale of the former site or lot, and the buildings thereon and appurtenances or any part thereof, at such price and upon such terms as they shall deem proper; and any deed duly executed by the trustees of such district, or a majority of them, in pursuance of such direction, shall be valid and effectual to pass all the estate or interest of such school district in the premises, and when a credit shall be directed to be given upon such sale for the consideration money, or any part thereof, the trustees are hereby authorized to take in their corporate name such security by bond and mortgage, or otherwise, for the payment thereof, as they shall deem best, and shall hold the same as a corporation, and account therefor to their successors in office and to the district, in the manner they are now required by law to account for moneys received by them; and the trustees of any such district for the time being may, in their name of office, sue for and recover the moneys due and unpaid upon any security so taken by them or their predecessors. *(Proceedings for the sale of lot and appurtenances. Security for the consideration money.)*

§ 22. All moneys arising from any sale made in pursuance of the last preceding section shall be applied to the expenses incurred in procuring a new site, and in *(Moneys arising from the sale to be applied to new houses, etc.)*

---

* As amended by sec. 8, chap. 647, Laws of 1865, and by sec. 4, of chap. 331, Laws of 1868.

removing or erecting thereon a school-house and improving and furnishing such site and house, and their appendages, so far as such application shall be necessary; and the surplus, if any, shall be devoted to the purchase of school apparatus and the support of the school, as the inhabitants at any annual meeting shall direct.

Third Article.

Of the qualification, election, choice and terms of office of district and neighborhood officers; and of vacancies in such offices.

Trustees who may not hold the office of.

§ 23. No school commissioner or supervisor is eligible to the office of trustee, nor can either be a member of any board of education within his district or town; and no trustee can hold the office of district clerk, collector or librarian.

District officer must reside in the district.

* § 24. Every district and neighborhood officer must be a resident of his district or neighborhood, and qualified to vote at its meetings.

Terms of office.

§ 25. From one annual meeting to the next is a year, within the meaning of the following provisions: The term of office of a trustee of a neighborhood, and a sole trustee of a district is one year. The full term of a joint trustee is three years, but a joint trustee may be elected for one or two years as herein provided. The term of office of all other district and neighborhood officers is one year. Every district and neighborhood officer shall hold his office unless removed, during his term of office, and until his successor shall be elected or appointed.

Officers of new districts.

† § 26. The terms of all officers elected at the first meeting of a newly erected neighborhood or district, except of a union free school district, shall expire on the *fourth* Tuesday of August, next thereafter.

School trustees, number, how fixed and elected.

‡ § 27. On the *fourth* Tuesday of August next after the erection of a district, at its first annual meeting, the electors shall determine by resolution, whether the district shall have one or three trustees, and if they resolve to have three trustees, shall elect the three for one, two and three years, respectively, and shall designate by their votes, for which term each is elected; thereafter in such district, one trustee shall be elected at each annual meeting

Annual elections.

---

* See also chap. 9. Laws of 1880, on page 150, *post*, entitled "An act to declare women eligible to serve as school trustees."
† As amended by sec. 4, chap. 413, Laws of 1883, and by sec. 4 of chap. 245 Laws of 1889, and by sec. 7, chap. 500, Laws of 1893.
‡ As amended by chap. 173, Laws of 1878, and by sec. 5, chap. 413, Laws of 1883, and by sec. 5 of chap. 245, Laws of 1889, and by sec. 8, chap. 500, Laws of 1893.

OF THE QUALIFICATIONS, ETC., OF SCHOOL OFFICERS. 45

to fill the office of the outgoing trustee. The electors of any district having three trustees, shall have power to decide by resolution, at any annual meeting, whether the district shall have a sole trustee or three trustees, and if they resolve to have a sole trustee, the trustee or trustees in office shall continue in office until their term or terms of office shall expire, and no election of a trustee shall be had in the district until the offices of such trustee or trustees shall become vacant by the expiration of their terms of office or otherwise, and thereafter but one trustee shall be elected for said district, until the electors of a district having decided to have but one trustee shall determine at an annual meeting, by a two-thirds vote of the legal voters present thereat, to have three trustees; in which case they shall, upon the adoption of such resolution, proceed to elect three trustees or such number as may be necessary to form a board of three trustees, in the same manner as provided in this section for the election of three trustees at the first annual meeting after the erection of a district; and thereafter in such district, one trustee shall be elected for three years, at each annual meeting, to fill the office of the outgoing trustee. *[TITLE 7. Number, how reduced. Number, how increased.]*

* § 28. It shall be the duty of the district clerk, and of the neighborhood clerk, or of any person who shall act as clerk at any district or neighborhood meeting, when any officer shall be elected, forthwith to give the person elected notice thereof in writing; and such person shall be deemed to have accepted the office, unless, within five days after the service of such notice, he shall file his written refusal of it with the clerk. The presence of any such person at the meeting which elects him to office, shall be deemed a sufficient notice to him of his election. *[Clerk to notify persons elected to office. Acceptance and refusal.]*

§ 29. The collector vacates his office by not executing a bond to the trustees, as hereinafter required, and the trustees may supply the vacancy. *[Collector vacates his office by not executing bond.]*

† § 30. In case the office of a trustee shall be vacated by his death, refusal to serve, incapacity, removal from the district or neighborhood, or by his being removed from the office, or in any other manner, and the vacancy be not supplied by a district or neighborhood meeting within one month thereafter, the school commissioner of the commissioner district, within which the school-house or principal school-house of the district is, or within which *[Vacancy in office of trustee, how filled.]*

---

* As amended by sec. 11, chap 406, Laws of 1867.
† As amended by sec. 7 of chap. 331, Laws of 1888.

TITLE 7.

Neglect of duty or refusal to serve vacates office.

Trustees may fill vacancies in other offices.

Appointment to be filed with district clerk.

Penalty for refusal to serve or neglect of duty.

School commissioner may accept resignation.

It may be made to a district meeting.

Duty of neighborhood clerk

the neighborhood or any part thereof is, may, by a writing under his hand, appoint a competent person to fill it.

§ 31. A trustee who publicly declares that he will not accept or serve in the office of trustee, or who refuses or neglects to attend three successive meetings of the board, of which he is duly notified, without rendering a good and valid excuse therefor to the other trustees, or trustee, where there are but two, vacates his office by refusal to serve.

§ 32. Any vacancy in the office of district clerk, collector, or librarian, may be supplied by appointment under the hands of the trustees of the district, or a majority of them, and the appointees shall hold their respective offices until the next annual meeting of the district, and until others are elected and take their places.

*§ 33. Every appointment to fill a vacancy shall be forthwith filed, by the commissioner or trustees making it, in the office of the district clerk, who shall immediately give notice of the appointment to the person appointed.

§ 34. Every person chosen or appointed to a school district office, who, being duly qualified to fill the same, shall refuse to serve therein, shall forfeit five dollars; and every person so chosen or appointed, who, not having refused to accept the office, shall willfully neglect or refuse to perform any duty thereof, shall by such neglect or refusal vacate his office and shall forfeit the sum of ten dollars. These penalties are for the benefit of common schools of the town.

† § 35. But the commissioner of the district wherein any such person resides may accept his written resignation of the office, and the filing of such resignation and acceptance in the office of the district clerk shall be a bar to the recovery of either penalty in the last preceding section mentioned; or such resignation may be made to and accepted by a district meeting.

FOURTH ARTICLE.

Of the duties of the neighborhood clerk, and of the district clerk and librarian.

§ 36. The neighborhood clerk shall keep a record of the proceedings of his neighborhood, and of the reports of the trustee, and deliver the same to his successor. In case such neighborhood shall be annexed to a district within the state, its records shall be filed in the office of the clerk of such district.

---

* As amended by sec. 8 of chap. 331, Laws of 1888.
† As amended by sec. 9, chap. 331, Laws of 1899.

DUTIES OF CLERKS AND LIBRARIAN.

§ 37. It shall be the duty of the clerk of each school district: *(Clerk of school district, his duties.)*

1. To record the proceedings of his district in a book to be provided for that purpose by the district, and to enter therein true copies of all reports made by the trustees to the school commissioner. *(To record proceedings and enter reports in a record book.)*

2. To give notice, in the manner prescribed by the sixth section of this title, or by the inhabitants, pursuant to such section, of the time and place of holding special district meetings called by the trustees. *(To give notice of meetings.)*

3. To affix a notice in writing of the time and place of any adjourned meeting, when the meeting shall have been adjourned for a longer time than one month, in at least four of the most public places of such district, at least five days before the time appointed for such adjourned meeting. *(To affix notice of adjourned meeting.)*

4. To give the like notice of every annual district meeting.

*5. To give notice immediately to every person elected or appointed to office of his election or appointment; and also to report to the town clerk of the town in which the school-house of his district is situated, the names and post-office address of such officers, under a penalty of five dollars for neglect in each instance. *(To notify persons elected and report the names and post-office addresses of such officers to town clerk.)*

6. To notify the trustees of every resignation duly accepted by the supervisor. *(Notice of resignations.)*

7. To keep and preserve all records, books and papers belonging to his office and to deliver the same to his successor. For a refusal or a neglect so to do, he shall forfeit fifty dollars for the benefit of the district, to be recovered by the trustees. *(To keep all records, and penalty for neglect.)*

8. In case his district shall be dissolved, to obey the order of the commissioner or commissioners as to depositing the books, papers and records of his office in the town clerk's office.

9. To attend all meetings of the board of trustees when notified, and keep a record of their proceedings in a book provided for that purpose. *(To attend all meetings of trustees.)*

10. To call special meetings of the inhabitants whenever all the trustees of the district shall have vacated their office. *(To call special meetings.)*

§ 38. The librarian, subject to the provisions of this act, shall have the charge and supervision of the district library. *(Librarian.)*

---

* As amended by sec. 10, chap. 647, Laws of 1865.

CONSOLIDATED SCHOOL ACT OF 1864.

TITLE 7.

FIFTH ARTICLE.

Of the pupils and teachers.

Schools free to pupils over five and under twenty-one years.

* § 39. Common schools in the several school districts of this state shall be free to all persons over five and under twenty-one years of age residing in the district as hereinafter provided; but non-residents of a district, if otherwise competent, may be admitted into the school of a district, with the written consent of the trustees, or of a majority of them, upon such terms as the trustees shall prescribe; provided that if such non-resident pupils, their parents or guardians shall be liable to be taxed for the support of said schools in the district, on account of owning property therein, the amount of any such tax paid by a non-resident pupil, his parent or guardian, during the current school year, shall be deducted from the charge for tuition. † ‡ ||

Non-residents may be admitted.

Tuition of non-resident pupils.

No Indian pupils admitted.

§ 40. If a school district include a portion of an Indian reservation, whereon a school for Indian children has been established by the superintendent of public instruction, and is taught, the school of the district is not free to Indian children resident in the district or on the reservation, nor shall they be admitted to such school except by the permission of the superintendent.

Qualified teachers, what constitutes.

** § 41. No teacher is a qualified one, within the meaning of this act, unless he possesses an unannulled diploma granted to him by the state normal school, or an unrevoked and unannulled certificate of qualification given to him by the superintendent of public instruction, or an unexpired certificate of qualification given to him by the school commissioner within whose district he is employed or by the school officer of the city or village in which he is employed, authorized by special act to grant such certificate. After August twentieth, eighteen hundred and eighty-five, no person shall be deemed to be qualified who is under the age of sixteen years.††

Unqualified teachers cannot be paid by public money or district tax.

‡‡ § 42. No part of the school moneys apportioned to a district can be applied or permitted to be applied to the payment of the wages of an unqualified teacher nor can

---

* As amended by sec. 3, chap. 528, Laws of 1881.
† NOTE.— Compulsory education act on page 95, *post*.
‡ NOTE.— Vaccination of children. See chap. 661, Laws of 1893, on page 139, *post*.
|| NOTE.— See chap. 413, Laws of 1884, page 134, *post*.
** As amended by sec. 7, chap. 340, Laws of 1885.
†† NOTE.— Examination in physiology and hygiene required by chap. 30, Laws of 1884, on page 150, *post*.
‡‡ As amended by sec. 12, chap. 406, Laws of 1867.
NOTE.— When children may be taught in an adjoining district. See chap. 219, Laws of 1877, on page 133, *post*.

his wages, or any part of them, be collected by a district tax.

§ 43. Any trustee who applies, or directs, or consents to the application of any such money to the payment of an unqualified teacher's wages, thereby commits a misdemeanor; and any fine imposed upon him therefor shall be for the benefit of the common schools of the county. Their payment to unqualified teachers a misdemeanor.

§ 44. Teachers shall keep, prepare and enter in the books provided for that purpose, the school lists and accounts of attendance hereinafter mentioned, and shall be responsible for their safe-keeping and delivery to the clerk of the district at the close of their engagements or terms. Teachers to keep lists of attendance.

Sixth Article.

Of the trustees, their powers and duties; and of school taxes and annual reports.

§ 45. All property which is now vested in, or shall hereafter be transferred to the trustee or trustees of a district, for the use of schools in the district, shall be held by him or them as a corporation. Trustees hold district property as a corporation.

§ 46. A sole trustee of the district shall have all the powers, and be subject to all the duties, liabilities and penalties conferred and imposed by law upon or against any trustee or trustees, or the majority of the trustees, of a district. A sole trustee has the same power as a board.

§ 47. The trustees of a district compose a board, and when two only meet to deliberate upon a matter, and the third, if notified, does not attend, or the three meet and deliberate thereon, the conclusion of two upon the matter, and their order, act or proceeding in relation thereto, shall be as valid as though it were the conclusion, order, act or proceeding of the three; and a recital of the two in their minute of the conclusion, act or proceeding, or in their order, act or proceeding of the fact of such notice, or of such meeting and deliberation, shall be conclusive evidence thereof. A meeting of the board may be ordered by any member thereof, by giving not less than twenty-four hours' notice of the same. Trustees must meet for official action. Any member of the board may call a meeting.

§ 48. While there is one vacancy in the office of trustee, the two trustees have all the powers and are subject to all the duties and liabilities of the three. And while there are two such vacancies, the trustee in office shall have all the powers and be subject to all the duties and liabilities of the three, as though he were a sole trustee. When there are vacancies in the board the remaining trustee or trustees may act.

CONSOLIDATED SCHOOL ACT OF 1864.

TITLE 7.

Powers and duties of trustees.

*§ 49. It shall be the duty of the trustees of every school district, and they shall have power:

To call special meetings.
1. To call special meetings of the inhabitants of such districts whenever they shall deem it necessary and proper.

To give notice in certain cases.
2. To give notice of special, annual and adjourned meetings in the manner prescribed in the sixth section of this title, if there be no clerk of the district, or he be absent or incapable of acting, or shall refuse to act.

To make out tax lists.
3. To make out a tax list of every district tax voted by any such meeting, or authorized by law, containing the names of all the taxable inhabitants residing in the district at the time of making out the list, and the amount of tax payable by each inhabitant, set opposite to his name.

To issue warrant for collection.
4. To annex to such tax list a warrant, directed to the collector of the district, for the collection of the sums in such list mentioned.

To purchase or lease sites, etc.
† 5. To purchase or lease a site for the district school-house or school-houses, as designated by a meeting of the district, and to build, hire or purchase such school-house as may be so designated, and to keep in repair and furnish such school-house with necessary fuel and appendages and to pay the expense thereof by tax, but such expense shall not exceed fifty dollars in any one year, unless authorized by the district or by law.‡

To have custody of the school-house.
6. To have the custody and safe-keeping of the district school-house or houses, their sites and appurtenances.

To insure school-house, etc.
7. When thereto authorized by a meeting of the district to insure the school-house or school-houses, and their furniture, and the school apparatus, in some company created by or under the laws of this state, and to comply with the conditions of the policy, and raise the premiums by a district tax.

To insure library.
8. To insure the district library in such a company in a sum fixed by a district meeting, and to raise the premium by a district tax, and comply with the conditions of the policy.

To contract with and employ teachers.
‖ 9. To contract with and employ all teachers in the district school or schools, but no person who is within two degrees of relationship by blood or marriage to any such trustee shall be so employed, except with the approval of two-thirds of the voters of such district present and voting upon the question at an annual or special meeting of the district; nor shall any sole trustee of a district make any contract for the employment of a teacher in and for said

---

* As amended by sec. 13, chap. 406, Laws of 1867.
† As amended by sec. 13, chap. 406, Laws of 1867.
‡ Plans for school buildings provided. See chap. 675, Laws of 1867, on page 132, *post*.
‖ As amended by section 9, chapter 647, Laws of 1865, and by chapter 264, Laws of 1879 and by section 2 of chapter 328, Laws of 1889, and by section 1, chapter 73, Laws, of 1890.

OF THE TRUSTEES, THEIR POWERS AND DUTIES. 51

school district beyond the close of the school term commencing next preceding the expiration of his term of office, and continuing not longer than sixteen weeks, except with the approval of a majority of the voters of such district present and voting upon the question at any annual or special meeting of the district; nor shall the trustees of any school district, having three or more trustees, make any contract for the employment of a teacher or teachers for more than one year in advance. Nor shall any trustee or trustees, employ any teacher for a shorter time than ten weeks unless for the purpose of filling out an unexpired term of school; nor shall any teacher be dismissed in the course of a term of employment, except for reasons which, if appealed to the superintendent of public instruction, shall be held to be sufficient cause for such dismissal. Any failure on the part of a teacher to complete an agreement to teach a term of school without good reason therefor, shall be deemed sufficient ground for the revocation of the teacher's certificate. Any person employed in disregard of the foregoing provisions shall have no claim for wages against the district, but may enforce the specific contract made against the trustee or trustees consenting to such employment as individuals. *

† 10. To pay, towards the wages of such teachers as are qualified, the public moneys apportioned to the district and legally applicable thereto, by giving them orders therefor on the supervisor, or on the collector of such district when duly qualified to receive and disburse the same, and to collect, as herein provided, the residue of such wages by direct tax. But no trustee shall issue any order or draw a draft upon a supervisor or collector for any money unless there shall be at the time a sufficient amount of money in the hands of such supervisor or collector belonging to the district, to meet such order or draft, and a violation of this provision by any trustee shall be a misdemeanor and punishable as such. If, at the time of the employment of a qualified teacher for a term of school, there shall be no public moneys in the hands of the district collector applicable to the payment of teachers' wages, or if there shall not be a sufficient amount in the hands of both

---
* NOTE. — Written contracts required. Chap. 335, Laws of 1887, on page 134, post.
† As amended by section 10 of chapter 331, Laws of 1888, and by section 3 of chapter 328, Laws of 1889, and by sec. 2, chap. 175, Laws of 1890.
‡ NOTE.—See chap. 692, Laws of 1893, to take effect Oct. 1, 1893, amending Penal Code.
§ 485a. School district trustee not to draw draft on supervisor in certain cases.— A school district trustee who issues an order or draws a draft on a supervisor or collector for any money, unless there is at the time sufficient money in the hands of such supervisor or collector belonging to the district to meet such order or draft, is guilty of a misdemeanor.

52   CONSOLIDATED SCHOOL ACT OF 1864.

TITLE 7.

officers to enable the trustee or trustees to pay the teachers' wages as they fall due, and the district meeting has failed or neglected to authorize a tax to pay the same, the trustee or trustees of such school district are hereby authorized and empowered, and it shall be their duty, to collect by district tax an amount sufficient to pay the wages of such teacher for such term, but not to exceed four months in advance. *

To divide the public money into equal parts for each term.

† 11. To divide such public moneys apportioned to the district, whenever authorized by a vote of their district into two or more portions for each year; to assign and apply one of such portions to each term during which a school shall be kept in such district, for the payment of teachers' wages during such term; and to collect the residue of such wages not paid by the proportion of public money allotted for that purpose, by district tax as herein provided.

To pay library money for teachers' wages when less than $3.

12. If the library money apportioned to the district be less than three dollars, to apply it to the payment of teachers' wages.

Drawing of moneys.

‡ 13. To draw upon the supervisor or the collector when duly qualified, to receive and disburse the same, for the school and library moneys, in the manner and form prescribed by subdivisions one and two of section six of title four of this act.

Balance of wages, collection of, by tax.

Orders on collector therefor.

When forbidden, etc.

|| 14. After having paid toward the wages of such teachers as are qualified the public moneys of the district legally applicable thereto, by giving them orders on the supervisor or collector therefor, to collect the residue of such wages by a district tax, or, if the same shall have been already collected, to give such teacher an order on the district collector for the balance of his or her wages still remaining unpaid. But it shall be a misdemeanor, and punishable as such, for a trustee to give an order upon the collector unless there shall be in the hands of the collector at the time sufficient money belonging to the district to meet the same.

Moneys trustees can expend without vote of district meeting.

¶ § 50. The trustees may expend in necessary and proper repairs of each school-house under their charge a sum not exceeding twenty dollars in any one year; and they may

---
* NOTE.—Teachers to be paid as often as once each month. See chap. 335, Laws of 1887, on page 134, post.
† As amended by sec. 13, chap. 406, Laws of 1867.
‡ As amended by sec. 3, chap. 175, Laws of 1890.
| As amended by sec. 13, chap. 406, Laws of 1867, and by sec. 11 of chap. 331, Laws of 1888, and by sec. 4, chap. 175, Laws of 1890.
¶ As amended by sec. 14, chap. 406, Laws of 1867, and by sec. 19, chap. 567, Laws of 1875; by sec. 1, chap. 179, Laws of 1894, and sec. 1, chap. 292, Laws of 1896, and by sec. 9, chap. 500, Laws of 1893.

OF THE TRUSTEES, THEIR POWERS AND DUTIES. 53

also expend a sum, not exceeding fifty dollars, in the erection of necessary outbuildings, when the district is wholly unprovided with such buildings, upon the direction of the school commissioner in whose district such school-house is situated, or of the state superintendent of public instruction. They may also make any repairs, and abate any nuisances, pursuant to the direction of the school commissioner as hereinbefore provided, and provide fuel, pails, brooms and other implements necessary to keep the school-house or houses clean and make them reasonably comfortable for use, and not provided for by a vote of the district; and may also provide for building fires and cleaning the school-room by arrangement with the teacher or otherwise. They shall provide the bound blank-books for the entering of their accounts and the keeping of the school lists, the records of the district and the proceedings of district and trustee meetings, and they may expend in the purchase of dictionary, maps, globes or other school apparatus, a sum not exceeding fifteen dollars in any one year. Whenever it shall be necessary for the due accommodation of the children of the district, *by reason of any considerable number of said children residing in portions of said districts remote from the school-house in said district, thereby rendering it difficult for them in inclement weather and in winter to attend school at such school-house, or by reason of the room or rooms in said school-house being over-crowded, or for any other sufficient reason the due accommodation of said children cannot be made in said school-house, they may establish temporary or branch school or schools in such place or places in said district as shall best accommodate such children, and hire any room or rooms for the keeping of said temporary or branch school or schools, and fit up and furnish said room or rooms in a suitable manner for conducting such school or schools therein.* Any expenditure made or liability incurred in pursuance of this section shall be a charge upon the district.*

TITLE 7.
Repairs.
Outbuildings.
Nuisances.
Fuel, etc.
Cleaning school-room.
Books for their accounts.
Dictionary, apparatus, etc.
Temporary and branch schools and school-rooms.

§ 51. When trustees are required or authorized by law, or by a vote of their district, to incur any expense for such district, and when any expenses incurred by them are made, by express provision of law, a charge upon such district, they may raise the amount thereof by tax in the same manner as if the definite sum to be raised had been voted by a district meeting.

May raise any legal sum by tax.

---

*NOTE.— To maintain separate water-closets. Chap. 538, Laws of 1887, on age 135, *post*.

TITLE 7.

School-house by consent of trustee may be used for instruction in any branch of learning or music.

§ 52. The trustees, or any one of them, if not forbidden by another, may freely permit the school-house, when not in use for the district school, to be used by persons assembling therein for the purpose of giving and receiving instruction in any branch of education or learning, or in the science or practice of music.

Trustees to procure account books, etc.

* § 53. They shall procure two bound blank books for the district, and, when necessary, others in their place. In one of them, at or before each annual district meeting, they shall enter at large and sign a statement of all movable property belonging to the district, and their accounts of all moneys received or drawn for or paid by them, and they shall deliver this book to their successors. In the other, the teachers shall enter the names of the pupils attending school, their ages, the names of the persons who send them, and the number of days each pupil attends; and, also, the facts and the dates of each inspection of the school by the school commissioner or other official visitor, and any other facts, and in such form as the superintendent of public instruction shall require;

Teacher must keep lists and verify record, and trustees shall not pay teacher until record is verified.

and each teacher shall, by his oath or affirmation, verify his entries in such book, and the entries shall constitute the school lists from which the average daily attendance shall be determined; and such oath or affirmation may be taken by the district clerk, but without charge. Until the teacher shall have so made and verified such entries, the trustees shall not draw on the supervisor for any portion of his wages.

To notify the treasurer and superintendent of money withheld by supervisor or collector.

† § 54. If any portion of the moneys apportioned to the district shall not be paid by the supervisor or the collector, upon the due requirement of the trustees, they shall forthwith notify the treasurer of the county, and the superintendent of public instruction, of the fact.

To render an account of all moneys received and paid, etc.

§ 55. The trustees shall, once in each year, render to the district, at its annual district meeting, a just, full and true account in writing, under their hands, of all moneys received by them respectively for the use of the district, and of the manner in which the same shall have been expended, and showing to which of them an unexpended balance, or any part thereof, is chargeable; and of all drafts or orders made by them upon the supervisor, collector, or other custodian of moneys of the district; and a full statement of all suits and proceedings brought by

---

* As amended by sec. 15, chap. 406, Laws of 1867.
† As amended by sec. 5, chap. 175, Laws of 1890.

OF THE TRUSTEES, THEIR POWERS AND DUTIES.

or against them, and of every special matter touching the condition of the district.

§ 56. An outgoing trustee shall forthwith pay, to his successor or any other trustee of the district in office, any such unexpended balance, or part of such balance, remaining in his hands. *(Out-going trustee to pay any balance to his successor.)*

* § 57. (Provided a penalty for neglect or refusal to render account. Repealed by section 1, subdivision 39 of chapter 593, Laws of 1886.) *(Penalty for refusal or neglect to render account.)*

§ 58. By a willful neglect or refusal to render such account, a trustee also forfeits any unexpired term of his office, and becomes liable to the trustees for any district moneys in his hands. *(Forfeits his office, etc.)*

§ 59. The trustees in office shall sue for and recover any district moneys in the hands of any former trustee, or of his personal representatives, and apply them to the use of the district. *(Trustee to sue any former trustee.)*

† § 60. The trustees of each school district shall, between the twenty-fifth day of July and the first Tuesday of August, in *the year eighteen hundred and ninety-three, make to the school commissioner a report in writing, dated on the twenty-sixth day of July; and on the first day of August in each year thereafter, make to the school commissioner a report in writing for the period ending with the date of such report; such report to cover the month of August in the preceding year.* In every case the trustee or trustees shall sign and certify to said report and deliver it to the clerk of the town in which the schoolhouse of the district is situated; and every such report shall certify: ‡ *(To report to commissioner between the twenty-fifth day of July and the first day of August, 1893, and on first day of August annually thereafter.)*

1. The whole time any school has been kept in their district during the year ending on the day previous to the date of such report, and distinguishing what portion of the time such school has been kept by qualified teachers, and the whole number of days, including holidays, in which the school was taught by qualified teachers. *(Items of annual report.)*

¶ 2. The amount of their drafts upon the supervisor or collector, for the payment of teachers' wages during such year, and the amount of their drafts upon him for the purchase of books and school apparatus during such year, and the manner in which such moneys have been expended. *(Amount of drafts upon supervisor or collector.)*

---
* Sections 470 and 471 of Penal Code applicable to such violations of law. See page 25, *ante.*
† As amended by sec. 16, chap. 406, Laws of 1867, and by chap. 413, Laws of 1883, and sec. 1, chap. 49, Laws of 1884, and by sec. 6 of chap. 245, Laws of 1889, and by sec. 10, chap. 500, Laws of 1893.
‡ NOTE.— Trustees to report annually number of children of school age who are vaccinated. See chap. 438, Laws of 1860, page 136, *post.*
¶ As amended by sec. 6, chap. 175, Laws of 1890.

TITLE 7.

Attendance of children.

*3. The number of children taught in the district school or schools during such year by qualified teachers, and the sum of the days' attendance of all such children upon the school.

Number of children residing in the district on the thirtieth of June previous to making the report.

†4. The number of children residing in the district on the thirtieth day of June previous to the making of such report, and the names of the parents or other persons with whom such children did respectively reside, and the number of children residing with each.

Amount paid for teachers' wages, and for other expenses.

5. The amount of money paid for teachers' wages, in addition to the public money paid therefor, the amount of taxes levied in said district for purchasing school-house sites, for building, hiring, purchasing, repairing and insuring school-houses, for fuel, for district libraries, or for any other purpose allowed by law, and such other information in relation to the schools and the district as the superintendent of public instruction may, from time to time, require.

Children included in trustees' report.

‡§ 61. The annual reports of trustees of school districts, of children residing in their district, shall include all over five and under twenty one years of age, who shall have been, on the thirtieth day of June last preceding the date of such report, actually in the district, comprising a part of the family of their parents or guardians or employers, if such parents, guardians or employers resided at the time in such district, although such residence was temporary; but such report shall not include children belonging to the family of any person who shall be an inhabitant of any other district in this state, in which such children may by law be included in the report of its trustees; nor any children who are supported at a county poor-house or an orphan asylum; nor any Indian children residing on reservations where schools provided by law for their education are taught.

Joint district to report to each commissioner.

§ 62. Where a school district lies in two or more counties, its trustees shall make such an annual report for each part of it lying in a different county, and file each in the office of the clerk of the town in which the part of the district to which it especially relates lies; and such report shall be in the form and contain all such special matters as the superintendent of public instruction shall from time to time prescribe.

---

* As amended by sec. 11, chap. 647, Laws of 1865.
† As amended by sec. 7, chap. 413, Laws of 1883.
‡ As amended by sec. 8, chap. 413, Laws of 1883.

OF THE ASSESSMENT OF DISTRICT TAXES.

* § 63. The trustee of every separate neighborhood shall every year, within the time aforesaid, in like manner, make his annual report to the school commissioner, and file it in the office of the clerk of the town in which the neighborhood is a part. Such report shall specify the whole amount of public moneys received during the year, and from what public officer, and the manner in which it was expended; the whole number of such children as can be included in the district trustees' report residing in the neighborhood on the thirtieth day of June previous to the making of the report; and any other matters which the superintendent of public instruction may require. *[TITLE 7. Separate neighborhood report of its trustees.]*

§ 64. (Provided a penalty for false reports by trustees. Repealed by sec. 1, sub. 39 of chap. 593, Laws of 1886.) Sections 470 and 471 of Penal Code provide a penalty for such an offense. *[Repealed.]*

SEVENTH ARTICLE.

Of the assessment of district taxes, and the collection of such taxes; and of the collector, his powers, duties and liability.

§ 65. Within thirty days after a tax shall have been voted by a district meeting, the trustees shall assess it, and make out the tax list therefor, and annex thereto their warrant for its collection. But they may at the same time assess two or more taxes so voted, and any tax or taxes they are authorized to raise without such vote, and make out one tax list and one warrant for the collection of the whole. They shall also prefix to their tax list a heading showing for what purpose the different items of the tax is levied. *[Assessment of taxes by trustees. Two or more taxes may be included under one warrant.]*

† § 66. School district taxes shall be apportioned by the trustees upon all real estate within the boundaries of the district which shall not be by law exempt from taxation, except as hereinafter provided, and such property shall be assessed to the person or persons, or corporation owning or possessing the same at the time such tax list shall be made out, but land lying in one body and occupied by the same person, either as owner or agent for the same principal, or as tenant under the same landlord, if assessed as one lot on the last assessment-roll of the town after *[Tax lists how made out. Taxation of land lying in one body.]*

---

* As amended by sec. 9, chap. 413, Laws of 1883.
† As amended by sec. 20, chap. 567, Laws of 1875, and by sec. 4 of chap. 328, Laws of 1889. See law in relation to the taxation of railroad companies on pages 146 and 147, *post;* also, law in relation to taxation of bank shares, in the general banking act, tit. 12 of chap. 409, Laws of 1882, on page 140, *post,* and taxation of forest preserve, chap. 280, Laws of 1886, on page 145. *post.*

TITLE 7.

Non-resident lands.

Personal estate.

Bank stock.

Valuation, how ascertained.

Of reduction of valuation.

Equalization of valuation.

revision by the assessors, shall, though situated partly in two or more school districts, be taxable in that one of them in which such occupant resides. This rule shall not apply to land owned by non-residents of the district, and which shall not be occupied by an agent, servant or tenant residing in the district. Such unoccupied real estate shall be assessed as non-resident, and a description thereof shall be entered in the tax list. The trustees shall also apportion the district taxes upon all persons residing in the district, and upon all corporations liable to taxation therein, for the personal estate owned by them and liable to taxation. They shall also apportion the same upon non-resident stockholders in banks or banking associations situated in their districts for the amount of stock owned by them therein, and upon individual bankers doing business in their district in accordance with the provisions of chapter * seven hundred and sixty-one of the laws of one thousand eight hundred and sixty-six.

§ 67. The valuations of taxable property shall be ascertained, so far as possible, from the last assessment-roll of the town, after revision by the assessors; and no person shall be entitled to any reduction in the valuation of such property, as so ascertained, unless he shall give notice of his claim to such reduction to the trustees of the district before the tax list shall be made out.

§ 68. Where such reduction shall be duly claimed and where the valuation of taxable property cannot be ascertained from the last assessment-roll of the town, the trustees shall ascertain the true value of the property to be taxed from the best evidence in their power, giving notice to the persons interested, and proceeding in the same manner as the town assessors are required by law to proceed in the valuation of taxable property.

† § 69. When a district embraces parts of more than one town, it shall be the duty of the supervisors of such towns so in part embraced, upon receiving a written notice from the trustee or trustees of such district, or from three or more persons liable to pay taxes upon real estate therein, to meet at a time and place to be named in such notice, which time shall not be less than five or more than ten days from the service thereof, and a place within the bounds of the towns so in part embraced, and proceed to inquire and determine whether the valuation of real prop-

---

* NOTE.—Chap. 761, Laws of 1866, was repealed by part 27 of sec. 1, chap. 402, Laws of 1882, and its provisions incorporated in the title on taxation in the general banking act, chap. 409. Laws of 1882. See page 140, post.

† As amended by sec. 21, chap. 567, Laws of 1875.

OF THE ASSESSMENT OF DISTRICT TAXES. 59

erty upon the several assessment-rolls of said towns are substantially just as compared with each other, so far as said districts are concerned, and if ascertained not to be so, they shall determine the relative proportion of taxes that ought to be assessed upon the real property of the parts of such district lying in different towns, and the trustees of such district shall thereupon assess the proportion of any tax·thereafter to be raised, according to the determination of such supervisors, until new assessment-rolls of the town shall be perfected and filed, using the assessment-rolls of the several towns to distribute the said proportion among the persons liable to be assessed for the same. In cases when such supervisors shall be unable to agree, they shall summon a supervisor from some adjoining town, who shall unite in such inquiring, and the finding of a majority shall be the determination of such meeting.

§ 70. Any person working land under a contract for a share of the produce of such land, shall be deemed the possessor, so far as to render him liable to taxation therefor in the district where such land is situate. *Persons working land on shares liable.*

§ 71. Every person owning or holding any real property within any school district, who shall improve and occupy the same by his agent or servant, shall, in respect to the liability of such property to taxation, be considered a taxable inhabitant of such district, in the same manner as if he actually resided therein. *Taxable inhabitants.*

§ 72. Where any district tax, for the purpose of purchasing a site for a school-house, or for purchasing or building, keeping in repair, or furnishing such school-house with necessary fuel and appendages, shall be lawfully assessed, and paid by any person on account of any real property whereof he is only tenant at will, or for three years, or for a less period of time, such tenant may charge the owner of such real estate with the amount of the tax so paid by him, unless some agreement to the contrary shall have been made by such tenant. *Of tenant at will, etc., liability of the owner.*

§ 73. Every taxable inhabitant of a district who shall have been, within four years, set off from any other district without his consent, and shall, within that period, have actually paid in such other district, under a lawful assessment therein, a district tax for building a school-house, shall be exempted by the trustees·of the district where he shall reside from the payment of any tax for building a school-house therein. *When exempt from tax for school-house.*

§ 74. When any real estate within a district so liable to taxation shall not be occupied and improved by the owner, *Taxes on non-resident lands.*

CONSOLIDATED SCHOOL ACT OF 1864.

TITLE 7.

his servant or agent, and shall not be possessed by any tenant, the trustees of any district, at the time of making out any tax list by which any tax shall be imposed thereon, shall make and insert in such tax list a statement and description of every such lot, piece or parcel of land so owned by non-residents therein, in the same manner as required by law from town assessors in making out the assessment-roll of their towns; and if any such lot is known to belong to an incorporated company liable to taxation in such district, the name of such company shall be specified, and the value of such lot or piece of land shall be set down opposite to such description, which value shall be the same that was affixed to such lot or piece of land in the last assessment-roll of the town; and if the same was not separately valued in such roll, then it shall be valued in proportion to the valuation which was affixed in the said assessment-roll to the whole tract of which such lot or piece shall be part.

Incorporated companies, etc.

Collector to return uncollected taxes; method of procedure.

* § 75. If any tax on real estate placed upon the tax list and duly delivered to the collector, or the taxes upon non-resident stockholders in banking associations organized under the laws of congress, shall be unpaid at the time the collector is required by law to return his warrant, he shall deliver to the trustees of the district an account of the taxes remaining due, containing a description of the lands upon which such taxes were unpaid as the same were placed upon the tax list, together with the amount of the tax so assessed, and upon making oath before any justice of the peace or judge of court of record, notary public or any other officer authorized to administer oaths, that the taxes mentioned in any such account remain unpaid, and that, after diligent efforts, he has been unable to collect the same, he shall be credited by said trustees with the amount thereof.

Trustees shall send it to treasurer of county.

§ 76. Upon receiving any such account from the collector, the trustees shall compare it with the original tax list, and, if they find it to be a true transcript, they shall add to such account their certificate, to the effect that they have compared it with the original tax list and found it to be correct, and shall immediately transmit the account, affidavit and certificate to the treasurer of the county.

Treasurer shall pay the taxes, and lay the account before the board of supervisors who shall levy tax, etc.

† § 77. Out of any moneys in the county treasury, raised

* As amended by sec. 22, chap. 567, Laws of 1875, and by sec. 1, chap. 250, Laws of 1883, and sec. 1, chap. 74, Laws of 1890.
† As amended by sec. 1, chap. 455, Laws of 1880, and by sec. 1, chap. 333, Laws of 1887.

OF THE ASSESSMENT OF DISTRICT TAXES.

TITLE 7.

for contingent expenses, the treasurer shall pay to the collector the amount of the taxes so returned as unpaid, and if there are no moneys in the treasury applicable to such purpose, the board of supervisors, at the time of levying said unpaid taxes, as provided in the next section, shall pay to the collector of the school district the amount thereof by voucher or draft on the county treasurer, in the same manner as other county charges are paid, and the collector shall be again charged therewith by the trustees.

* § 78. Such account, affidavit and certificate shall be laid by the county treasurer before the board of supervisors of the county, who shall cause the amount of such unpaid taxes, with seven per cent of the amount in addition thereto, to be levied upon the lands on which the same were imposed; and if imposed upon the lands of any incorporated company, then upon such company; and when collected the same shall be returned to the county treasurer to reimburse the amount so advanced, with the expenses of collection; and if imposed upon the stock of a non-resident stockholder in a banking association organized under the laws of congress, then the same, with seven per cent of the amount in addition thereto, shall be a lien upon any dividends thereafter declared upon such stock, and, upon notice by the board of supervisors to the president and directors of such bank of such charge upon such stock, the president and directors shall thereafter withhold the amount so stated from any future dividends upon such stock, and shall pay the same to the collector of the town duly authorized to receive the same.

County treasurer to lay the account before the supervisors; their powers and duties thereon.

§ 79. Any person whose lands are included in any such account may pay the tax assessed thereon to the county treasurer, at any time before the board of supervisors shall have directed the same to be levied.

Any person may make payment before said levy.

§ 80. The same proceedings in all respects shall be had for the collection of the amount so directed to be raised by the board of supervisors as are provided by law in relation to the county taxes; and, upon a similar account, as in the case of county taxes of the arrears thereof uncollected, being transmitted by the county treasurer to the comptroller, the same shall be paid on his warrant to the treasurer of the county advancing the same; and the amount so assumed by the state shall be collected for its benefit, in the manner prescribed by law in respect to the arrears of county taxes upon land of non-residents;

Proceedings as for county taxes.

---

* As amended by sec. 23, chap. 567, Laws of 1875, and by sec. 2, chap. 250, Laws of 1883.

CONSOLIDATED SCHOOL ACT OF 1864.

TITLE 7.

or if any part of the amount so assumed consisted of a tax upon any incorporated company, the same proceedings may also be had for the collection thereof as provided by law in respect to the county taxes assessed upon such company.

Warrant, form and effect of.

* § 81. The warrant for the collection of a district tax shall be under the hands of the trustees, or a majority of them, with or without their seals; and it shall have the like force and effect as a warrant issued by a board of supervisors to a collector of taxes in the town; and the collector to whom it may be delivered for collection shall be thereby authorized and required to collect from every person in such tax list named, the sum set opposite to his name, or the amount due from any person or persons specified therein, in the same manner that collectors are authorized to collect town and county charges.

Delivery of the warrant.

† § 82. A warrant for the collection of a tax voted by the district shall not be delivered to the collector until the thirty-first day after the tax was voted. A warrant for the collection of any tax not so voted may be delivered to the collector whenever the same is completed.

Collectors to execute a bond.

‡ § 83. Within such time, not less than ten days, as the trustees shall allow him for the purpose, the collector, before receiving the first warrant for the collection of money, shall execute a bond to the trustees, with one or more sureties, to be approved by a majority of the trustees, in such amount as the district meeting shall have fixed, or if such meeting shall not have fixed the amount, then in such amount as the trustees shall deem reasonable, conditioned for the due and faithful execution of the duties of his office. The trustees, upon receiving said bond, shall, if they approve thereof, indorse their approval thereon, and forthwith deliver the same to the town clerk of the town in which said collector resides, and said clerk shall file the same in his office and enter in a book to be kept by him for that purpose, a memorandum showing the date of said bond, the names of the parties and sureties thereto, the amount of the penalty thereof, and the date and time of filing the same, and said town clerk is authorized to receive as a fee for such filing and memorandum, the sum of twenty-five cents, which sum is

Bond to be filed with town clerk.

Clerk's fees for filing bond.

---

* As amended by sec. 18, chap. 406, Laws of 1867.
† As amended by sec. 19, chap. 406, Laws of 1867.
‡ As amended by sec. 24, chap. 567, Laws of 1875, and by sec. 1, chap. 334, Laws of 1887, and by sec. 7, chap. 175, Laws of 1890.

OF THE ASSESSMENT OF DISTRICT TAXES.

hereby made a charge against the school district interested in said bond; and in case the trustees of any school district, other than those within the limits of any city or incorporated village, shall deem it for the best interests of the district or the public to have the collector of such district disburse to teachers the money apportioned by the state for teachers' wages, they shall so direct, by resolution to be entered upon the minutes of their proceedings, and thereupon the said collector, before receiving any such money for such purpose, shall execute a bond to the trustees, with two or more sureties, in double the amount of the last apportionment, with like conditions of sureties, approval of trustees, and amount and like directions as to filing as are required above for a bond for the collection of taxes, and conditioned also for the due and faithful execution of the duties of his office as such disbursing agent.

*§ 84. The collector, on the receipt of a warrant for the collection of taxes, shall give notice to the taxpayers of the district by publicly posting written or printed, or partly written and partly printed, notices in at least three public places in such district, one of which shall be on the outside of the front door of the school-house, stating that he has received such warrant and will receive all such taxes as may be voluntarily paid to him within two weeks from the time of posting said notice. Such collector shall also give a like notice, either personally or by mail, at least ten days previous to the expiration of the two weeks aforesaid, to the ticket agent at the nearest station of any railroad corporation assessed for taxes upon the tax list delivered to him with the aforesaid warrant, and where the amount of the tax is one dollar or more the collector shall also give a like notice to all non-resident taxpayers on said list whose residence or post-office address may be known to such collector, or which may be ascertained by him upon inquiry of the trustees and clerk of his district, and no school collector shall be entitled to recover from any railroad corporation or non-resident taxpayer more than one per cent fees on the taxes assessed against such corporation or non-resident, unless such notice shall have been given as aforesaid; and in case the whole amount of taxes shall not be so paid in the collector shall forthwith proceed to collect the same. He shall receive for his services, on all sums paid in as aforesaid, one per cent, and upon all sums collected by him, after the expiration

---

* As amended by chap. 33, Laws of 1877, and by sec. 1, chap. 526, Laws of 1890.

TITLE 7.

of the time mentioned, five per cent, except as hereinbefore provided; and in case a levy and sale shall be necessarily made by such collector, he shall be entitled to traveling fees, at the rate of ten cents per mile, to be computed from the school-house in such district. *

Warrant may be executed in any other town, etc.

†§ 85. Any collector to whom any tax list and warrant may be delivered for collection may execute the same in any other district or town in the same county, or in any other county where the district is a joint district and composed of territory from adjoining counties, in the same manner and with the like authority as in the district in which the trustees issuing the said warrant may reside, and for the benefit of which said tax is intended to be collected; and the bail or sureties of any collector, given for the faithful performance of his official duties, are hereby declared and made liable for any moneys received or collected on any such tax list and warrant.

Trustees may sue for unpaid taxes in certain cases.

‡ § 86. If the sum or sums of money, payable by any person named in such tax list * * * shall not be paid by him or collected by such warrant within the time therein limited, it shall and may be lawful for the trustees to renew such warrant in respect to such delinquent person; or in case such person shall not reside within their district at the time of making out a tax list, or shall not reside therein at the expiration of such warrant, or in case the property assessed be real estate belonging in an incorporated company, and no goods or chattels can be found whereon to levy the tax, the trustees may sue for and recover the same in their name of office. ‖

Trustees may correct error in tax list by consent of superintendent.

¶ § 87. Whenever the trustees of any school district shall discover any error in a tax list made out by them, they may, with the approbation and consent of the superintendent of public instruction, after refunding any amount that may have been improperly collected on such tax list, if the same shall be required by him, amend and correct such tax list, as directed by the superintendent, in conformity to law; and whenever more than one renewal of a warrant for the collection of any tax list may become necessary in any district, the trustees may make such further renewal, with the written appobation of the

If more than one renewal must have consent of supervisor.

---

*NOTE. — For the collection of taxes against railroad companies, see chap. 675, Laws of 1881, as amended by sec. 1, chap. 319, Laws of 1882, and by chap. 533, Laws of 1885, on page 147, *post*.
† As amended by sec. 20, chap. 406, Laws of 1867.
‡ As amended by sec. 25, chap. 567, Laws of 1875.
‖ NOTE. — Tax by rate bill abolished. Sec. 28 of chap. 406, Laws of 1867, on page 139, *post*.
¶ As amended by sec. 22, chap. 406, Laws of 1867.

OF SCHOOL DISTRICT LIBRARIES.

supervisor of any town in which a school-house of said district shall be located, to be indorsed upon such warrant.

* § 88. The collector shall keep in his possession all moneys received or collected by him by virtue of any warrant, or received by him from the county treasurer or board of supervisors for taxes returned as unpaid, or moneys apportioned by the state or raised by direct taxation for teachers' wages or library, to be by him paid out upon the order of a majority of the trustees; and he shall report in writing, at the annual meeting, all his collections, receipts and disbursements, and shall report to the supervisor on or before the first Tuesday of March in each year the amounts of school moneys in his hands not paid out on trustees' orders, and shall pay over to his successor in office, when he has duly qualified and given bail, all moneys in his hands belonging to the district.

§ 89. If by the neglect of any collector any moneys shall be lost to any school-district, which might have been collected within the time limited in the warrant delivered to him for their collection, he shall forfeit to such district the amount of the moneys thus lost, and shall account for and pay over the same to the trustees of such district, in the same manner as if they had been collected.

§ 90. For the recovery of all such forfeitures, and of all balances, in the hands of the collector, which he shall have neglected or refused to pay to his successor, the trustees, in their name of office, shall have their remedy upon the official bond of the collector, or any action and any remedy given by law; and they shall apply all such moneys, when recovered, in the same manner as if paid without suit.

† § 91. Within fifteen days after any tax list and warrant shall have been returned by a collector to the trustees of any school district, the trustees shall deliver the same to the town clerk of the town in which the collector resides, and said town clerk shall file the same in his office.

TITLE 7.

Custody of moneys by the collector.

Shall report at annual meeting.

Collector to make up any loss.

Trustees to sue for recovery of money in collector's hands.

Trustee to file tax list and warrant when returned.

---

* As amended by sec. 2, chap. 333, Laws of 1887, and by sec. 8, chap. 175, Laws of 1890.
† As amended by sec. 2, chap. 334, Laws of 1887.
NOTE.— By sec. 11 chap. 573, Laws of 1892, sec. 4, chap. 237, Laws of 1838 is repealed, and sections 1 to 9 of chap. 573, Laws of 1892, are substituted for title 8 of chap. 555, Laws of 1864, entitled "Of school district libraries, and the application of library moneys;" and said title 8 is repeated. All other acts repugnant to or inconsistent with the provisions of chap. 573, Laws of 1892, are, by said chapter, so far as they are so inconsistent, repealed.
Sections 1 to 8, inclusive, are given as constituting title 8.
Sections 9, 10 and 11 of chapter 573, Laws of 1892, are as follows:
§ 9. The sum of fifty-five thousand dollars directed to be distributed to the several cities and school districts of the state by section four of chapter two hundred and thirty-seven of the laws of eighteen hundred and thirty-eight, shall continue to be appropriated and shall be known as school library moneys, and shall be applied to the purchase of books for the formation or extension of common school libraries.—[Continued on next page.

TITLE VIII.

FOR THE ENCOURAGEMENT OF COMMON SCHOOLS AND PUBLIC LIBRARIES.

School library moneys, apportionment and expenditure of.

SECTION 1. So much of the school library money as shall be needed for that purpose shall be apportioned among the several cities and school districts by the state superintendent of public instruction, who may, so far as consistent with law, make, alter or repeal any rules that he may deem proper for regulating the expenditure of the school library money and the administration and care of school libraries established or maintained under authority of this act; provided that no portion of the school library money shall be expended except for books approved by the said superintendent. Said school libraries shall consist of reference books for use in the school room, suitable supplementary reading books for children, or books relating to branches of study being pursued in the school and pedagogic books as aids to teachers. And no city or school district shall share in the apportionment unless it shall raise and use for the same purpose an equal amount from taxation or other local sources, and shall also comply with the requirements of the superintendent as to the care of such libraries and otherwise.

School libraries, what books to constitute.

Requirements for share in apportionment.

Use, etc. of school library.

§ 2. The school library shall be a part of the school equipment and shall be kept in the school building at all times, and shall not be used as a circulating library, except that, so far as the rules fixed by the state superintendent shall allow, teachers and school officers or pupils, with the leave of the librarian, may borrow from said library any book not needed for reference in the school-room, but such persons shall not borrow more than one volume at a time

---

§ 10. For the fiscal year beginning October first, eighteen hundred and ninety-two, but not thereafter, out of said fifty-five thousand dollars school library money, there shall be paid twenty-five thousand dollars for public library money, and said twenty-five thousand dollars shall be paid by the treasurer, on the warrant of the comptroller, according to an apportionment to be made for the benefit of free libraries by the regents in accordance with their rules and authenticated by the university seal; provided that none of this money shall be spent for books except those approved or selected and furnished by the regents; that no locality shall share in the apportionment unless it shall raise for the same purpose not less than an equal amount from taxation or other local sources; that for any part of the apportionment not payable directly to the library trustees the regents shall file with the comptroller proper vouchers showing that it has been spent in accordance with law exclusively for books for free public libraries or for proper expenses incurred for their benefit; and that books paid for by the state shall be subject to return to the regents whenever the library shall neglect or refuse to conform to the ordinances under which it secured them.

§ 11. Repeals.— Section four, chapter two hundred and thirty-seven of the laws of eighteen hundred and thirty-eight is hereby repealed, and sections one to nine of this act are hereby substituted for title eight, of chapter five hundred and fifty-five of the laws of eighteen hundred and sixty-four, which said title eight is hereby repealed; and all other acts repugnant to or inconsistent with the provisions of this act are, so far as they are so inconsistent, hereby repealed.

OF SCHOOL DISTRICT LIBRARIES.   67

and shall not keep the same more than two weeks. The board of education or trustees shall appoint a teacher of the schools under their charge as librarian, who, with the trustees, shall be responsible for the safety and proper care of the books, and shall annually, and whenever required, make such reports concerning the library as the state superintendent may direct. *[TITLE 8. Librarian.]*

§ 3. Rules. — All existing provisions of law and rules established by the superintendent of public instruction for the management of district libraries shall hold good as to the management of school libraries till altered by or in pursuance of law. *[Rules.]*

§ 4. Each city and school district in the state is hereby authorized to raise moneys by tax in the same manner as other school moneys are raised, or to receive moneys by gift or devise, for starting or extending or caring for the school library. *[Tax for school library.]*

§ 5. Any board of education in any city or union free school district, or any duly constituted meeting in any other district, is hereby authorized to give any or all of its books or other library property to any township or other free public library under state supervision, or to aid in establishing such free public library, provided it is free to the people of such city or district. A receipt from the officers of the said free public library, and an approval of the transfer under seal by the regents of the university, shall forever thereafter relieve the said school authorities of further responsibility for the said library and property so transferred. *[Transfer of books, etc., to free public libraries. Release of school authorities.]*

§ 6. Any books or other library property belonging to any district library, and which have not been in direct charge of a librarian duly appointed within one year, may be taken and shall thereafter be owned by any public library under state supervision, which has received from the regents of the university written permission to collect such books or library property, and to administer the same for the benefit of the public; provided that said books or other library property shall be found in the territory for which such public library is maintained, as defined in its charter or in the permission granted by the regents; and further provided that, on written request of the school authorities, any dictionaries, cyclopedias and pedagogic books shall be placed in the school library of the district to which such books originally belong. Any person, association or corporation having possession of books or other property belonging to any school, district or other *[Public libraries may take books, etc., of district libraries.]*

TITLE 9. Delivery of books and property to libraries.

public library, except books regularly borrowed and charged for a period not yet expired, shall deliver the same within one month from the passage of this law to the legally appointed librarian of such library, or of the free public library, duly authorized to take the same as provided in this section, and willful neglect or refusal to comply with this provision shall be a misdemeanor.

Public not to use school library.

§ 7. The public shall not be entitled to use any library, now or hereafter in the custody of the school authorities, but said authorities may appoint three trustees who shall have the powers, duties and responsibilities of trustees of public libraries incorporated by the regents, and there-

Transfer of property for circulating library.

after the school authorities may transfer to the custody of said trustees for the purposes of a circulating library any of their library property as provided in section five.

Withholding of moneys by state superintendent.

§ 8. The state superintendent of public instruction is hereby authorized to withhold its share of public school moneys from any city or district which uses school library moneys for any other purpose than that for which they are provided, or for any willful neglect or disobedience of the law or the rules or orders of said superintendent in the premises.

TITLE IX.

OF UNION FREE SCHOOLS.

Call for special meeting to form district.

SECTION 1. Whenever fifteen persons entitled to vote at any meeting of the inhabitants of any school district in the state, shall sign a call for a meeting, to be held for the purpose of determining whether a union free school shall be established therein, in conformity with the provisions of this title, it shall be the duty of the trustees of such district, within ten days after such call shall have been presented to them, to give public notice that a meeting of the inhabitants of such district, entitled to vote thereat, will be held for such purpose as aforesaid, at the school-house, or other more suitable place, in such district, on a day and at an hour in such notice to be specified, not more than twenty days after the publication of such notice.

When superintendent may give notice.

If the trustees shall refuse to give such notice, or shall neglect to give the same for twenty days, the superintendent of public instruction may authorize and direct any inhabitant of said district to give the same. The

Qualification of voters.

qualifications of the inhabitants, entitled to vote at such meeting as now by law expressed, shall be sufficiently set forth in the notice aforesaid.

OF UNION FREE SCHOOLS.   69

TITLE 9.

* § 2. Whenever such district shall correspond wholly or in part with an incorporated village, in which there shall be published a daily or weekly newspaper, the notice aforesaid shall be given by posting at least five copies thereof, severally, in various conspicuous places in said district, at least twenty days prior to such meeting, and by causing the same to be published once a week for three consecutive weeks before such meeting, in all the newspapers published in said district. In other districts the said notice shall be given by posting the same as aforesaid, and in addition thereto, the trustees of such district shall authorize and require any taxable inhabitant of the same, to notify every other inhabitant (qualified to vote as aforesaid), of such meeting, to be called as aforesaid, who shall give such notification in the manner and subject to the penalty prescribed in the case of the formation of a new school district by title seven of this act. Formation of union free schools in incorporated villages.
In other districts.

§ 3. The reasonable expense of such notices, and of their publication and service, shall be chargeable upon the district, in case a union free school is established by the meeting so convened, to be levied and collected by the trustees, as in case of taxes now levied for school purposes; but in the event that such union free school shall not be established, then the said expense shall be chargeable upon the inhabitants signing the call, jointly and severally, to be sued for, if necessary, in any court having jurisdiction of the same. Expense of notices, how paid.

† § 4. Whenever fifteen persons, entitled as aforesaid, from each of two or more adjoining districts shall unite in a call for a meeting of the inhabitants of such districts, to determine whether such districts shall be consolidated by the establishment of a union free school therefor and therein, it shall be the duty of the trustees of such districts, or a majority of them, to give like public notice of such meeting, at some convenient place within such districts and as central as may be, within the time, and to be published and served in the manner set forth in the second section of this title, in each of such districts. The reasonable expenses of preparing, publishing and serving such notices shall be chargeable upon the union free school district, and be collected by tax, if a union free school shall be established pursuant to such call, but otherwise the signers of the call shall be jointly and severally liable for such expenses. The superintendent of public Union free schools of two or more districts.
Nature of.
Superintendent may order meeting.

---

* As amended by sec. 1. chap. 50, Laws of 1876.
† As amended by sec. 15, chap. 647, Laws of 1865.

TITLE 9.

instruction may order such meeting under the conditions and in the manner prescribed in the first section of this title.

Proceedings of meeting, to determine as to formation of union free school.

* § 5. Any such meeting held as aforesaid shall be organized by the appointment of a chairman and secretary, and may be adjourned from time to time by a majority vote, provided that such adjournment shall not be for a longer period than ten days; and whenever any such meeting, at which not less than fifteen persons entitled to vote thereat shall, by the affirmative vote of a majority present and voting, determine to establish a union free school in said district, pursuant to such notice, it shall thereupon be lawful for such meeting to proceed to the election, by ballot, of not less than three or more than nine trustees, who shall, by the order of such meeting, be divided into three several classes, the first to hold until one, the second until two, the third until three years from the *fourth* Tuesday in August next following, except in the cases in the next section provided for; and when the trustees so elected shall enter upon their office, the office of any existing trustee or trustees shall cease, except for the purposes stated in section eleven of title six of this act. The said trustees and their successors in office shall constitute the board of education of and for the union free school district for which they are elected, and the designation of such district as union free school district number   of the town of   shall be made by the school commissioner having jurisdiction of the district; and the said board shall have the name and style of the board of education of (adding the designation aforesaid); copies of said call, minutes of said meeting or meetings, duly certified by the chairman and secretary thereof, shall be by them, or either of them, transmitted and deposited, one to and with the town clerk, one to and with the school commissioner in whose jurisdiction said districts are located, and one to and with the superintendent of public instruction; but when, at any such meeting, the question as to the establishment of a union free school shall not be decided in the affirmative, as aforesaid, then all further proceedings at such meeting, except a motion to reconsider or adjourn, shall be dispensed with, and no such meeting shall be again called within one year thereafter.

Election of trustees, to form board of education.

Designation of board.

Proceedings, how certified and deposited.

Effect of negative action.

---

* As amended by sec. 2, chap. 50 Laws of 1876, and by sec. 10, chap. 413, Laws of 1883, and by sec. 2, chap. 49, Laws of 1884, and by sec. 7 of chap. 245, Laws of 1889.

OF UNION FREE SCHOOLS. 71

TITLE 9.

* § 6. Whenever said board of education shall be constituted for any district or districts whose limits correspond with those of any incorporated village or city, the trustees so elected shall, by the order of such meeting, be divided into three several classes : the first class to serve until one, the second until two, and the third until three years after the day of the next charter election in such village or city, and their regular term of service shall be computed from the several days of such charter elections, and not from the second Tuesday in October. And thereafter there shall be annually elected in such villages and cities, by separate ballot, to be indorsed " School Trustee," in the same manner as the charter officers thereof, trustees of the said union free schools, to supply the places of those whose terms by the classification aforesaid are about to expire. *Where district limits correspond with those of incorporated village or city; election of trustees in.*

† § 7. The said boards of education are hereby severally created bodies corporate, and each shall, at its first meeting, and at each annual meeting thereafter, elect one of their number president. They may, with the advice and consent of a majority of the legal voters entitled to vote on questions of taxation, to be had at an annual meeting of the inhabitants, appoint a clerk to the board. Such appointed clerk must be a resident of the district, and a person other than a trustee or a teacher in the employ of the board. The clerk so appointed shall be the general librarian of the district, and also perform all the clerical and other duties pertaining to his office. For his services he shall be entitled to receive a salary, which shall not be greater than twenty-five cents a year for each scholar, to be computed from the actual average daily attendance for the previous year, as set forth in the annual report to the school commissioner, or less, as in the best judgment of said legal voters to be had at such annual meeting ; such consent and approval not to be for a longer period of time than one year. In case no provision is made at an annual meeting of the inhabitants for the appointment and payment of a clerk, then and in that case the board will appoint one of their own number to act as clerk. In districts other than those whose limits correspond with those of any city or incorporated village, said board shall have power to appoint one of the taxable inhabitants *Boards of education created bodies corporate. Clerk, appointment of, etc. Salary. Districts other than those whose limits correspond with those of cities and villages, appointment of treasurer and collector for.*

· * NOTE. — In relation to election of officers in districts having more than 300 children of school age, see chap. 248, Laws of 1878, on page 129, *post.*
† As amended by chap. 161, Laws of 1877. This section (7), as amended, not to affect the towns of Cortlandt and White Plains, Westchester county.

TITLE 9.

Bonds of, etc.

of their district treasurer, and another collector of the moneys to be raised within the same for school purposes, who shall severally hold such appointments during the pleasure of the board. Such treasurer and collector shall each, and within ten days after notice in writing of his appointment, duly served upon him, and before entering upon the duties of his office, execute and deliver to the said board of education a bond, with such sufficient penalty and sureties as the board may require, conditioned for the faithful discharge of the duties of his office. And in case such bond shall not be given within the time specified, such office shall thereby become vacant, and said board shall thereupon, by appointment, supply such vacancy.

Vacancies, etc.

Corporate authorities, to raise by tax, etc.

* § 8. The corporate authorities of any incorporated village or city, in which any such union free school shall be established, shall have power, and it shall be their duty, to raise, from time to time, by tax, to be levied upon all the real and personal property in said city or village, as by law provided for the defraying of the expenses of its municipal government, such sum or sums as the board of education established therein shall declare necessary for teachers' wages and the ordinary contingent expenses of supporting the schools of said district. The sums so declared necessary shall be set forth in a detailed statement in writing, addressed to the corporate authorities by the board of education, giving the various purposes of anticipated expenditure, and the amount necessary for each; and the said corporate authorities shall have no power to withhold the sums so declared to be necessary, and such further sum or sums to be set forth in a detailed statement in writing, addressed to the corporate authorities by the board of education, giving the various purposes of the proposed expenditure, and the amount necessary for each which may have been or which may hereafter be authorized by a majority of the voters of such union free school district present and voting at any special district meeting duly convened, for making additions, alterations or improvements to or on the sites or structures belonging to the district, or for the purchase of other sites or structures, or for a change of sites, or for the erection of new buildings, or for buying apparatus or fixtures, or for such other purpose relating to the support and welfare of the school as they may, by resolution, approve; and they may direct the moneys so voted to be levied in one sum, or by installments, but no addition to or change of site or purchase of

Board to submit statement to corporate authorities.

Sums set forth and voted at special meeting not to be withheld.

Tax for money voted.

---
* As amended by sec. 1, chap.548, Laws of 1890.

a new site or tax for the purchase of any new site or structure, or for the purchase of an addition to the site of any school-house, or for building any new school-house or for the erection of an addition to any school-house already built shall be voted at any such meeting unless a notice by the board of education stating that such tax will be proposed, and specifying the amount and object thereof shall have been published once in each week for the four weeks next preceding such district meeting, in two newspapers, if there shall be two, or in one newspaper if there shall be but one, published in such district. But if no newspaper shall then be published therein, the said notice shall be posted up in at least ten of the most public places in said district twenty days before the time of such meeting. No vote to raise money shall be rescinded, nor the amount thereof be reduced at any subsequent meeting, unless the same be done within ten days after the same shall have been first voted. For the purpose of giving effect to these provisions, the corporate authorities are hereby authorized, whenever a tax shall have been voted to be collected in installments for the purpose of building a new school-house or building an addition to a school-house, or making additions, alterations or improvements to buildings or structures belonging to the district, or for the purchase of a new site, or for an addition to a site, or to borrow so much of the sum voted as may be necessary at a rate of interest not exceeding six per cent, and to issue bonds or other evidences of indebtedness therefor, which shall be a charge upon the district, and be paid at maturity, and which shall not be sold below par. Said bonds or other evidences of indebtedness shall be prepared by the board of education, signed by the president and secretary thereof, and delivered to the treasurer of the incorporated village or city, who shall countersign the same and give due notice of the time and place of the sale of such bonds, at least ten days prior thereto, by publication twice in two newspapers, if there shall be two, or in one newspaper, if there shall be but one published in such district. But if no newspaper shall then be published therein, the said notice shall be posted up in at least ten of the most public places in said district ten days before the day of sale. The proceeds of the sale of said bonds shall be paid into the treasury of said incorporated village or city to the credit of the board of education of such district.

TITLE 9.

Annual meetings of boards of education.

* § 9. The annual meeting of the board of education of every union free school district shall be held on the *first Tuesday of September of each year.*

Powers of annual and special meetings.

† § 10. A majority of the voters of any union free school district, other than those whose limits correspond with an incorporated city or village, present at any annual or special district meeting, duly convened, may authorize such acts and vote such taxes as they shall deem expedient for making additions, alterations or improvements to or in the sites or structures belonging to the district, or for the purchase of other sites or structures, or for a change of sites, or for the erection of new buildings, or for buying apparatus or fixtures, or for paying the wages of teachers and the necessary expenses of the school, or for such

Moneys to be raised in installments.

other purpose relating to the support and welfare of the school as they may, by resolution, approve; and they may direct the moneys so voted to be levied in one sum, or by installments, but no addition to or change of site or purchase of a new site or tax for the purchase of any new site or structure, or for the purchase of an addition to the site of any school-house, or for building any new school-house or for the erection of an addition to any school-

The notice of the proposed action must be given; manner of giving notice.

house already built, shall be voted at any such meeting unless a notice by the board of education stating that such tax will be proposed, and specifying the amount and object thereof, shall have been published once in each week for the four weeks next preceding such district meeting, in two newspapers if there shall be two, or in one newspaper if there shall be but one, published in such district. But if no newspaper shall then be published therein, the said notice shall be posted up in at least ten of the most public places in said district twenty days before the time of such meeting. And whenever a tax for any of the objects hereinbefore specified shall be legally voted the board of education shall make out their tax list, and attach their warrant thereto, in the manner provided in article seven of title seven of this act, for the collection of school district taxes, and shall cause such taxes or such installments to be collected at such times as they shall

---

* As amended by sec. 11, chap. 413, Laws of 1883, and by sec. 8 of chap. 245, Laws of 1889, and by sec. 2, chap. 548, Laws of 1890, and by sec. 12, chap. 500, Laws of 1893.
† As amended by sec. 3, chap. 49, Laws of 1884, and by sec. 1, chap. 595 Laws of 1886, and by chap. 27, Laws of 1888, and by sec. 3, chap. 548, Laws of 1890.
NOTE.—By section 4 of chapter 548, Laws of 1890, it is provided that sections 8, 9 and 10 of title 9 of chapter 555, Laws of 1864, as theretofore amended, and as in said chapter 548 of Laws of 1890, amended, were made applicable to all school districts established by and organized under special statutes, except those of cities. By section 5 of chapter 548, Laws of 1890, all acts, or parts of acts, inconsistent with or repugnant to such provisions were thereby repealed.

OF UNION FREE SCHOOLS.

become due. No vote to raise money shall be rescinded, nor the amount thereof be reduced at any subsequent meeting, unless the same be done within ten days after the same shall have been first voted. For the purpose of giving effect to these provisions, trustees or boards of education are hereby authorized, whenever a tax shall have been voted to be collected in installments for the purpose of building a new school-house or building an addition to a school-house, or making additions, alterations or improvements to buildings or structures belonging to the district, or for the purchase of a new site or for an addition to a site, to borrow so much of the sum voted as may be necessary at a rate of interest not exceeding six per cent, and to issue bonds or other evidences of indebtedness therefor, which shall be a charge upon the district, and be paid at maturity, and which shall not be sold below par; due notice of the time and place of the sale of such bonds shall be given by the board of education at least ten days prior thereto by publication twice in two newspapers, if there shall be two, or in one newspaper if there shall be but one published in such district. But if no newspaper shall then be published therein, the said notice shall be posted up in at least ten of the most public places in said district ten days before the day of sale.* †

§ 11. Any moneys required to pay teachers' wages in a union free school, or in the academical department thereof, after the due application of the school moneys thereto, shall be raised by tax and not by rate bill.

§ 12. Every union free school district shall, for all the purposes of the apportionment and distribution of school moneys, be regarded and recognized as a school district.

§ 13. The said board of education of every union free school district shall severally have power:

1. To pass such by-laws as they may deem proper for the regulation and exercise of their lawful business and power.

2. To establish such rules and regulations concerning the order and discipline of the school or schools, in the several departments thereof, as they may deem necessary to secure the best educational results.

3. To grade and classify the school or schools of the district, and to regulate the admission of pupils and their

---

* NOTE.— Title to sites, how acquired. Chap. 800, Laws of 1866, on page 122, *post*.
† Plans for school buildings. See chap. 675, Laws of 1897, on page 132, *post*.

TITLE 9.

To prescribe and furnish text-books.

transfer from one class or department to another, as their scholarship shall warrant.

4. To prescribe the text-books to be used in the schools, and to compel a uniformity in the use of the same, and to furnish the same to pupils out of any moneys provided for that purpose.

To have charge of all properties.

5. To take charge and possession of the school-houses, sites, lots, furniture, books, apparatus, and all school property within their respective districts; and the title of the same shall be vested respectively in said board of education, and the same shall not be subject to taxation for any purpose.

To hold real estate.

6. To take and hold for the use of the said schools or of any department of the same, any real estate transferred to it by gift, grant, bequest or devise, or any gift, legacy or annuity, of whatever kind, given or bequeathed to the said board, and apply the same, or the interest or proceeds thereof, according to the instructions of the donor or testator.

To establish an academical department.

* 7. To have, in all respects the superintendence, management and control of said union free schools, and to establish in the same an academical department, whenever in their judgment the same is warranted by the demand for such instruction; to receive into said union free schools any pupils residing out of said district, and to regulate and establish the tuition fees of such non-resident pupils in the several departments of said schools; provided, that if such non-resident pupils, their parents or guardians, shall be liable to be taxed for the support of said schools in the districts, or either of them, on account of owning property therein, the amount of any such tax paid by a non-resident pupil, his parent or guardian shall be deducted from the charge for tuition; to provide fuel, furniture, apparatus and other necessaries for the use of said schools, and to appoint such librarians as they may from time to time, deem necessary.

To regulate tuition fees of non-resident pupils.

To contract with and employ teachers and remove them.

† 8. To contract with and employ qualified teachers in the several departments of instruction, in all not less than one for every fifty pupils attending such schools; to remove them at any time for neglect of duty or for immoral conduct, and to pay the wages of such teachers out of the moneys appropriated for that purpose. ‡ ‖

---

* As amended by chap. 134, Laws of 1879; also, see chap. 413, Laws of 1884, on Page 134, *post.*
† As amended by sec. 17 chap. 647, Laws of 1865.
‡ NOTE.— Contracts to be in writing. Chap. 335. Laws of 1887, on page 134, *post.*
‖ Teachers to be paid as often as once each month. Idem.

OF UNION FREE SCHOOLS.

*9. To fill any vacancy which may happen in said board by reason of the death, resignation, removal or refusal to serve of any member or officer of said board; and the person so appointed in the place of any such member of the board shall hold his office until the next election of trustees, as by this act provided. In case of the failure of such board to fill such vacancy, and in case no special election is ordered for filling the same for a period of thirty days, the same may be filled by the school commissioner having jurisdiction. The superintendent of public instruction may order a special election to be held in any district for the purpose of filling such vacancy and when such special election is ordered the vacancy shall not be filled otherwise.

10. To remove any member of their board for official misconduct. But a written copy of all charges made of such misconduct shall be served upon him at least ten days before the time appointed for a hearing of the same; and he shall be allowed a full and fair opportunity to refute such charges before removal.

11. And generally to possess all the powers and privileges, and be subject to all the duties in respect to the common schools, or the common school departments in any union free school in said districts, which the trustees of common schools now possess or are subject to, not inconsistent with the provisions of this title; and to enjoy, whenever an academical department shall be by them established, all the immunities and privileges now enjoyed by the trustees of academies in this state.

†12. In any incorporated village having a population of five thousand and upwards, or in any union free school district having a like population, which fact shall in either case be determined by the state superintendent of public instruction, as provided in section six of title three of this act, the board of education in any such village or union free school district may appoint a superintendent of schools. Such superintendent shall be under the direction of the board of education, which shall prescribe his powers and duties. He shall be paid a salary from the teachers' fund to be fixed by the board of education, and he may be removed from office by a vote of the majority of all the members of such board. Whenever such superintendent shall be appointed, the said union free school district shall be entitled to the benefits of the provisions of section six

---
*As amended by chap. 331, Laws of 1888.
† Added by sec. 2 of chap. 90, Laws of 1889.

TITLE 9.

of title three of chapter five hundred and fifty-five of the laws of one thousand eight hundred and sixty-four, and the amendments thereto.

Special and annual meetings in certain union districts, how called.

* § 14. In union free school districts, other than those whose limits correspond with any city or incorporated village, the board of education shall have power to call special meetings of the inhabitants, in the manner provided in *section ten of title nine of this act, and shall in like manner* give notice of the time and place of holding the annual school district meeting, which shall be held on the *fourth* Tuesday of August in each year. The proceedings of no such special meeting shall be held illegal for want of a due notice to all the persons qualified to vote thereat unless it shall appear that the omission to give such notice was willful and fraudulent.

Boards to keep record of proceedings open to public inspection.

Boards to publish annually detailed statement of receipts and disbursements.

† § 15. *It shall be the duty of said board to keep an accurate record of all its proceedings in books provided for that purpose, which books shall be open for public inspection at all reasonable hours. It shall be the duty of said board to cause to be published once in each year, and twenty days next before the annual meeting of the district, in at least one public newspaper printed in such district, a full and detailed account of all moneys received by the board or the treasurer of said district, for its account and use, and of all the money expended therefor, giving the items of expenditure in full; should there be no paper published in said district said board shall publish such account by notice to the taxpayers, by posting copies thereof in five public places in said district. No member of said board shall be personally interested in any contract made by said board.* It shall be the duty of the board, at the annual meeting of the district, besides any other report or statement required by law, to present a detailed statement in writing of the amount of money which will be required for the ensuing year for school purposes, exclusive of the public moneys, specifying the several purposes for which it will be required, and the amount for each, but nothing in this section contained shall be construed to prevent the board from presenting such statement at any special meeting called for the purpose, nor from presenting a supplementary and amended statement or estimate at any time.

Board to report estimate of expenses to annual meeting.

May make such statement at any time.

Powers of inhabitants thereupon.

§ 16. After the presentation of such statement, the

---

* As amended by chap. 413, Laws of 1883, and by sec. 9, chap. 245, Laws of 1889, and by sec. 13, chap. 500, Laws of 1893.
† As amended by sec. 1, chap. 485, Laws of 1894.

OF UNION FREE SCHOOLS.

question shall be taken upon voting the necessary taxes to meet the estimated expenditures, and when demanded by any voter present, the question shall be taken upon each item separately, and the inhabitants may increase the amount of any estimated expenditures or reduce the same, except for teachers' wages, and the ordinary contingent expenses of the school or schools.

* § 17. If the inhabitants shall neglect or refuse to vote the sum or sums estimated necessary for teacher's wages, after applying thereto the public school moneys, and other moneys received or to be received for that purpose, or if they shall neglect or refuse to vote the sum or sums estimated necessary for ordinary contingent expenses, the board of education may levy a tax for the same, in like manner as if the same had been voted by the inhabitants. *When board may levy tax without vote of the inhabitants.*

§ 18. If any question shall arise as to what are ordinary contingent expenses the same may be referred to the superintendent of public instruction, by a statement in writing, signed by one or more of each of the opposing parties upon the question, and the decision of the superintendent shall be conclusive. *Superintendent to decide any question as to what are "contingent expenses."*

§ 19. It shall be the duty of each of the said boards of education, elected pursuant to the provisions of this title, to have a regular meeting at least once in each quarter, and at such meetings to appoint one or more committees, to visit every school or department under the supervision of said board, and such committees shall visit all said schools at least twice in each quarter, and report at the next regular meeting of the board on the condition and prospects thereof. *Board to meet once in each quarter. Visit schools, etc.*

§ 20. It shall also be the duty of said boards, respectively, to have reference in all their expenditures and contracts to the amount of moneys which shall be appropriated, or subject to their order or drafts, during the current year, and not to exceed that amount. And said boards shall severally apply all the moneys apportioned to the common school districts under their charge, to the departments below the academical; and all moneys from the literature fund or otherwise, appropriated for the support of the academical department, to the latter departments. *Expenditure of money.*

§ 21. All moneys raised for the use of the union free schools in any city or incorporated village, or apportioned to the same from the income of the literature, common school or United States deposit funds, or otherwise, shall be paid into the treasury of such city or village, to the *Money to be paid into village or city treasury.*

---
* As amended by sec. 5 of chap. 328, Laws of 1889.

TITLE 9.

Additional security to be given by officer.

credit of the board of education therein; and the funds so received into such treasury shall be kept separate and distinct from any other funds received into the said treasury. And the officer having the charge thereof shall give such additional security for the safe custody thereof as the corporate authorities of such city or village shall require.

Moneys, how drawn.

No money shall be drawn from such funds, credited to the several boards of education, unless in pursuance of a resolution or resolutions of said board, and on drafts drawn by the president and countersigned by the secretary, payable to the order of the person or persons entitled to receive such money, and stating on their face the purpose or service for which such moneys have been authorized to be paid by the said board of education.

Payment, disbursements and accounting for school moneys.

§ 22. All moneys raised for the use of said union free schools, other than those whose limits correspond with those of any cities and incorporated villages, or apportioned from the income of the literature or common school or United States deposit funds, or otherwise, shall be paid to the respective treasurers of the said several boards of education entitled to receive the same, and be by them applied to the uses of said several boards, who shall annually render their accounts of all moneys received and expended by them for the use of said schools, with every voucher for the same, and certified copies of all orders of the said boards touching the same, to the school commissioner of the town in which the principal school-house of the district is located.

Academical department subject to regents.

§ 23. Every academical department, established as aforesaid, shall be under the visitation of the regents of the university, and shall be subject, in its course of education and matters pertaining thereto (but not in reference to the buildings or erections in which the same is held), to all the regulations made in regard to academies by the said regents.

Qualifications of pupils.

In such departments the qualifications for the entrance of any pupil shall be as high as those established by the said regents for participation in the literature fund of any academy of the state under their supervision.

May adopt existing academy procedure therefor.

§ 24. Whenever a union free school shall be established under the provisions of this title, and there shall exist within its district an academy, the board of education, if thereto authorized by a vote of the voters of the district, may adopt such academy as the academical department of the district, with the consent of the trustees of the academy, and thereupon the trustees, by a resolution to be attested by the signatures of the officers of the board, and filed in the office of the clerk of the county, shall declare their offices vacant, and thereafter the said academy shall be the academical department of such union free school.

*§ 25. Every union free school district, in all its departments, shall be subject to the visitation of the superintendent of public instruction. He is charged with the general supervision of its board of education and their management and conduct of all its departments of instruction. And every board of education shall annually, between the twenty-fifth day of July, and the first Tuesday of August, make to the commissioner having jurisdiction, and deposit in the town clerk's office, a report for the preceding school year of all matters and things which trustees of a school district are required to report, and of all such other matters and things as the superintendent shall, from time to time, require; and shall also, whenever thereto required by the superintendent of public instruction, report fully to him upon any particular matter or thing; and such report shall be in such form, and so authenticated, as the superintendent shall, from time to time, require.

§ 26. For cause shown, and after giving notice of the charge and opportunity of defense, the superintendent of public instruction may remove any member of a board of education. Willful disobedience of any lawful requirement of the superintendent, or a want of due diligence in obeying such requirement is cause of removal.

§ 27. The provisions of this title shall apply to all union free schools heretofore organized pursuant to the provisions of chapter four hundred and thirty-three of the laws of eighteen hundred and fifty-three.†

TITLE X.

‡ OF SCHOOLS FOR COLORED CHILDREN.

SECTION 1. The school authorities of any city or incorporated village, the schools of which are or shall be organized under title nine of this act, or under special act, may, when they shall deem it expedient, establish a separate school or separate schools for the instruction of children and youth of African decent, resident therein,

---
* As amended by chap. 413, Laws of 1883, and by chap. 340, Laws of 1885, and by sec. 10 of chap. 245, Laws of 1889.
† NOTE.— Proceedings to dissolve union free school districts. See chap. 210, Laws of 1880, as amended, on page 127, *post*.
‡ See chap. 248, Laws of 1884, on page 100, *post*, in relation to colored schools in New York city.

and over five and under twenty-one years of age; and such school or schools shall be supported in the same manner and to the same extent as the school or schools supported therein for white children, and they shall be subject to the same rules and regulations, and be furnished with facilities for instruction equal to those furnished to the white schools therein.

Colored schools in union free school district.

§ 2. The trustees of any union school district, or of any school district organized under a special act, may, when the inhabitants of any such district shall so determine, by resolution, at any annual meeting, or at a special meeting called for that purpose, establish a separate school or separate schools for the instruction of such colored children resident therein, and such schools shall be supported in the same manner and receive the same care, and be furnished with the same facilities for instruction, as the white schools therein.

Teacher must be legally qualified.

§ 3. No person shall be employed to teach any of such schools who shall not, at the time of such employment be legally qualified.

Repealed.

§ 4. (Section 4 repeals section 147 of chapter 480, Laws of 1847.)

TITLE XI.
TEACHERS' INSTITUTES.

Commissioner to hold institute.

SECTION 1. It shall be the duty of every school commissioner, at least once in each year, to organize in his own district or, in concert with one or more commissioners in the same county, to organize in and for the combined districts, a teachers' institute, and to induce, if possible, all the teachers in his district to be present and take part in its exercises.

To give due notice, etc.

§ 2. The commissioner or commissioners, subject always to the advice and direction of the superintendent of public instruction, shall, in such form and manner as may be deemed most effectual, give public notice to the teachers of the district, or combined districts, and to all others who may desire to become such, of the time when and the place where the institute will be organized.

Superintendent to advise, employ teachers, etc.

§ 3. The superintendent of public instruction shall advise and co-operate with the school commissioners in fixing the times and places of holding the teachers' institute; and he shall have power to employ, or cause the school commissioner to employ, suitable persons, at a reasonable compensation, to conduct and teach the institutes; and he shall visit, or cause to be visited by persons employed in

OF TEACHERS' INSTITUTES.

the department of public instruction, such and so many of the institutes as he possibly can, for the purpose of examining into the course and manner of instruction pursued, and of rendering such assistance as he may find expedient; and he shall establish the basis upon which the yearly appropriation for the support of teachers' institutes shall be distributed to the several institutes, and the term or terms during which the same may be held, having reference, in the establishment of such regulations, to the number of teachers in the county, district or combined districts, and in attendance at the institute, to the length of time during which they shall be held, to the facilities for attendance upon them, and to local disadvantages requiring especial consideration. *To establish the basis of apportionment.*

* § 4. The superintendent of public instruction may establish such regulations in regard to certificates of qualification or recommendation, which may be issued by school commissioners, as will, in his judgment, furnish incentives and encouragement to teachers to attend the institutes; and the closing of his school by a teacher for the time during which an institute shall be held in and for the county or school commissioner district in which his school is, and which institute he shall have attended during the time for which he closed his school, shall not work a forfeiture of the contract under which he is teaching. *Superintendent may establish regulations. Teachers may close school and not vitiate contract.*

† § 5. The trustees of every school district are hereby directed to give the teacher or teachers employed by them the whole of the time spent by such teacher or teachers in attending at any regular session or sessions of an institute in a county embracing the school district, or a part thereof, without deducting anything from his or their wages for the time so spent, and in order to secure to teachers the full exercise of this privilege (after the twentieth day of August, eighteen hundred and eighty-five), all schools in school districts and parts of school districts, not included within the boundaries of an incorporated city, or certain union free school districts hereinafter referred to, shall be closed during the time a teachers' institute shall be in session in the same county in which such schools are situated. In union free school districts having a population of more than five thousand, and employing a superintendent whose time is exclusively devoted to the supervision of the schools therein, the schools may be closed or not, at the option of the board of education in said dis *Trustees directed to give teachers time spent at institute. Schools shall be closed during the time an institute is being held in the county. Average pupil attendance during the time the school is so closed.*

---

* As amended by sec. 9, chap. 340, Laws of 1885.
† As amended by sec. 23, chap. 406, Laws of 1867, and by sec. 10, chap. 340, Laws of 1885, and by sec. 1, chap. 524, Laws of 1890.

TITLE 11.

tricts. In the apportionment of public school money, the schools thus closing in any school term shall be allowed the same average pupil attendance during such time, as was the average weekly aggregate during that part of the term when the school was not thus closed, and any school continuing its sessions in violation of the above provision shall not be allowed any public money based upon the aggregate pupil attendance during the days the school was thus kept in session. Trustees and boards of education in such school districts and parts of school districts shall report, in their annual reports to the school commissioners, the number of days and the dates thereof on which a teachers's institute was held in their counties during the school year, and whether schools under their charge were or were not closed during such days; and whenever the trustees' report shows a district school has been supported for the full time required by law, including the time spent by the teacher or teachers in their employ in attendance upon such institute, and that the trustees have given the teacher or teachers the time of such absence, and have not deducted anything from his or their wages on account thereof, the superintendent of public instruction may include the district in his apportionment of the state school moneys, and direct that it be included by the school commissioner or commissioners in their apportionment of school moneys; provided, always, that such school district be in all other respects entitled to be included in such apportionment.

Trustees to report, etc.

When district has complied with the law superintendent may include the district in the apportionment of public money.

Mode of payment.

§ 6. The treasurer shall pay, on the warrant of the comptroller, to the order of any one or more of the school commissioners, such sum or sums of money as the superintendent of public instruction shall certify to be due to them for expenses in holding a teachers' institute; and, upon the like warrant and certificate, to the order of any persons employed by the superintendent to conduct and teach any teachers' institute, his reasonable compensation as certified by the superintendent.

To transmit catalogue and report to the superintendent.

§ 7. The school commissioner or commissioners by whom any teachers' institute shall be organized, shall transmit to the superintendent of public instruction a catalogue of the names of all persons who shall have attended such institute, with such other 'statistical information in such form and within such time, as may be prescribed by said superintendent.

TITLE XII.

APPEALS TO THE SUPERINTENDENT OF PUBLIC INSTRUCTION.

SECTION 1. Any person conceiving himself aggrieved in consequence of any decision made: *Any person may appeal.*

1. By any school district meeting; *From what.*
2. By any school commissioner or school commissioners and other officers, in forming or altering, or refusing to form or alter, any school district, or in refusing to apportion any school moneys to any such district or part of a district.
3. By a supervisor in refusing to pay any such moneys to any such district;
4. By the trustees of any district in paying or refusing to pay any teacher, or in refusing to admit any scholar gratuitously into any school;
5. By any trustees of any school district library concerning such library, or the books therein, or the use of such books; *Ibid.*
6. By any district meeting in relation to the library; *Ibid.*
7. By any other official act or decision concerning any other matter under this act, or any other act pertaining to common schools, may appeal to the superintendent of public instruction, who is hereby authorized and required to examine and decide the same; and his decision shall be final and conclusive, and not subject to question or review in any place or court whatever. *Ibid.* *Superintendent's decision final.*

§ 2. The superintendent, in reference to such appeals, shall have power: *Power of superintendent.*

1. To regulate the practice therein;
2. To determine whether an appeal shall stay proceedings, and prescribe conditions upon which it shall or shall not so operate; *When appeal shall stay proceedings.*
3. To decline to entertain or to dismiss an appeal, when it shall appear that the appellant has no interest in the matter appealed from, and that the matter is not a matter of public concern, and that the person injuriously affected by the act or decision appealed from is incompetent to appeal. *When appeal will not be entertained.*
4. To make all orders, by directing the levying of taxes or otherwise, which may, in his judgment, be proper or necessary to give effect to his decision.

§ 3. The superintendent shall file, arrange in the order of time, and keep in his office, so that they may be at all times accessible, all the proceedings on every appeal to *Superintendent shall file papers.*

him under this title, including his decision and orders founded thereon; and copies of all such papers and proceedings, authenticated by him under his seal of office, shall be evidence equally with the originals.

TITLE XIII.

MISCELLANEOUS PROVISIONS.

School moneys, penalties for their loss.

SECTION 1. Whenever the share of school moneys or any portion thereof, apportioned to any town, school district or separate neighborhood, or any money to which a town, school district or separate neighborhood would have been entitled, shall be lost, in consequence of any willful neglect of official duty by any school commissioner, town clerk, trustees or clerks of school districts, the officer or officers guilty of such neglect shall forfeit to the town, school district or separate neighborhood so losing the same, the full amount of such loss with interest thereon.

Penalty for neglect to prosecute.

§ 2. Where any penalty for the benefit of a school district, or of the schools of any school district, town, school commissioner district or county, shall be incurred, and the officer or officers, whose duty it is by law to sue for the same, shall willfully and unreasonably refuse or neglect to sue for the same, such officer or officers shall forfeit the amount of such penalty to the same use, and it shall be the duty of their successor or successors in office to sue for the same.

Repealed.

* § 3. (This section, which provided a penalty for disturbing a school meeting, was repealed by subdivision 39 of section 1 of chapter 593, Laws of 1886.)

Procedure.

† § 4. It shall be the duty of the trustees of the district, or the teacher of the school, and he shall have power, to enter a complaint against such offender before any justice of the peace of the county, or the mayor or any alderman, recorder or other magistrate of the city wherein the offense was committed. The magistrate or other officer before whom the complaint is made shall thereupon by his warrant, directed to any constable or person, cause the person complained of to be arrested and brought before him for trial. If such person, on the charge being stated to him, shall plead guilty, the magistrate shall convict him; and if he demands a trial by the magistrate, shall summarily try him; and, if he demands a trial by jury, the magistrate shall issue a venire, and impanel a jury for

---

* Section 448 of the Penal Code applies in such cases.
† NOTE.—This section refers to a person who shall willfully disturb, interrupt or disquiet any school or school meeting.

his trial, and he shall be tried in the same manner as in a court of special sessions.

§ 5. If any person convicted of the said offense do not immediately pay the penalty, with the costs of the prosecution, or give security to the satisfaction of the magistrate for the payment thereof within twenty days, the magistrate or other officer shall commit him to the common jail of the county, there to be imprisoned until the penalty and costs be paid, but not exceeding thirty days. *Penalty.*

§ 6. In any action against a school officer or officers, including supervisors of towns, in respect to their duties and powers under this act, for any act performed by virtue of or under color of their offices, or for any refusal or omission to perform any duty enjoined by law, and which might have been the subject of an appeal to the superintendent, no costs shall be allowed to the plaintiff, in cases where the court shall certify that it appeared on the trial that the defendants acted in good faith. But this provision shall not extend to suits for penalties, nor to suits or proceedings to enforce the decisions of the superintendent. *Actions against school officers.*

* § 7. Whenever the trustees of any school district, or any school district officer or officers, have been or shall be instructed by a resolution of the district, at a meeting called for that purpose, to defend any action brought against them, or to bring or defend an action or proceeding touching any district property or claim of the district, or involving its rights or interests, or to continue any such action or defense, all their costs and reasonable expenses, as well as all costs and damages adjudged against them, shall be a district charge and shall be levied by tax. If the amount claimed by them be disputed by a district meeting, it shall be adjusted by the county judge of any county in which the district or any part of it is situated. *Actions by school officers, costs and expenses allowed.*

§ 8. Whenever such trustees or any school district officer shall have brought or defended any such action or proceeding, without any such resolution of the district meeting, and after the final determination of such suit or proceeding, shall present to any regular meeting of the inhabitants of the district an account in writing of all costs, charges and expenses paid by him or them, with the items thereof, and verified by his or their oath or affirmation, and a majority of the voters at such meeting shall so direct, it shall be the duty of the trustees to cause the same to be assessed upon and collected of the taxable property of said district, in the same manner as other *Action without direction of district, expenses, how paid.*

---

* As amended by chap. 174, Laws of 1878.

TITLE 13.

taxes are by law assessed and collected; and, when so collected, the same shall be paid over, by an order upon the collector, to the officer or officers entitled to receive the same; but this provision shall not extend to suits for penalties, nor to suits or proceedings to enforce the decisions of the superintendent of public instruction.

When the district refuse, what action.

* § 9. Whenever an officer or officers mentioned in the last preceding section of this act shall have complied with the provisions of said section, and the inhabitants shall have refused to direct the trustees to levy a tax for the payment of the costs, charges and expenses therein mentioned, it shall be lawful for him or them,

Notice to be given.

then and there, to give notice orally and publicly, that he will appeal to the county judge of the county; and in case of his disability to act in the matter by reason of being disqualified, or otherwise, then to the district attorney of the county in which the school-house of said district is located, from the refusal of said meeting to vote a tax for the payment of said claim, and the inhabitants may, then or there, or at any subsequent

District may appoint inhabitant to protect interests.

district meeting, appoint one or more of the inhabitants of the district to protect the rights and interest of the district upon said appeal. And the officer or officers before mentioned shall thereupon, within ten days, serve upon the clerk of said district (or if there be no such clerk, upon the town clerk of the town) a copy of the aforesaid account, so sworn to, together with a notice, in writing, that on a certain day therein specified he or they intend to present such account to the county judge or to the district attorney, as the case may be, for settlement. And the clerk shall record such notice, together with the copy of the account, and the same shall be subject to the inspection of the inhabitants of the district. And it shall be the duty of the person or persons appointed by any district meeting for that purpose, to appear before the county judge or the district attorney, as the case may be, on the day mentioned in the notice aforesaid, and to protect the rights of the

Expenses incurred a district charge.

district upon such settlement; and the expenses incurred in the performance of this duty shall be a charge upon said district, and the trustees, upon presentation of the account of such expenses, with the proper voucher therefor, may levy a tax therefor, or add the same to any other tax to be levied by them; and their refusal to levy said tax for the payment of said expenses, shall be subject to an appeal to the superintendent of public instruction.

* As amended by sec. 1, chap. 746, Laws of 1871.

Miscellaneous Provisions. 89

*§ 10. Upon the appearance of the parties, or upon due proof of service of the notice and copy of the account, the county judge shall examine into the matter and hear the proofs and allegations propounded by the parties, and decide by order whether or not the account, or any and what portion thereof, ought justly be charged upon the district, with costs and disbursements to such officer or officers, in his discretion, which costs and disbursements shall not exceed the sum of thirty dollars, and the decision of the county judge shall be final; but no portion of such account shall be so ordered to be paid which shall appear to such judge to have arisen from the willful neglect or misconduct of the claimant. The account with the oath of the party claiming the same shall be *prima facie* evidence of the correctness thereof. The county judge may adjourn the hearing from time to time, as justice shall seem to require.

_{TITLE 13.}
_{County judge to hear proofs and decide.}

§ 11. It shall be the duty of the trustees of any school district, within thirty days after service of a copy of such order upon them, or upon the district clerk, and notice thereof to them, or any two of them, to cause the same to be entered at length in the book of record of said district, and to raise the amount thereby directed to be paid, by a tax upon the district, to be by them assessed and levied in the same manner as a tax voted by the district.

_{Order to be recorded.}

§ 12. For the support of the Indian schools, already established and which may be established, under authority of chapter seventy-one of the laws of eighteen hundred and fifty-six, the superintendent of public instruction, in his annual general apportionment of the state school moneys appropriated for the support of common schools, shall make an equitable apportionment, as provided by section six of title three of this act; and the moneys which shall be thus apportioned, and those which have been apportioned for their support, under authority of section four, chapter seventy one of the laws of eighteen hundred and fifty-six, shall be paid out of the treasury for expenditures authorized by law and actually incurred in the support of such schools, upon the warrant of the superintendent, countersigned by the comptroller.

_{Indian schools.}

§ 13. The superintendent of public instruction, so soon as may be after the passage of this act, shall prepare and cause to be printed, and distribute among the school districts of the state, to each one copy, an edition of this statute, with brief annotations embodying such of the

_{Publication of this statute, etc.}

---

* As amended by chap. 514, Laws of 1874.

TITLE 13.

decisions of the courts of the state, and of the superintendents of common schools and the superintendents of public instruction as are applicable thereto, and such comments, explanations and instructions as he shall deem necessary or expedient, and the same shall be deposited with the district clerk, and kept by him for the use of the inhabitants. *

Repeal of other acts.

§ 14. All provisions of law repugnant to or inconsistent with the provisions of this act are hereby repealed, saving always all rights of action vested under such prior provisions, and proceedings commenced for the assertion thereof; but nothing herein contained, unless it be so expressed, shall be construed, unless by inevitable implication, to revive any act or portion of an act heretofore repealed; nor to impair or in any manner affect or change any special law touching the schools or school system of any city or incorporated village of the state.

---

* NOTE.— Chap. 672, Laws of 1837, provides that trustees shall be the custodians o' the Code (edition of 1887), and they are made responsible for its safe-keeping. See page 152, *post*.

GENERAL STATUTES.

The following provisions of law while not amending any particular title of the consolidated school act, chapter 555, Laws of 1864, relate thereto by separate and distinct enactments, and form a part of the general school law:

AMERICAN MUSEUM OF NATURAL HISTORY.

CHAP. 428.

AN ACT to provide for a course of free instruction in natural history, and making an appropriation for the support thereof.

PASSED May 20, 1886.

SECTION 1. The state superintendent of public instruction is hereby authorized and empowered to make and enter into an agreement with the American Museum of Natural History in the city of New York, for a term not to exceed two years, to supply, furnish and maintain in connection with said museum a course of free instruction to be given and illustrated by the curators of said museum, on human and comparative anatomy, physiology, zoology, physical geography, and such other subjects as the said superintendent of public instruction may require, to the teachers of the common schools, the normal schools of the State, the normal college of the city of New York, and the training school for teachers in the city of Brooklyn, who may desire to avail themselves of this training, and to provide for at least one lecture every year during the term of said agreement, to be delivered on one or more of said subjects at each of the several normal schools of the State, the normal college of the city of New York and the training school for teachers in the city of Brooklyn, and to supply to the said normal schools and said normal college and training school, and to the public schools of the city of New York and Brook-

State superintendent authorized to contract with American Museum of Natural History for a course of free instruction to teachers.

lyn, and to any common school, on the application of its trustees, all such appliances, plates and apparatus as may be necessary for the proper presentation to their teachers and pupils of this instruction.

§ 2. The state superintendent of public instruction is hereby authorized also to make and enter into a contract with said museum for repeating the aforesaid information to artisans, mechanics and other citizens, when a lecture hall capable of seating at least one thousand persons, and other necessary rooms shall have been erected by said city as an extension of the building now in possession of said museum.

§ 3. The sum of eighteen thousand dollars is hereby appropriated for the support and maintenance of said course of free instruction for the fiscal year beginning on the first day of October, eighteen hundred and eighty-six, and said sum of eighteen thousand dollars shall be appropriated annually for the support and maintenance of said course of free instruction during the term of said agreement.

§ 4. This act shall take effect immediately.

CHAP. 337.

AN ACT to continue free instruction in natural history to certain institutions and making an appropriation therefor.

PASSED May 19, 1888.

SECTION 1. The state superintendent of public instruction is hereby authorized to enter into an agreement with the American Museum of Natural History, in the city of New York, for continuing the instruction in natural history to the several state normal schools, the normal college of the city of New York, the training school for teachers in the city of Brooklyn, and the teachers in the common schools of the city of New York, Brooklyn and vicinity, authorized by chapter four hundred and twenty-eight of the laws of eighteen hundred and eighty-six, for the further term of two years from the termination of the agreement authorized by said act; and he may also extend such instruction to the teachers' institutes in the different counties of the state, if he shall think advisable.

§ 2. The sum of fifteen thousand dollars, payable from the free school fund, is hereby appropriated for the support and maintenance of said course of instruction, for the year beginning on the first day of October, eighteen hundred and eighty-eight, and the sum of fifteen thousand dollars shall be appropriated annually for the support and maintenance of said course of instruction during the term of the agreement authorized by this act.

CHAP. 6.

AN ACT to continue free instruction in natural history, geography and kindred subjects to certain institutions, and making an appropriation therefor.

APPROVED by the Governor January 26, 1893. Passed, three fifths being present.

SECTION 1. The state superintendent of public instruction is hereby authorized to enter into an agreement with the American Museum of Natural History, in the city of New York, for continuing the instruction in natural history, geography and kindred subjects to the several state normal schools, the normal college of the city of New York, the training school for teachers in the city of Brooklyn, the teachers' institutes in the different counties of the state, and to the teachers in the common schools of the city of New York, Brooklyn and vicinity, authorized by chapter four hundred and twenty-eight of the laws of eighteen hundred and eighty-six, by chapter three hundred and thirty-seven of the laws of eighteen hundred and eighty-eight, and by chapter forty-three of the laws of eighteen hundred and ninety-one for the further term of four years from the first day of January, eighteen hundred and ninety-three.

§ 2. Said instruction may include free illustrated lectures to artisans, mechanics and other citizens, on such legal holidays as the state superintendent and museum authorities may agree upon.

§ 3. The sum of eighteen thousand dollars, payable from the free school fund, is hereby appropriated for the preparation for and the support and maintenance of said course of instruction, for the year beginning on the first day of January, eighteen hundred and ninety-three; and the said sum of eighteen thousand dollars shall be appropriated annually thereafter in the general appropriation bill for the preparation for and the support and maintenance of said course of instruction during the term of the agreement authorized by this act.

*ARBOR DAY.

CHAP. 196.

AN ACT to encourage arboriculture.

PASSED April 30, 1888.

Arbor Day established.

SECTION 1. The Friday following the first day of May in each year shall hereafter be known throughout this state as Arbor Day.

Duty of school authorities.

§ 2. It shall be the duty of the authorities of every public school in this state to assemble the scholars in their charge on that day in the school building, or elsewhere, as they may deem proper, and to provide for and conduct, under the general supervision of the city superintendent or the school commissioner, or other chief officers having the general oversight of the public schools in each city or district, such exercise as shall tend to encourage the planting, protection and preservation of trees and shrubs, and an acquaintance with the best methods to be adopted to accomplish such results.

State superintendent may prescribe a course of exercises.

§ 3. The state superintendent of public instruction shall have power to prescribe from time to time, in writing, a course of exercises and instruction in the subjects hereinbefore mentioned which shall be adopted and observed by the public school authorities on Arbor Day, and upon receipt of copies of such course, sufficient in number to supply all the schools under their supervision, the school commissioner or city superintendent aforesaid shall promptly provide each of the schools under his or their charge with a copy, and cause it to be adopted and observed.

§ 4. This act shall take effect immediately.

---

* NOTE.—Arbor Day is not a legal holiday in any sense. If the day is not observed or school taught a teacher will not be entitled to pay for the same, nor can the day be included in the school week.

COMPULSORY EDUCATION.

CHAP. 421.

AN ACT to secure to children the benefits of elementary education.

PASSED May 11, 1874.

SECTION 1. All parents and those who have the care of children shall instruct them, or cause them to be instructed, in spelling, reading, writing, English grammar, geography and arithmetic. And every parent, guardian or other person having control and charge of any child between the ages of eight and fourteen years shall cause such child to attend some public or private day school at least fourteen weeks in each year, eight weeks at least of which attendance shall be consecutive, or to be instructed regularly at home at least fourteen weeks in each year in spelling, reading, writing, English grammar, geography and arithmetic, unless the physical or mental condition of the child is such as to render such attendance or instruction inexpedient or impracticable. *Children to be instructed at school or at home, for at least fourteen weeks in each year.*

* § 2. No child under the age of fourteen years shall be employed by any person to labor in any business whatever during the school hours of any school day of the school term of the public school in the school district or the city where such child is, unless such child shall have attended some public or private day school where instruction was given by a teacher qualified to instruct in spelling, reading, writing, geography, English grammar and arithmetic, or shall have been regularly instructed at home in said branches by some person qualified to instruct in the same, at least fourteen weeks of the fifty-two weeks next preceding any and every year in which such child shall be employed, and shall, at the time of such employment, deliver to the employer a certificate in writing, signed by the teacher or a school trustee of the district or of a school, and countersigned by such officer as the board of education or public instruction, by whatever name it may be known in any city, incorporated village or town, shall designate, certifying to such attendance or instruction; and any person who shall employ any child contrary to the provisions of this section, shall, for each offense, forfeit and pay a penalty of fifty dollars to the treasurer or chief *Employment of children under fourteen years of age prohibited.*

---

* As amended by sec. 1, chap. 372, Laws of 1876.

GENERAL ACTS RELATING TO SCHOOLS.

CHAP. 421, 1874.

fiscal officer of the city, or supervisor of the town in which such offense shall occur; the said sum or penalty, when so paid, to be added to the public school money of the school district in which the offense occurred.

Trustees to examine for and report violations of this act.

* § 3. It shall be the duty of the trustee or trustees of every school district, or public school, or union school, or of officers appointed for that purpose by the board of education or public instruction, by whatever name it may be known, in every town and city, in the months of September and of February in each year, and at such other times as may be deemed necessary, to examine into the situation of the children employed in all manufacturing and other establishments in such school district where children are employed; and in case any town or city is not divided into school districts, it shall for the purposes of the examination provided for in this section, be divided by the school authorities thereof into districts, and the said trustees or other officers as aforesaid notified of their respective districts on or before the first day of January of each year; and the said trustee or trustees, or other officers as aforesaid, shall ascertain whether all the provisions of this act are duly observed, and report all violations thereof to the treasurer or chief fiscal officer of said city, or supervisor of said town. On such examination the proprietor, superintendent or manager of said establishment shall, on demand, exhibit to said examining trustee, or other officer as aforesaid, a correct list of all children between the ages of eight and fourteen years employed in said establishment, with the said certificates of attendance on school or of instruction.

List of children employed.

Children temporarily discharged from employment to attend school.

§ 4. Every parent, guardian or other person having control and charge of any child between the ages of eight and fourteen years, who has been temporarily discharged from employment in any business, in order to be afforded an opportunity to receive instruction or schooling, shall send such child to some public or private school, or shall cause such child to be regularly instructed as aforesaid at home for the period for which such child may have been so discharged, to the extent of at least fourteen weeks in all in each year, unless the physical or mental condition of the child is such as to render such an attendance or instruction inexpedient or impracticable.

Trustees to enforce act.

† § 5. The trustee or trustees of any school district or public school, or the president of any union school, or

---

* As amended by sec. 2, chap. 372, Laws of 1876.
† As amended by sec. 3, chap. 372, Laws of 1876.

such officer as the board of education of said city, incorporated village or town may designate, is hereby authorized and empowered to see that sections one, two, three, four and five of this act are enforced, and to report in writing all violations thereof to the treasurer or chief fiscal officer of his city, or to the supervisor of his town; any person who shall violate any provision of sections one, three and four of this act shall, on written notice of such violation from one of the school officers above named, forfeit, for the first offense, and pay to the treasurer or chief fiscal officer of the city, or to the supervisor of the town in which he resides, or such offense has occurred, the sum of one dollar, and, after such first offense, shall, for each succeeding offense in the same year, forfeit and pay to the treasurer of said city or supervisor of said town, the sum of five dollars for each and every week, not exceeding thirteen weeks in any one year, during which he, after written notice from said school officer, shall have failed to comply with any of said provisions; the said penalties, when paid, to be added to the public school money of said school district in which the offense occurred.

§ 6. In every case arising under this act where the parent, guardian, or other person having the control of any child between the said ages of eight and fifteen* years, is unable to provide such child for said fourteen weeks with the text-books required to be furnished to enable such child to attend school for said period, and shall so state in writing to the said trustee, the said trustee shall provide said text-books for said fourteen weeks at the public schools for the use of such child, and the expense of the same shall be paid by the treasurer of said city or the supervisor of said town on the certificate of the said trustee, specifying the items furnished for the use of such child.

† § 7. In case any person having the control of any child, between the ages of eight and fourteen years, is unable to induce said child to attend school for the said fourteen weeks in each year, and shall so state in writing to said trustee, or said other officers appointed by the board of education or public instruction by whatever name it may be known, the said child shall, from and after the date and delivery to said trustee, or other officer as aforesaid, of said statement in writing, be deemed and dealt with as an habitual truant, and said person shall be relieved of all

---
* So in the original.
† As amended by sec. 4, chap. 372, Laws of 1876.

CHAP. 421, 1874

penalties incurred for said year after said date, under sections one, four and five of this act, as to such child.

Rules concerning truants.

* § 8. The board of education or public instruction, by whatever name it may be called, in such city and incorporated village, and the trustees of the school districts and union school in each town, by an affirmative vote of a majority of said trustees, at a meeting or meetings to be called for this purpose, on ten days' notice in writing to each trustee, said notice to be given by the town clerk, are for each of their respective cities and towns hereby authorized and empowered and directed, on or before the first day of January, eighteen hundred and seventy-seven, to make all needful provisions, arrangements, rules and regulations concerning habitual truants and children between said ages of eight and fourteen years of age, who may be found wandering about the streets or public places of such city or town during the school hours of the school day of the term of the public school of said city or town, having no lawful occupation or business, and growing up in ignorance; and said provisions, arrangements, rules and regulation shall be such as shall, in their judgment, be most conducive to the welfare of such children, and to the good order of such city or town; and shall provide suitable places for the discipline and instruction and confinement, when necessary, of such children, and may require the aid of the police of cities or incorporated villages, and constables of towns, to enforce their said rules and regulations, provided, however, that such provisions, arrangements, rules and regulations shall not go into effect, as laws for said several cities and towns, until they shall have been approved, in writing, by a justice of the supreme court for the judicial district in which said city, incorporated village or town is situated; and, when so approved, he shall file the same with the clerk of the said city, incorporated village or town, who shall print the same, and furnish ten copies thereof to each trustee of each school district, or public or union school of said city, incorporated village or town. The said trustee shall keep one copy thereof posted in a conspicuous place in or upon each school-house in his charge during the school terms each year. In like manner the same in each city, incorporated village or town may be amended or revised within six months after the passage of this act, and thereafter annually as the trustee or trustees of any school

Approval of by a justice of the supreme court.

Copy on school-house.

Amendments.

---

* As amended by sec. 5, chap. 372, Laws of 1876.

district or public school, or the president of any union school, or the board of education or public instruction, or by whatever name it may be known, in any city, incorporated village or town, may determine.

§ 9. Justices of the peace, civil justices, and police justices shall have jurisdiction, within their respective towns and cities, of all offenses and all actions for penalties or fines described in this act, or that may be described in said provisions, arrangements, rules and regulations authorized by section eight of this act. All actions for fines and penalties under this act shall be brought in the name of the treasurer or chief fiscal officer of the city or supervisor of the town to whom the same is payable, but shall be brought by and under the direction of the said trustee or trustees, or said officer designated by the board of education

§ 10. Two weeks' attendance at a half-time or evening school shall, for all purposes of this act, be counted as one week at a day school.

§ 11. This act shall take effect on the first day of January, eighteen hundred and seventy-five.

Justices to have jurisdiction.
Actions for fines.
Evening scholars.

HOLIDAYS.

CHAP. 677.

AN ACT relating to the construction of statutes constituting chapter one of the general laws.

PASSED May 18, 1892.

§ 24. The term holiday includes the following days in each year: The first day of January, known as New Year's Day; the twenty-second day of February known as Washington's Birthday; the thirtieth day of May, known as Memorial Day; the fourth day of July, known as Independence Day; the first Monday of September, known as Labor Day, and the twenty-fifth day of December, known as Christmas day, and if either of such days is Sunday, the next day thereafter; each general election day and each day appointed by the president of the United States or by the governor of this state as a day of general thanksgiving, general fasting and prayer, or other general religious observance.

The term half-holiday includes the period from noon to midnight of each Saturday which is not a holiday.

Public holidays.
Half-holidays

NOTE.— By section 7 of title 3, chapter 555 Laws of 1864, as amended by section 2 of chapter 500 Laws of 1893, all legal holidays that may occur during the terms of school during every school year, commencing August 1, 1893, of one hundred and sixty days of school, are included as parts of said one hundred and sixty days, and exclusive of Saturdays. No Saturday shall be counted as part of said one hundred and sixty days of school, and no school shall be in session on a legal holiday.

SCHOOLS.

COLORED SCHOOLS.

CHAP. 248.

AN ACT in relation to public education in the city of New York.

PASSED May 5, 1884.

Colored schools to be classed as ward schools.

SECTION 1. The colored schools in the city of New York, now existing and in operation, shall hereafter be classed and known and be continued as ward schools, and primaries, with their present teachers, unless such teachers are removed in the manner provided by law, and such schools shall be under the control and management of the school officers of the respective wards in which they are located in the same manner and to the same extent as other ward schools, and shall be open for the education of pupils for whom admission is sought, without regard to race or color.

§ 2. All acts or parts of acts inconsistent with the provisions of this act are hereby repealed.

§ 3. This act shall take effect immediately.

CORNELL UNIVERSITY — STATE SCHOLARSHIPS IN.

CHAP. 291.

AN ACT to amend chapter five hundred and eighty-five of the laws of eighteen hundred and sixty-five, entitled "An act to establish Cornell university, and to appropriate to it the income of the sale of public lands granted to this state by congress, on the second day of July, eighteen hundred and sixty-two, also to restrict the operation of chapter five hundred and eleven of the laws of eighteen hundred and sixty-three."

PASSED May 7, 1887.

SECTION 1. Section nine of chapter five hundred and eighty-five of the laws of eighteen hundred and sixty-five is hereby amended so as to read as follows:

Open to applicants.

§ 9. The several departments of study in the said university shall be open to applicants for admission thereto at the lowest rates of expense consistent with its welfare

STATE SCHOLARSHIPS IN CORNELL UNIVERSITY.

CHAP. 291, 1887.

Free scholarships in.

and efficiency, and without distinction as to rank, class, previous occupation or locality. But, with a view to equalize its advantages to all parts of the state, the institution shall receive students to the number of one each year from each assembly district in this state, to be selected as hereinafter provided, and shall give them instruction in any or in all the prescribed branches of study in any department of said institution, free of any tuition fee or of any incidental charges to be paid to said university, unless such incidental charges shall have been made to compensate for materials consumed by said students or for damages needlessly or purposely done by them to the property of said university. The said free instruction shall, moreover, be accorded to said students in consideration of their superior ability, and as a reward for superior scholarship in the academies and public schools of this state. Said students shall be selected as the legislature may from time to time direct, and until otherwise ordered as follows:

Competitive examinations.

1. A competitive examination, under the direction of the department of public instruction, shall be held at the county court-house in each county of the state, upon the first Saturday of June, in each year, by the city superintendents and the school commissioners of the county.

Qualifications of applicants.

2. None but pupils of at least sixteen years of age and of six months standing in the common schools or academies of the state, during the year immediately preceding the examination, shall be eligible.

3. Such examination shall be upon such subjects as may be designated by the president of the university. Question papers prepared by the department of public instruction shall be used, and the examination papers handed in by the different candidates shall be retained by the examiners and forwarded to the department of public instruction.

Selection of candidates.

4. The examiners shall, within ten days after such examination, make and file in the department of public instruction a certificate, in which they shall name all the candidates examined and specify the order of their excellence, and such candidates shall, in the order of their excellence, become entitled to the scholarships belonging to their respective counties.

Vacancies, how filled.

5. In case any candidate who may become entitled to a scholarship shall fail to claim the same, or shall fail to pass the entrance examination at such university, or shall die, resign, absent himself without leave, be expelled

CHAP. 291, 1887.

or, for any other reason, shall abandon his right to or vacate such scholarship either before or after entering thereupon, then the candidate certified to be next entitled in the same county shall become entitled to the same. In case any scholarship belonging to any county shall not be claimed by any candidate resident in that county, the state superintendent may fill the same by appointing thereto some candidate first entitled to a vacancy in some other county, after notice has been served on the superintendent or commissioners of schools of said county. In any such case, the president of the university shall at once notify the superintendent of public instruction, and that officer shall immediately notify the candidate next entitled to the vacant scholarship of his right to the same.

Leave of absence, how obtained.

6. Any state student who shall make it appear to the satisfaction of the president of the university that he requires leave of absence for the purpose of earning funds with which to defray his living expenses, while in attendance, may, in the discretion of the president, be granted such leave of absence, and may be allowed a period not exceeding six years from the commencement thereof for the completion of his course at said university.

Preference to soldiers' children.

7. In certifying the qualifications of the candidates, preference shall be given (where other qualifications are equal) to the children of those who have died in the military or naval service of the United States.

Notice of examinations, how given.

8. Notices of the time and place of the examinations shall be given in all the schools, having pupils eligible thereto, prior to the first day of January in each year, and shall be published once a week for three weeks in at least two newspapers in each county immediately prior to the holding of such examinations. The cost of publishing such notices and the necessary expenses of such examination shall be a charge upon each county respectively, and shall be audited and paid by the board of supervisors thereof. The state superintendent of public instruction shall attend to the giving and publishing of the notices hereinbefore provided for. He may, in his discretion, direct that the examination in any county may be held at some other time and place than that above specified, in which case it shall be held as directed by him.

Record to be kept by state superintendent.

He shall keep full records in his department of the reports of the different examiners, showing the age, post-office address and standing of each candidate, and shall notify candidates of their rights under this act. He shall determine any controversies which may arise under the provisions of this act. He is hereby charged with the general supervision and direction of all matters in connection with the filling of such scholarships. Students enjoying the privileges of free scholarships shall in common with the other students of said university be subject to all of the examinations, rules and requirements of the board of trustees or faculty of said university except as herein provided.

INDIAN SCHOOLS.

CHAP. 71.

AN ACT to facilitate education and civilization among the Indians residing in this state.

PASSED April 1, 1856.

SECTION 1. The superintendent of public instruction shall be charged with providing the means of education for all the Indian children in the state. He shall cause to be ascertained the condition of the various bands in the state in respect to education; he shall establish schools in such places, and of such character and description as he shall deem necessary; he shall employ superintendents for such schools, and shall, with the concurrence of the comptroller and secretary of state, cause to be erected, where necessary, convenient buildings for their accommodation. *Duty of the superintendent of public instruction.*

§ 2. In the discharge of the duties imposed by this act, the said superintendent shall endeavor to secure the co-operation of all the several bands of Indians, and for this purpose, shall visit, by himself or his authorized agent, all the reservations where they reside, lay the matter before them in public assembly, inviting them to assist either by appropriating their public moneys to this object, or by setting apart lands and erecting suitable buildings, or by furnishing labor or materials for such buildings, or in any other way which he or they may suggest as most effectual for the promotion of this object. *Indians to co-operate.*

§ 3. In any contract which may be entered into with said Indians, for the use or occupancy of any land for school grounds, sites or buildings, care shall be taken to protect the title of the Indians to their lands, and to reserve to the state the right to remove or otherwise dispose of all improvements made at the expense of the state. *Indian title to be protected.*

§ 4. The Indian children in the state, between the ages of four and twenty-one years, shall be entitled to draw public money the same as white children. The superin- *Children to draw public money.*
Enumeration

GENERAL ACTS RELATING TO SCHOOLS.

CHAP. 410, 1882

tendent shall cause an annual enumeration of said Indian children to be made, and shall see that the public money, to which they are ratably entitled, is devoted exclusively to their education.

$5,000 appropriated.

§ 5. To carry into effect the provisions of this act, the sum of five thousand dollars is hereby appropriated out of the surplus income of the United States deposit fund, to be paid by the treasurer, on the warrant of the comptroller, from time to time, to the order of the superintendent of public instruction.

Vouchers to be taken and filed.

§ 6. The superintendent shall take and file in his office, vouchers and receipts for all the expenditures made under this act, subject to the inspection of the joint committee to examine the accounts of the auditor and treasurer; and shall annually report to the legislature all his doings, by virtue of the authority vested in him; and for this purpose said superintendent may require full and detailed reports in such form as he may prescribe, from those having the immediate supervision of any Indian schools in this state.

§ 7. This act shall take effect immediately.

NOTE.— State superintendent may select ten Indian youth in each year fo education in State Normal School. See chap. 89, Laws of 1850, page 113, *post*.

---

* NAUTICAL SCHOOL.

The following provision of chapter 410, Laws of 1882 entitled an act to consolidate in one act the laws affecting the city of New York, authorize the board of education of said city to establish a nautical school:

Board of education to establish nautical school.

SECTION 1068. The board of education (for the city of New York) are authorized and directed to provide and maintain a nautical school in said city, for the education and training of pupils in the science and practice of navigation; to furnish accommodations for said school, and make all needful rules and regulations therefor, and for the number and compensation of instructors and others employed therein; to prescribe the government and discipline thereof, and the terms and conditions upon which pupils shall be received and instructed therein, and discharged therefrom, and provide in all things for the good management of said nautical school. And the said board

Books, etc.

shall have power to purchase the books, apparatus, stationery and other things necessary or expedient to enable

---

* NOTE.— This is a substantial re-enactment of chap. 288, Laws of 1873.

said school to be properly and successfully conducted, and may cause the said school or the pupils or parts of the pupils thereof to go on board vessels in the harbor of New York, and take cruises in or from said harbor for the purpose of obtaining a practical knowledge in navigation and of the duties of mariners. And the said board are hereby authorized to apply to the United States government for the requisite use of vessels and supplies for the purpose above mentioned.

§ 1070. The said board of education shall appoint annually at least three of their number, who shall, subject to the control, supervision and approbation of the board, constitute an executive committee, for the care, government and management of such nautical school, under rules and regulations so prescribed, and whose duty it shall be, among other things, to recommend the rules and regulations which they deem necessary and rpoper for such school. *Executive committee.*

§ 1071. After the establishment and organization of the said school, the expense thereof, and of carrying out of the provisions of this chapter, shall be defrayed from the moneys raised by law for the support of common schools in the city and county of New York. *Expenses of, how provided for.*

§ 1072. The chamber of commerce of New York is authorized to provide for and appoint a committee of its members to serve as a council of the nautical school, whose duty it shall be, as far as may be, to advise and co-operate with the board of education in the establishment and management of such schools, and from time to time to visit and examine the same, and to communicate in respect thereof with the board of education or such executive committee thereof, and to make reports to the chamber of commerce, which may transmit to the state superintendent of public instruction such reports or any thereof, or an abstract of the same, with such recommendations as may be deemed advisable. *Committee of chamber of commerce.* *Reports.*

NORMAL SCHOOLS.

CHAP. 311.

[1. ALBANY.]

AN ACT for the establishment of a normal school.

PASSED May 7, 1844.

SECTION 1. The treasurer shall pay on the warrant of the comptroller, to the order of the superintendent of common schools, from that portion of the avails of the *Appropriation for the establishment of a normal school at Albany.*

CHAP. 311, 1844.

literature fund appropriated by chapter two hundred and forty-one of the laws of one thousand eight hundred and thirty-four, to the support of academical departments for the instructions of teachers of common schools, the sum of nine thousand six hundred dollars; which sum shall be expended under the direction of the superintendent of common schools and the regents of the university, in the establishment and support of a normal school for the instruction and practice of teachers of common schools in the science of education and in the art of teaching, to be located in the county of Albany.

Annual appropriation for support.

§ 2. The sum of ten thousand dollars shall, after the present year, be annually paid by the treasurer, on the warrant of the comptroller, to the superintendent of common schools, from the revenue of the literature fund, for the maintenance and support of the school so established, for five years, and until otherwise directed by law.

Supervision by state superintendent and the regents of the university.

§ 3. The said school shall be under the supervision, management and government of the superintendent of common schools and the regents of the university. The said superintendent and regents shall, from time to time, make all needful rules and regulations, to fix the number and compensation of teachers and others to be employed therein; to prescribe the preliminary examination and the terms and conditions on which pupils shall be received and instructed therein; the number of pupils from the respective cities and counties, conforming as nearly as may be to the ratio of population; to fix the location of the said school, and the terms and conditions on which the grounds and buildings therefor shall be rented, if the same shall not be provided by the corporation of the city of Albany, and to provide in all things for the good government and management of the said school.

Executive committee, duty of.

They shall appoint a board, consisting of five persons, of whom the said superintendent shall be one, who shall constitute an executive committee for the care, management and government of the said school under the rules and regulations prescribed as aforesaid, whose duty it shall be, from time to time, to make full and detailed reports to the said superintendent and regents, and, among other things, to recommend the rules and regulations which they deem necessary and proper for the said school.

Rules and regulations.

Annual report.

§ 4. The superintendent and regents shall annually transmit to the legislature a full account of their proceedings and expenditures of money under this act, together with a detailed report of said executive committee of the progress, condition and prospects of the school.

The foregoing was the first provision made by law in this state for the establishment of any normal school. Though general in the sense of being for the benefit of the state, the school was located at Albany, and to provide uniformity in arrangement, the act is inserted here with other local acts relating to normal schools.* The laws providing for the establishment of normal schools generally will follow.

The preceding act was regarded as experimental and for a term of five years only. At the expiration of the term, the institution, still at the time the only one in the state, was permanently established by the following act:

CHAP. 318.
AN ACT for the permanent establishment of the normal school.

PASSED April 12, 1848.

SECTION 1. The treasurer shall pay, on the warrant of the comptroller, to the order of the state superintendent of common schools, from the general fund, a sum not exceeding fifteen thousand dollars, to be expended in the erection of a suitable building for the accommodation of the state normal school for the instruction and practice of teachers of common schools in the science of education and the art of teaching. *Appropriation for erection of normal school building at Albany.*

§ 2. The said building shall be erected, under the direction of the executive committee of the school, upon the ground owned by the state, and lying in the rear of the geological rooms. *How to be erected.*

§ 3. The said school shall be, as heretofore, under the supervision, management and government of the state superintendent of common schools and the regents of the university. The said superintendent and regents shall, from time to time, make all needful rules and regulations to fix the number and compensation of teachers and others to be employed therein; to prescribe the preliminary examination and the terms and conditions on which pupils shall be received and instructed therein, the number of pupils from the respective counties conforming as nearly as may be to the ratio of population; and to provide in *Supervision, management and government of.*

---

* At a meeting of the regents of the university held March 13, 1890, the corporate name of the Albany Normal School was changed to the New York State Normal College.

all things for the good government and management of the said school. They shall appoint a board consisting of five persons, of whom the said superintendent shall be one who shall constitute an executive committee for the care, management and government of said school, under the rules and regulations prescribed as aforesaid, whose duty it shall be, from time to time, to make full and detailed reports to the said superintendent and regents, and, among other things, to recommend the rules and regulations which they deem necessary and proper for the said school.

§ 4. The superintendent and regents shall annually transmit to the legislature a full account of their proceedings, and of the expenditures of money under this and previous acts, together with a detailed report of the progress, condition and prospects of the school.

CHAP. 466.

AN ACT in regard to normal schools.

PASSED April 7, 1866.

SECTION 1. The governor, the lieutenant-governor, the secretary of state, the comptroller, the state treasurer, the attorney-general and the superintendent of public instruction shall constitute a commission to receive proposals in writing in regard to the establishment of normal and training schools for the education and discipline of teachers for the common schools of this state from the board of supervisors of any county in this state; from the corporate authority of any city or village; from the board of trustees of any college or academy, and from one or more individuals. Such commission shall have power to accept or refuse such proposals, but the number accepted shall not exceed four. Such proposals shall contain specifications for the purchase of lands and the erection thereon of suitable buildings for such schools, or for the appropriation of land and buildings to such use, and also the furnishing of such schools with furniture, apparatus, books and everything necessary to their support and management. Such proposals may have in view, either the grant and conveyance of such land and premises to the state, or the use of the same for a limited time, and for the gift to the state of furniture, apparatus, books and other things necessary to conduct such schools.

§ 2. If the proposals made by any board of supervisors, or by the corporate authorities of any city or village, shall be accepted, said board or corporate authorities shall have power to raise, by tax, and expend the money necessary to carry the same into effect; and if, in their judgment, it shall be deemed expedient, they shall have power to borrow money for such purpose, for any time not exceeding ten years, and at a rate of interest not exceeding seven per cent, and issue the corporate bonds of said county, city or village therefor.

CHAP. 466, 1866.
Power to raise money by tax or borrow.

§ 3. When the said commission shall have accepted proposals and determined the location of any one of such schools, and when suitable grounds and buildings have been set apart and appropriated for such schools, and all needful preparations made for opening same in accordance with the proposals accepted, the commission shall certify the same in writing, and then their power under this act in relation to such school shall cease, and thereupon the superintendent of public instruction shall appoint a local board, consisting of not less than three persons, who shall, respectively, hold their offices until removed by the concurrent action of the chancellor of the university and the superintendent of public instruction, and who shall have the immediate supervision and management of such school, subject, however, to his general supervision and to his direction in all things pertaining to the school. Such local board shall have power to appoint one of their number chairman, and another secretary, of the board. Two-thirds of each of said boards shall form a quorum for the transaction of business, and in the absence of any officer of the board, another member may be appointed *pro tempore* to fill his place and perform his duties. It shall be the duty of such board to make and establish, and from time to time to alter and amend, such rules and regulations for the government of such schools under their charge, respectively, as they shall deem best, which shall be subject to the approval of the superintendent of public instruction. They shall also severally transmit through him, and subject to his approval, a report to the legislature on the first day of January in each year, showing the condition of the school under their charge during the year next preceding, and which report shall be in such form and contain such an account of their acts and doings as the superintendent shall direct, including, especially an account in detail of their receipts and expenditures, which shall be duly verified by the oath or affirmation of their chairman and secretary.

Commissioners to certify acceptance of proposals.

Superintendent of public instruction to appoint local board.

Powers and duties of local boards.

Report to the legislature.

CHAP. 466, 1866.
Course of study to be prescribed.
Powers and duties of superintendent.

§ 4. It shall be the duty of the local board, subject to the approval of the superintendent of public instruction, to prescribe the course of study to be pursued in each of said schools. It shall be the duty of the superintendent of public instruction to determine what number of teachers shall be employed in each school, and their wages, whose employment shall also be subject to his approval; to

Selection of pupils.

order, in his discretion, that one or more of said schools shall be composed exclusively of males, and one or more of females; to decide upon the number of pupils to be admitted to each of said schools, and to prescribe the time and manner of their selection, but he shall take care in such selection to provide that every part of the state shall have its proportionate representation in such school as near as may be, according to population; but if any school commissioner district, or any city, shall not, for any cause, be fully represented in either of said schools, then the superintendent of public instruction may cause the maximum number of such pupils to be supplied from any part of the state, giving preference, however, to those living in the county, city or village where such school is situated.

Admission of pupils.

* § 5. All applicants for admission shall be residents of this state, or, if not, they shall be admitted only upon the payment of such tuition fees as shall be, from time to time, prescribed by the superintendent of public instruction.

Examination.

Applicants shall present such evidence of proficiency or be subject to such examination at the school as shall be prescribed by said superintendent. From and after the twentieth day of August, one thousand eight hundred and eighty-nine, it shall not be lawful for any such school to receive, into any academic department connected therewith, any pupil not a resident of the territory, for the benefit or advantage of whose residents the state has pledged itself to maintain such academic department.

Privileges and liabilities.

When admitted, students, unless they are students in the academic or practice department or are non-residents, shall be entitled to all the privileges of the school, free from all charges for tuition or for the use of books or apparatus, but every pupil shall pay for books lost by him, and for any damages to books in his possession; any pupil may be dismissed from the school by the local board for immoral or disorderly conduct, or for neglect or inability to perform his duties.

Diplomas to be granted.

§ 6. The superintendent of public instruction shall prepare suitable diplomas to be granted to the students of

---
* As amended by chapter 142, Laws of 1889.

such school who shall have completed one or more of the courses of study and discipline prescribed; and a diploma signed by him, the chairman and secretary of the local board, and the principal of the school, shall be of itself a certificate of qualification to teach common schools; but such diploma may be annulled for the immoral conduct of its holder, in like manner as provided for the annulment of a diploma of state normal school, in title two, chapter five hundred and fifty-five of the laws of eighteen hundred and sixty-four. The provisions of this section shall be applicable to the Oswego normal training school. *CHAP. 466, 1866. To be a certificate of qualification to teach in the common schools. Diplomas may be annulled.*

§ 7. The sum of twelve thousand dollars shall be annually, and is hereby appropriated for the support of each of said normal and training schools to be organized under this act, payable out of the income of the common school fund, to be paid by the treasurer, on the warrant of the comptroller, upon the certificate of the superintendent of public instruction affixed to the proper accounts, verified by the oath or affirmation of the local board of each school; but none of the money hereby appropriated shall be paid for the purchase of any ground, site or buildings, for the use of such schools.

§ 8. Local boards appointed under this act shall consist of not more than thirteen persons, and the office of any member of any such local board, which now consists of more than thirteen members, is hereby declared vacant; and the said superintendent of public instruction shall appoint a new local board, and may fill, by appointment, all vacancies occurring in said local boards. Until the appointment of such new local board, and until a quorum of such board shall have entered upon the discharge of its duties, and during such time as any local board shall omit to discharge its duties, the said superintendent is authorized to discharge the duties of such local board or any of its officers; and the acts of said superintendent in the premises shall be as valid and binding as if done by a competent local board or its officers, or with their co-operation. This section added by Laws of 1869, chapter 18. *Local boards to consist of.*

State Normal and Training Schools were established under the provisions of the foregoing act and special acts, as follows:

Brockport — Chaps. 21 and 96, Laws of 1867.
Buffalo — Chap. 583, Laws of 1867.
Cortland — Chap. 199, Laws of 1867; chap. 174, Laws of 1868.

Fredonia — Chap. 223, Laws of 1867.
Geneseo — Chap. 195, Laws of 1867; chap. 601, Laws of 1868, and chap. 294, Laws of 1871.
Oswego — Chap. 418, Laws of 1863, as amended by chap. 445, Laws of 1865; chap. 170, Laws of 1867.
Potsdam — Chap. 6, Laws of 1867.
New Paltz — Chap. 287, Laws of 1885.
Oneonta — Chap. 374, Laws of 1887.
Plattsburgh — Chap. 517, Law of 1889.
Jamaica — Chap. 553, Laws of 1893.

NOTE.—There is also a Normal College in the city of New York and training schools in other cities of the state, maintained by local authorities.

CUSTODY AND PRESERVATION OF BUILDINGS.

CHAP. 348.

AN ACT concerning the grounds, buildings and property of the state provided for normal schools, the custody, protection and preservation of the same, and the powers of local boards in relation thereto.

PASSED May 20, 1880.

Local boards to have custody, etc., of grounds and buildings.

SECTION 1. The local boards of managers of the respective normal schools in this state shall have the custody, keeping and management of the grounds and buildings provided or used for the purposes of such schools, respectively, and other property of the state pertaining thereto, with power to protect, preserve and improve the same.

Willful trespass upon, a misdemeanor.

* § 2. (Section 2 providing for the punishment for willful trespass, repealed by subdivision 55 of sec. 1 of chap. 593, Laws of 1886.)

Special policeman may be appointed.

§ 3. For the purpose of protecting and preserving such buildings, grounds and other property, and preventing injuries thereto, and preserving order, preventing disturbances, and preserving the peace in such buildings and upon such grounds, the local boards of managers of each of said normal schools shall have power, by resolution or otherwise, to appoint, from time to time, one or more special policemen, and the same to remove at pleasure, who shall be police officers, with the same powers as constables of the town or city where such school is located, whose duty it shall be to preserve order, and prevent disturbances and breaches of the peace in and about the buildings, and on and about the grounds used for said school, or pertaining thereto, and protect and preserve the

---

* Chapter XIV of the Penal Code provides a penalty for such offenses.

same from injury, and to arrest any and all persons making any loud or unusual noise, causing any disturbance, committing any breach of the peace, or misdemeanor, or any willful trespass upon such grounds, or in or upon said buildings, or any part thereof, and convey such person or persons so arrested, with a statement of the cause of the arrest, before a proper magistrate to be dealt with according to law.

CHAP. 89, 1850. Arrest of offenders.

§ 4. This act shall take effect immediately.

INSURANCE.

CHAP. 116.

AN ACT authorizing the boards of the state normal schools of this state to insure the buildings and property belonging to said schools for the benefit of the state.

PASSED May 2, 1882.

SECTION 1. The local boards of the state normal schools of this state are each hereby authorized to insure and keep insured the normal school buildings connected with and belonging to said schools, at a risk not exceeding seventy-five thousand dollars, for the benefit of the state, and to pay for said insurance out of any money or moneys appropriated and set apart, from time to time, for the use and benefit of said schools by the state of New York.

Insurance of buildings.

§ 2. This act shall take effect immediately.

INDIANS — APPOINTMENTS TO NORMAL SCHOOLS.

CHAP. 89.

AN ACT to provide for the support and education of a limited number of Indian youth, of the state of New York, at the state normal school.

PASSED March 23, 1850.

SECTION 1. The treasurer shall pay, on the warrant of the comptroller, to the order of the state superintendent of common schools, from the general fund, a sum not exceeding one thousand dollars per year for the support and education of ten Indian youth in the state normal school, which moneys are hereby appropriated for the purpose of this act.

Appropriation.

§ 2. The selection of such youth shall be made by the state superintendent of common schools, from the several Indian tribes located within this state and, in making

Selection of pupils.

CHAP. 261, 1850.

such selection, due regard shall be had to a just participation in the privileges of this act by each of the said several tribes, and, if practicable, reference shall also be had to the population of each of said tribes in determining such selection.

Age of pupils. § 3. Such youth shall not be under sixteen year of age, nor shall any such youth be supported or educated at said normal school for a period exceeding three years.

Their guardians and expenses. § 4. The executive committee of the state normal school shall be the guardian of such Indian youth, during the period of their connection with the school, and shall pay their necessary expenses, not to exceed one hundred dollars per year for each pupil, to be defrayed out of the money appropriated by the first section of this act.

To enjoy all privileges. § 5. The Indian pupils selected in pursuance of this act, and attending said normal school, shall enjoy the same privileges, of every kind, as the other pupils attending said school, including the payment of traveling expenses, not exceeding ten dollars to each pupil.

TUITION MONEY — HOW TO BE USED.

*CHAP. 492.

Tuition money, how to be expended. Tuition money may be expended for current expenses, etc. The local boards of the several state normal schools are hereby authorized to expend, under the direction of the superintendent of public instruction, the moneys now on hand, received for tuition in any of the departments of the respective schools, and the moneys hereafter to be received for such tuition, for apparatus, repairs, insurance, furniture, or other improvements upon the grounds or buildings, or for the ordinary expenses of the respective schools.

ORPHAN SCHOOLS.

CHAP. 261.

AN ACT to provide for the better education of the children in the several orphan asylums in this state, other than in the city of New York.

PASSED April 10, 1850.

To participate in the distribution of the public money. SECTION 1. The schools of the several incorporated orphan asylum societies in this state, other than those in the city of New York, shall participate in the distribution of the school moneys, in the same manner and to the same

---

* From the Supply Bill, Laws of 1870.

extent, in proportion to the number of children educated therein, as the common schools in their respective cities or districts.

§ 2. The schools of said societies shall be subject to the rules and regulations of the common schools in such cities or districts, but shall remain under the immediate management and direction of the said societies as heretofore.

{sidenote: CHAP. 170, 1890.}
{sidenote: Rules and management of.}

* TEACHERS' TRAINING CLASSES.

CHAP. 170.

AN ACT in regard to the professional instruction of common school teachers in academies and union schools.

PASSED April 23, 1890.

The People of the State of New York, represented in Senate and Assembly, do enact as follows:

SECTION 1. There shall be annually appropriated out of the income of the United States deposit fund not otherwise appropriated, the sum of thirty thousand dollars and out of the free school fund the sum of thirty thousand dollars for the instruction of competent persons in academies and union schools, in the science and practice of common school teaching, under a course to be prescribed by the superintendent of public instruction.

{sidenote: Annual appropriation for instruction of teachers.}

§ 2. The superintendent of public instruction shall designate the academies and union schools in which such instruction shall be given, distributing them among the school commissioner districts of the state, as nearly as may well be, having reference to the number of school districts in each, to location and to the character of the institutions selected.

{sidenote: Designation of academies and schools therefor.}

§ 3. Every academy and union school so designated shall instruct a class of not less than ten nor more than twenty-five scholars, and every scholar admitted to such class shall continue under instruction not less than sixteen weeks. The superintendent shall prescribe the conditions of admission to the classes, the course of instruction and the rules and regulations under which said instruction shall be given, and shall, in his discretion, determine the number of classes which may be formed in any one year, in any academy or union school, and the length of time exceeding sixteen weeks during which such instruction may be given.

{sidenote: Teachers' classes.}
{sidenote: Supervision thereof.}

---

* By the provisions of chapter 137, Laws of 1889, the management and supervision of the teachers' classes was transferred to the superintendent of public instruction. See page 116 *post*.

CHAP. 137.
1889.

Instruction free.

§ 4. Instruction shall be free to all scholars admitted to such classes, and who have continued in them the length of time required by the third section of this act.

Payments to trustees.

§ 5. The trustees of all academies and union schools in which such instruction shall be given shall be paid from the appropriations mentioned in the first section of this act at the rate of one dollar for each week's instruction of each scholar, on the certificate of the superintendent to be furnished to the comptroller.

Expenses of inspection and supervision of instruction.

§ 6. The appropriation provided by this act, for the instruction in academies and union schools in the science and practice of common school teaching, shall be deemed to include, and shall include, the due inspection and supervision of such instruction by the superintendent of public instruction, and the expenses of such inspection and supervision for the present and each succeeding fiscal year, shall be paid out of said appropriation on vouchers certified by the superintendent.

Classes subject to visitation.

§ 7. Each class organized in any academy or union school under appointment by the superintendent for instruction in the science and practice of common school teaching, shall be subject to the visitation of the school commissioner of the district in which such academy or union school is situated; and it shall be the duty of said commissioner to advise and assist the principals of said academies or union schools in the organization and management of said classes, and at the close of the term of instruction of said classes, under the direction of the superintendent, to examine the students in such classes, and to issue teachers' certificates to such as show moral character, fitness and scholastic and professional qualifications, worthy thereof.

Duty of school commissioners.

Repeal.

§ 8. All acts or parts of acts inconsistent with the provisions of this act, are hereby repealed.

§ 9. This act shall take effect immediately.

CHAP. 137.

AN ACT to transfer the management and supervision of teachers' classes in academies and union schools from the board of regents to the superintendent of public instruction.

PASSED April 15, 1889.

Teachers' classes under supervision of state superintendent.

SECTION 1. The powers and duties conferred and imposed upon the regents of the university by chapter four hundred and twenty-five of the laws of one thousand eight hundred and seventy-seven, and chapter three hundred and eighteen of the laws of one thousand eight hundred and eighty-two, relative to the instruction of classes in academies and union schools in the science and practice of common school teaching, are hereby transferred to the superintendent of public instruction.

§ 2. This act shall take effect immediately.

INDUSTRIAL TRAINING IN THE PUBLIC SCHOOLS.

CHAP. 334.

AN ACT to authorize the establishment and maintenance of departments for industrial training and for teaching and illustrating the industrial or manual arts in the public schools and normal schools of this state.

PASSED May 19, 1888.

SECTION 1. Boards or departments of education of cities and villages, and of union free schools and trustees of public school districts, are hereby authorized and empowered to establish and maintain a department or departments in the schools under their charge for industrial training and for teaching and illustrating the manual or industrial arts, and the principles underlying the same; and for that purpose they are respectively authorized to purchase and use such material and apparatus, and to establish and maintain such shops, and to employ such instructor or instructors, in addition to the other teachers in said schools, as in their judgment shall be deemed necessary or proper whenever the authorities or electors respectively now authorized by law to raise money by taxation for school purposes, shall make provision for the maintenance of such departments. *Industrial training may be taught.*

§ 2. All authorities and electors, respectively, now authorized by law to levy and raise taxes for school purposes, are hereby authorized to levy and raise by taxation, in addition to any amount or amounts which they are now, respectively, in any city, village or district, authorized by law to raise for school purposes, and in the same manner, and at a regular or special meeting, the necessary funds to establish and maintain such industrial departments as aforesaid. *Taxes may be levied to purchase material, etc., and pay instructors.*

§ 3. The state normal and training schools which are or hereafter may be established in this state, hereby are and shall be required to include in their courses of *Normal schools to include in courses of*

CHAP. 484, 1893.
study instruction in principles of manual or industrial arts as prescribed by state superintendent.

instruction the principles underlying the manual or industrial arts, and also the practical training in the same, to such an extent as the superintendent of public instruction may prescribe, and to such further extent as the local boards, respectively, of said normal and training schools may prescribe.

§ 4. This act shall take effect immediately.

EVENING SCHOOLS — INDUSTRIAL DRAWING.

CHAP. 540.

AN ACT to provide for the establishment of evening schools for free instruction in industrial drawing.

PASSED June 7, 1887.

Evening schools for industrial drawing.

SECTION 1. The board of education, or other body having supervision of the public schools in any city or union free school district in this state, is hereby authorized to establish and maintain evening schools for free instruction in industrial drawing, whenever the city authorities in any city or the qualified electors duly convened in any union free school district shall so direct, and shall make provision for the maintenance of such schools. In addition to the powers now conferred by law upon the authorities of any city, or upon the electors of any union free school district in the state, such authorities and such electors shall also have power, whenever they shall think it advisable, to raise such moneys as shall be necessary to carry out the purposes of this act.

§ 2. This act shall take effect immediately.

FREE KINDERGARTEN SCHOOLS IN CITIES AND VILLAGES.

CHAP. 484.

AN ACT to encourage and promote the establishment and maintenance of free kindergarten schools in cities and villages.

APPROVED by the Governor April 29, 1893. Passed, three-fifths being present.

The People of the State of New York, represented in Senate and Assembly, do enact as follows:

Free Kindergarten school may be established in certain localities.

SECTION 1. The board of education, or the public school authorities of any city or village located in a county having less than one million inhabitants, and employing a superintendent of schools, may establish and maintain one or more free kindergarten schools. The money for the support of such schools shall be raised in like manner as for the support of the other public schools of the city or village.

§ 2. No child under the age of four years shall be admitted to these schools, and the local school authorities are hereby empowered to fix the highest age limit of children who may attend.

§ 3. All teachers employed in these schools shall be licensed in the same manner as teachers employed in the other public schools of this state, and shall be entitled to their distributive share in the district quotas.

§ 4. The attendance of children under the age of five years who may be enrolled in these schools shall be reported separately, and shall not be counted in the distribution of public money.

§ 5. This act shall take effect immediately.

VOCAL MUSIC — STUDY OF.

CHAP. 636.

AN ACT in relation to the study of vocal music in the public schools of the state of New York.

APPROVED by the Governor May 6, 1893. Passed, three-fifths being present.

The People of the State of New York, represented in Senate and Assembly, do enact as follows:

SECTION 1. In each of the state normal schools the course of study may embrace instruction in vocal music.

§ 2. The board of education in each city in this state may cause free instruction to be given in vocal music in the schools under their charge.

§ 3. The board of education of each union free school district, incorporated under the laws of this state, may cause free instruction to be given in vocal music in the schools under their charge.

§ 4. The superintendent of public instruction may provide instruction in vocal music in all teachers' institutes held throughout the state.

§ 5. This act shall take effect immediately.

DRAWING TO BE TAUGHT.

CHAP. 322.

AN ACT relating to free instruction in drawing.

Passed May 14, 1875.

Drawing to be taught in normal schools.

SECTION 1. In each of the state normal schools the course of study shall embrace instruction in industrial or free hand drawing.

In schools in cities.

§ 2. The board of education in each city in this state shall cause free instruction to be given in industrial or free hand drawing in at least one department of the schools under their charge.

In union free school districts.

State superintendent may excuse from.

§ 3. The board of education of each union free school district incorporated by special act of the legislature, shall cause free instruction to be given in industrial or free hand drawing in the schools under their charge, unless excused therefrom by the superintendent of public instruction.

§ 4. This act shall take effect October first, eighteen hundred and seventy-five.

SCHOOL COMMISSIONERS.

SALARIES, HOW PAYABLE.

CHAP. 1.

AN ACT to provide for the deficiency in the revenue of the United States deposit fund, and for the payment of the salaries of school commissioners.

Passed January 15, 1888.

Commissioners' salaries to be paid.

(SECTION 1. Omitted as temporary.)

§ 2. The salaries now due and hereafter to become due to the several school commissioners of the state shall be paid out of any unexpended balances in the treasury credited to the free school fund.

Superintendent to set apart a sum sufficient to pay salaries of school commissioners from the free school fund.

§ 3. In making the annual apportionment of school moneys, the superintendent of public instruction shall hereafter set apart a sum sufficient to pay the salaries of the several school commissioners from the free school fund, instead of from the United States deposit fund as heretofore.

§ 4. All acts and parts of acts inconsistent with this act are hereby repealed.

§ 5. This act shall take effect immediately.

TO DESCRIBE DEFINITELY DISTRICT LINES.

CHAP. 456

AN ACT requiring school district lines to be definitely described and recorded.

Passed April 16, 1860.

SECTION 1. It shall be the duty of the school commissioner or commissioners having jurisdiction to inquire into and ascertain whether the several school district lines within his or their commissioners' district, are definitely and plainly described in the book of records kept in the town clerk's office for that purpose, as now required by law. And in case any of them shall be found to be defective or indefinite, then he or they shall cause the same to be correctly and definitely described and recorded in said book, as required by law.

Duty of school commissioners to definitely describe district lines.

SCHOOL COMMISSIONER DISTRICTS.

CITIES NOT INCLUDED IN COMMISSIONER DISTRICTS — COUNTIES, HOW TO BE DIVIDED INTO DISTRICTS, IN CERTAIN CASES.

CHAP. 414.

AN ACT to amend section sixteen of chapter one hundred and seventy-nine of the laws of eighteen hundred and fifty-six, entitled "An act to provide for a more thorough supervision and inspection of common schools, and further to amend the statutes relating to public instruction in the state."

Passed May 16, 1883.

SECTION 1. Section sixteen of chapter one hundred and seventy-nine of the laws of eighteen hundred and fifty-six* is hereby amended so as to read as follows:

§ 16. The several cities which already or which shall hereafter, under special acts, elect superintendents of common schools, or whose board of education choose clerks doing the duty of supervision under direction of the board of education, shall not be included in any commissioner's district created by this act or authorized to be formed by the board of supervisors; and the several boards of supervisors in counties in which such cities are

Cities having a superintendent of schools not to be included in commissioner district.

Supervisors to divide county into commissioner districts.

---

* Chapter 179, Laws of 1856, was superseded by the provisions of chapter 555 Laws of 1864. This act is, therefore, regarded as a new and independent statute.

joined to towns in the formation of an assembly district may divide the county, exclusive of such cities, into school commissioner's district as they may deem advisable, but no town shall be divided in forming such districts.

DIVISION OF DISTRICTS — ERECTION OF.

CHAP. 686.
AN ACT in relation to counties, constituting chapter eighteen of the general laws.

PASSED MAY 18, 1892.

THE COUNTY LAW.

ARTICLE ELEVEN — BOARDS OF SUPERVISORS.

General powers.

§ 12. The board of supervisors shall:

Boards of supervisors may divide school commissioner districts containing more than two hundred school districts.

9. Divide any school commissioner's district within the county which contains more than two hundred school districts and erect therefrom an additional school commissioner's district, and when such district shall have been formed, a school commissioner for the district shall be elected in the manner provided by law for the election of school commissioners.

SCHOOL DISTRICTS.

ACQUISITION OF SITES.

*†CHAP. 800.
AN ACT to provide for the appraisal of and acquiring title to lands taken for or in addition to sites for district school-houses.

PASSED April 25, 1866.

Land, or additional land for site.

SECTION 1. Land for the site of a district school-house, or additional land adjoining to and for the enlargement of an established site, not exceeding one acre, may be acquired in cases where the owner or owners thereof, or some of them, shall not consent to sell the same for such purpose, or the trustee or trustees of the district cannot agree with such owner or owners, or some of them, upon the price or value thereof, as follows:

Mode of procedure.

A petition shall be prepared for presentation to the

---

* As amended by chap. 819, Laws of 1867, and chap. 329, Laws of 1871.

† NOTE.— So much of this chapter and the amendments thereof as prescribes a method of procedure in proceedings for the condemnation of real property for a public use, on lands taken for or in addition to sites for district school-houses is repealed in the amendment of section 3383 of the Code of Civil Procedure by sec. 1, chap. 247, Laws of 1890, and sections 3357 to 3383 (both inclusive) of the Code of Civil Procedure are substituted as a method of procedure in the taking of lands for school-house sites.

county court of the county in which the land is situated, at some regular term thereof, signed by the trustee or trustees of the district, or a majority of them, setting forth that the inhabitants of the district have designated or desire to obtain the land for the site of a district school-house, or in addition to and for the enlargement of that already established as such site, describing such land by its locality and by particular metes and bounds, stating the quantity thereof as nearly as may be, with the name or names and place or places of residence of owner or owners, and that the consent of such owner or owners, or some of them, to sell such land for said purpose, cannot be obtained, or that the trustee or trustees cannot agree with him or them, or some of them, upon a reasonable price therefor, and praying for the appointment of commissioners to appraise the same.

Said petition shall be filed in the office of the county clerk of the county in which the land is situated, and at the time of filing thereof, or at any time afterwards, the petitioners may cause a notice of the pendency of the proceedings to be filed in said office, which notice the county clerk shall file and record in the same manner that similar notices in actions in the supreme court are required to be filed and recorded; which notice shall state the object of the proceeding, and contain a description of the land and the names of the parties affected thereby. And all persons who shall acquire, in whatsoever way, any title to, interest in, lien or incumbrance upon said land, after the filing of the notice of the pendency of the proceedings as aforesaid, shall be bound and affected by said proceedings in the same manner and to the same extent as if they had been named in the petition as parties thereto; and said persons shall also be bound in the same manner, and to the same extent, by notice of the existence of said proceedings, whether notice of the pendency thereof has been filed or not. The petitioners may appear and prosecute such proceedings by an attorney.

A copy of said petition, with a notice thereto annexed of the time and place when and where the same will be presented to said county court, addressed to the owner or owners of the required lands, shall be served in all cases, except as hereinafter allowed, as follows: Upon each person to whom the notice is addressed, who resides in the county in which the land is situated, by delivering to each such person, or, in case of his absence, by leaving at his dwelling-house or usual place of abode or business, such

CHAP. 800, 1866.

copy and notice, at least thirty days before the day specified in the notice for the presentation of the petition. Upon each such person who shall reside out of such county, by depositing such copy and notice in one of the post-offices nearest to said land, directed to such persons at his reputed place of residence, and paying the proper postage thereon, at least forty days before the day specified in the notice, for the presentation of the petition, if such place of residence be within this state, and at least sixty days before that day if such place of residence be out of this state, except that if such place of residence be in the upper peninsula of Michigan, or in any state or territory of the United States west of the Mississippi river, except the states of Iowa, Missouri, Arkansas and Louisianna or any place out of the jurisdiction of the United States, then at least four months before such specified day of presentation. If any such owner or owners shall reside out of the state, and shall have an agent or attorney residing therein, authorized to convey or contract for the sale of his or their interest in said lands who shall not consent, or with whom the trustee or trustees cannot agree as aforesaid, then and in that case the service of the copy of petition and of notice aforesaid may be made upon such agent or attorney instead of upon such owner or owners, either personally or by depositing the same in a post-office as aforesaid, directed to such agent or attorney at his place of residence, and paying postage as aforesaid, the same number of days or months before the said specified day for the presentation of the petition, as if the service were upon such owner or owners, as hereinbefore required. If any such owner shall be an infant, under the age of twenty-one years, such service shall be made on his general guardian; if there be no such guardian, on the infant, if over fourteen years of age, and if under that age on the person with whom such infant shall reside, in each case in the same mode, and the same number of days or months before the specified day for the presentation of the petition, as if the service were upon an adult owner, according to the place of residence of such guardian, infant or person with whom such infant resides, upon whom service is made. If any such owner shall be an idiot, or of unsound mind, service shall be made upon the committee of his person or estate; or, if there be no such committee, then upon the person who shall have the care of such idiot or person of unsound mind, in the same mode and the same number of days before presentation of the petition, as in other

Notice may be served on agent.

On guardian.

If owner be an idiot.

cases. In all other cases service of copies of the petition, of notices, appointments of guardians or committees, orders or other papers in the proceedings under this act, or in connection therewith, shall be made as the court in which the proceedings are had shall direct.

CHAP. 800, 1866.

§ 2. On presenting such petition to the county court aforesaid, on the day specified for its presentation as aforesaid, with proof of service of a copy or copies thereof and notice, and of other papers as hereinbefore required, all persons whose estate or interest are to be effected by the proposed proceedings, relative to the land described in the petition, may appear in person or by attorney, or other proper representative, before the said court, and show cause against granting the prayer of the petitioners. The said court shall hear the proofs and allegations of the parties, and if no sufficient cause be shown against granting the prayer of the petitioner, shall make an order appointing three disinterested and suitable persons, residing in the same county, neither of whom shall be an inhabitant of the school district named in the petition, or interested in any taxable property therein, or who shall be within two degrees of relationship, by blood or marriage, to any owner of such taxable property, or to any owner of the land described in such petition, as commissioners to appraise the said land, and to award the compensation to be made to the owner or owners thereof for the same, for the purposes specified in said petition; and the said court shall specify and appoint in such order the time and place within said school district, for the first meeting of said commissioners, and also the time and place, when and where said county court will receive the report of said commissioners of their proceedings and award in the premises, for confirmation.

One may appear in person or by attorney.

Court to appoint commissioners by an order.

§ 3. The said commissioners, before entering upon their duties, shall be sworn before some officer, authorized to administer oaths, that they will fairly and impartially view the land in question, hear the proofs and allegations of the parties interested, and make a just and reasonable award of the compensation to be paid by the school district for the said land to be appropriated for a site or part of a site for a district school-house. The said commissioners shall have power to issue subpœnas and administer oaths to witnesses, and a majority of them may adjourn the proceedings from time to time, if necessary. They shall also view the land in question, hear the proofs and allegations of parties, reduce the testimony given, if any,

Commissioners must be sworn.

Powers of commissioners.

CHAP. 800, 1866.

to writing; and without unnecessary delay, they, or a majority of them, shall appraise the said land and determine and award the compensation which ought to be made therefor by said school district, to the party or parties owning the same. They shall make a written report of their proceedings and award in the case, signed by them, or a majority of them, which shall be accompanied by the minutes of the testimony taken by them, and shall deliver the same to the county judge of the county on or before the day named in the order appointing them, for receiving such report for confirmation. The said commissioners shall be entitled to two dollars per day for their services, which shall be a charge upon and be paid by the school district in whose behalf the land in question has been appraised by them as aforesaid.

Duty of commissioners.

Pay.

Court to make order on proceedings, and judge to give trustees a copy.

§ 4. On the day and at the time and place appointed in the order aforesaid for receiving such report, the county court aforesaid, on being satisfied of the regularity and fairness of the previous proceedings, shall make an order reciting the proceedings, giving a description of the land appraised, confirming the report and directing to whom the compensation awarded shall be paid, or where and with whom the same shall be deposited. A certified copy of the last-mentioned order shall, without unnecessary delay, be delivered by the judge holding said county court to the trustee or trustees aforesaid, or to one of them, whose duty it shall be forthwith to cause the same to be recorded at the expense of the said school district, in the office of the county clerk of the county in which the land therein described is situated. The trustee or trustees are hereby authorized and directed, on the filing of said order with the county clerk as aforesaid, forthwith to levy a district tax for a sum sufficient to pay the compensation named in said award and the expense of recording said order.

Trustees to levy tax.

Title to vest in district.

§ 5. Upon said order being recorded as aforesaid, and upon the payment or deposit of the amount of compensation awarded for said land, all the right, title and interest of the owner and owners aforesaid, in and to the said land, shall vest in the school district in whose behalf the proceedings aforesaid were instituted; and the trustee or trustees of such district shall be entitled to enter upon, take possession of, occupy and use said land for the purpose set forth in their petition aforesaid; and all land acquired by any school district pursuant to the provisions of this act, shall be deemed to be taken for public use.

ACQUISITION OF SITES.

§ 6. The proceeds of every such award shall be divided amongst the parties whose rights and interests shall have been sold, in proportion to their respective rights in the premises; and the share of such of the parties as are of full age shall be paid to them or their legal representatives by the commissioners, or shall be brought into court for their use. *(CHAP. 800, 1866. Proceeds, how divided.)*

§ 7. When any of such known parties are infants, the court may, in its discretion, direct the share of such infants to be paid over to the general guardian on proper security being filed, or to be invested in permanent securities at interest, in the name and for the benefit of such infants, or be deposited in some trust company or savings bank to abide the further order of the court. *(Share of infants, how disposed of.)*

§ 8. When any of the parties whose interests have been sold are absent from the state, or are not known or named in the proceedings, the court shall direct the shares of such parties to be invested in permanent securities at interest or to be deposited in some trust company or savings bank to abide the further order of the court, for the benefit of such parties, until claimed by them or their legal representatives. *(When proceeds to be invested.)*

§ 9. When the proceeds of a sale belonging to any tenant in dower, or by courtesy, or for life, shall be brought into court as hereinbefore directed, the court shall direct the same to be invested in permanent securities at interest, so that such interest shall annually be paid to the parties entitled to such estate during their lives respectively, unless such parties shall elect to accept a sum in gross in lieu thereof.

§ 10. The court may, in its discretion, require all or any of the parties, before they shall receive any share of the moneys arising from such sale, to give security to the satisfaction of such court to refund the said shares with interest thereon, in case it shall thereafter appear that such party was not entitled thereto. *(Court may require security.)*

§ 11. The amounts of all commissioners' fees, and of all expenses incurred by or in behalf of any school district, in pursuance of the provisions of this act, shall be a charge upon such district, and be levied and collected by tax in the same manner as other district taxes are levied and collected therein. *(Expenses a charge on district.)*

* § 12. This act shall not apply to cities of more than thirty thousand inhabitants; nor shall it be lawful under this act to acquire title to less than the whole of any city *(What lands may not be taken.)*

---

* As amended by sec. 1, chap. 329. Laws of 1871.

CHAP. 800,
1866.

or village lot, with the erections thereon, if any, nor to any premises occupied as a homestead by the owner or owners thereof, without the consent of such owner or owners; nor beyond the corporate limits of cities, to any garden or orchard, or any part thereof, nor to any part of any yard or inclosure necessary to the use and enjoyment of buildings, or any fixtures or erections for the purposes of trade or manufactures, without the consent of the owner or owners thereof.

Boards of education, when to be trustees.

* § 13. Boards of education in cities of not more than thirty thousand inhabitants are hereby clothed with all the powers of trustees under the act hereby amended, and the title to any and all lands acquired in any city under the provisions of said act, shall vest in the board of education thereof, or such other corporate body as is by law vested with the title to the school lands in such city. But nothing in the act hereby amended contained shall be construed to limit or circumscribe the powers and duties heretofore lodged in such board of education by law.

Provisions of this act extended to the city of Brooklyn.

† § 14. The provisions of this act, and of subsequent amendments thereto, shall be extended and apply to the city of Brooklyn, and the board of education of that city is hereby clothed with all the powers of trustees under the provisions of this act and the amendments thereto, and the title to any and all lands acquired in said city under the provisions of this act shall vest in the board of education thereof. The proceedings mentioned in section one of this act may be authorized by a vote of said board of education and the petition may be signed by the officers of said board. The commissioners provided for in section two of this act may be inhabitants of the city of Brooklyn and owners of taxable property therein, but shall not be owners of nor interested in the property proposed to be taken, nor related to the owners of the land proposed to be taken. The proceedings authorized by this act may be taken in the city of Brooklyn before the supreme court or city court of Brooklyn, and if taken in the latter court the petition shall be filed in the office of the clerk of that court, and the notice of *lis pendens* in the office of the clerk of Kings county. The compensation named in the award, the fees of the commissioners and the costs and expenses of said board of education of the city of Brooklyn in such proceeding shall be paid by said board out of the special fund in

---

* As amended by sec. 2, chap. 329, Laws of 1871.
† Added by sec. 1, chap. 121, Laws of 1886. See sec. 35 of title XXII. Chap. 583, Laws of 1888, relating to the city of Brooklyn.

their hands, and such fees, costs and expenses may be taxed and allowed in the final order.

_{CHAP. 248.}
_{1878.}

* The act hereby amended shall apply to union free school districts and to districts organized under special laws; and the trustees of such districts and the boards of education organized under special laws, shall be and are hereby clothed with all the powers vested in trustees under said act.

_{To apply to union free school districts and districts organized under special acts.}

* Nothing in this act contained shall prejudice or impair any right acquired or proceeding had or instituted under or by virtue of the act hereby amended.

§ 15. (Which was added by chapter 318, Laws of 1887, so as to make the law applicable to New York city, was by chapter 191, Laws of 1888, declared to be no longer applicable, and provision by said act was made for the acquisition of sites for school buildings in the city of New York.)

_{Repealed.}

ELECTIONS IN CERTAIN SCHOOL DISTRICTS.

CHAP. 248.

AN ACT in relation to the election of officers in certain school districts.

;PASSED May 13, 1878.

SECTION 1. In all school districts in this state in which the number of children of school age exceeds three hundred, as shown by the last annual report of the trustees to the school commissioner, all district officers, except the treasurer and collector of union free school districts, shall be elected by ballot.

_{Elections by ballot.}

† § 2. Such election shall be held on the Wednesday next following the first Tuesday in August in each year, between the hours of twelve o'clock mid-day and four o'clock in the afternoon at the principal school-house in the district, or at such other suitable place as the trustees may designate. When the place of holding such election is other than at the principal school-house, the trustees shall give notice thereof by the publication of such notice, at least one week before the time of holding such election, in some newspaper published in the district, or by posting the same in three conspicuous places in the district. The trustees may, by resolution extend the time of holding the election from four o'clock until sunset.

_{Election, when and where held.}

---

* These two paragraphs are added by chap. 819, Laws of 1867.
† As amended by chap. 405, Laws of 1879; chap. 115, Laws of 1882; chap. 413, Laws of 1883, and sec. 11 of chap. 245, Laws of 1889.

CHAP. 248, 1878.
Inspectors.

§ 3. The trustees or board of education, or such of them as may be present, shall act as inspectors of election, and immediately after the close of the polls shall proceed to canvass the votes and declare the result. If any such district shall have but one trustee, the district clerk shall be associated with him as inspector. If a majority of the trustees shall not be present at the time for opening the polls, those in attendance may appoint any of the legal voters of the district present, to act as inspectors in place of the absent trustees. If none of the trustees shall be present at the time for opening the polls, the legal voters may choose three of their number to act as inspectors.

Trustees to provide ballot box.

§ 4. The trustees shall, at the expense of the district, provide a suitable box in which the ballots shall be deposited as they are received. Such ballots shall contain the names of the persons voted for, and shall designate the office for which each one is voted. The ballots may be either written or printed, or partly written and partly printed.

Duties of clerk.

§ 5. The district clerk, or clerk of the board of education, as the case may be, shall attend to the election and record in a book to be provided for that purpose the name of each elector as he deposits his ballot. When the polls shall have been closed the inspectors shall first count the ballots to see if they tally with the number of names recorded by the clerk. If they exceed that number enough ballots shall be withdrawn to make them correspond. Any clerk who shall neglect or refuse to record the name of a person whose ballot is received by the inspectors, shall be liable to a fine of twenty-five dollars, to be sued for by the supervisor of the town. If the district clerk or clerk of the board of education shall be absent, or shall be unable or shall refuse to act, the trustees, inspectors of election, or board of education shall appoint some person to act in his place.

Challenges.

§ 6. If any person offering to vote at any such election shall be challenged as unqualified by any legal voter, the chairman of the inspectors shall require the person so offering to vote to make the following declaration: "I do declare and affirm that I am an actual resident of this school district, and that I am legally qualified to vote at this election." And every person making such declaration shall be permitted to vote; but if any person shall refuse to make such declaration his ballot shall not be received by the inspectors. Any person who upon being

ELECTIONS IN CERTAIN SCHOOL DISTRICTS.

so challenged shall willfully make a false declaration of his right to vote at such election, shall be deemed guilty of a misdemeanor and punished by imprisonment in the county jail for not less than six months nor more than one year. Any person who shall vote at such election, not being duly qualified, shall, though not challenged, forfeit the sum of ten dollars, to be sued for by the supervisor of the town for the benefit of the school or schools of the district.

CHAP. 248, 1878.
Penalties, for false declaration or illegal voting.

§ 7. All disputes concerning the validity of any such election, or of any votes cast thereat, or of any of the acts of the inspectors or clerk, shall be referred to the superintendent of public instruction, whose decision in the matter shall be final. Such superintendent may, in his discretion, order a new election in any district.

Disputes concerning the election to be referred to the superintendent of public instruction.

§ 8. The persons having the highest number of votes, respectively, for the several offices shall be declared elected, and the clerk shall record the declaration of the inspectors. In case two persons shall have an equal number of votes for the same office, the inspectors of election shall immediately choose one of such persons. If the inspectors cannot agree, the clerk shall decide the matter.

Result, how declared.

§ 9. The annual meeting, in the several districts shall be held as now provided by law for the purpose of transacting all business except the election of officers.

Annual meeting.

* § 10. This act shall not apply to cities nor to union free school districts whose boundaries correspond with those of an incorporated village, nor to any school district organized under a special act of the legislature, in which the time, manner and form of the election of district officers shall be different from that prescribed for the election of officers in common school districts, organized under the general law, nor to any of the school districts in counties of Richmond, Suffolk, Chenango, Westchester, Warren, Erie and St. Lawrence.

Districts exempted from the provisions of this act.

---

* Last amended by chapter 209, Laws of 1888.

PLANS FOR SCHOOL BUILDINGS.

CHAP. 675.

AN ACT to provide plans and specifications for the use of trustees in the erection of school-houses, and making an appropriation therefor.

PASSED June 24, 1887.

Plans for school buildings.

SECTION 1. The state superintendent of public instruction is hereby authorized and directed to procure architect's plans and specifications for a series of school buildings, to cost sums ranging from six hundred to ten thousand dollars, together with full detail working plans and directions *Arrangement of plans, etc.* for the erection of the same. After procuring said plans and specifications, he shall accompany the same with blank forms for builders' contracts and with suggestions in relation to the preparation of the grounds and the arrangement of the building with regard to lighting, heating, ventilating and the health and convenience of teachers and pupils, and then publish the whole in convenient form for distribution to trustees and others having use for the same.

Appropriation for.

§ 2. The sum of two thousand five hundred dollars, or so much thereof as may be necessary, payable out of the free school fund, is hereby appropriated for carrying out the purposes of this act.

§ 3. This act shall take effect immediately.

REQUIRING FIRE ESCAPES IN CONNECTION WITH CERTAIN SCHOOL BUILDINGS.

CHAP. 431.

AN ACT to require fire-escapes in connection with certain school buildings.

PASSED May 24, 1890.

Fire-escapes for school buildings.

SECTION 1. All school buildings which are more than two stories high shall have properly constructed stairways on the outside thereof with suitable door-ways leading thereto from each story above the first, for use in case of fire. Such stairways shall be kept in good order and free from obstruction. It shall be the duty of the board of education or the trustees having charge of such school-houses, to cause such stairways to be constructed and *Tax therefor.* maintained, and the reasonable and proper cost thereof, shall in each case be a legal charge upon the city or district, and shall be raised by tax, as other moneys are raised for school purposes. This act shall not apply to the cities of New York and Brooklyn.

§ 2. This act shall take effect immediately.

CERTAIN DISTRICTS MAY CONTRACT TO TEACH CHILDREN OF OTHER DISTRICTS.

CHAP. 219.

AN ACT for the relief of school districts wishing to contract with boards of education of cities, to educate their children in city schools.

PASSED May 3, 1877.

* SECTION 1. Whenever any school district adjoining a city or village of six thousand inhabitants, by a vote of a majority of the qualified voters of such district, shall empower the trustees thereof, the said trustees shall enter into a written contract with the board of education of such city or village, whereby all the children of such district may be entitled to be taught in the public schools of such city or village, for a period of not less than twenty-eight weeks in any school year, upon filing a copy of such contract duly certified by the trustees of such school district, and by the secretary of the board of education of said city or village, in the office of the superintendent of public instruction, such school district shall be deemed to have employed a competent teacher for such period, and shall be entitled to receive one distribution district quota each year, during which such contract shall be renewed and continued.

† § 2. The board of education of any city or village so contracting with any school district shall report the number of persons of school age in such district, together with those resident in the city or village the same as though they were actual residents of the city or village, and shall report for the pupils attending the city or village schools from such district to the superintendent of public instruction, the same as though they were residents of such city or village.

§ 3. It shall be the duty of the superintendent of public instruction to give to school commissioners such directions as may, in his judgment, be required and proper in relation to the reports to be made by the trustees of such districts to school commissioners.

§ 4. This act shall take effect immediately.

---

* As amended by sec. 1 of chap. 396, Laws of 1879.
† As amended by sec. 2 of chap. 396, Laws of 1879.

TUITION OF NON-RESIDENT PUPILS — TAX PAID TO BE DEDUCTED.

CHAP. 413.

AN ACT for the relief of non-resident taxpayers who, or whose children or wards are attendants at any free school.

PASSED May 31, 1884.

Non-resident pupils subject to the payment of tuition fee

* SECTION 1. Pupils attending any free school, whether the same be organized under chapter five hundred and fifty-five of the laws of eighteen hundred and sixty-four, entitled "An act to revise and consolidate the general acts relating to public instruction," or under any special act applying to a village or city, if residing out of the districts where said schools are kept, shall be subject to the payment of the tuition prescribed by the proper authorities;

Deduction to be made when pupil, parent or guardian pays tax in district where pupil attends school.

provided, that if such non-resident pupils, their parents or guardians, shall be liable to be taxed for the support of said schools in the said districts, on account of owning property therein, the amount of any such tax paid by a non-resident pupil, his parent or guardian, during the same school year in which the charge for tuition was incurred, shall be deducted from such charge for tuition.

EMPLOYMENT AND PAY OF TEACHERS.

CHAP. 335.

AN ACT in relation to the employment and pay of teachers in the public schools.

PASSED May 16, 1887.

Memorandum of hiring.

SECTION 1. From and after the passage of this act, all officers or boards of officers who shall employ any teacher to teach in any of the public schools of this state shall, at the time of such employment, make and deliver to such teacher, or cause to be made and delivered, a memorandum in writing, signed by said officer, or by the members of said board, or by some person duly authorized by said board, to represent them in the premises, in which the detail of the agreement between the parties, and particularly the length of the term of employment, the amount of compensation and the time or times when such compensation shall be due and payable shall be clearly and

---

* As amended by sec. 11, chap. 340, Laws of 1885.

definitely set forth. But nothing herein contained shall be deemed to abridge or otherwise affect the term of employment of any teacher now or hereafter employed in the public schools, nor to repeal or affect any provision of special laws concerning the employment or removal of teachers now in force in any particular locality.

§ 2. The pay of any teacher employed in the public schools of this state shall be due and payable at least as often as at the end of each calendar month of the term of employment. *Teachers to be paid at least monthly*

§ 3. This act shall take effect immediately.

CHAP. 538, 1887.

HEALTH AND DECENCY.

CHAP. 538.

AN ACT in relation to health and decency in the school districts of this state.

PASSED June 7, 1887.

SECTION 1. From and after the first day of September, eighteen hundred and eighty-seven, the board of education, or the trustee or trustees having supervision over any school district of this state, shall provide suitable and convenient water-closets or privies for each of the schools under their charge, at least two in number, which shall be entirely separated each from the other and having separate means of access, and the approaches thereto shall be separated by a substantial close fence not less than seven feet in height. It shall be the duty of the officers aforesaid to keep the same in a clean and wholesome condition, and a failure to comply with the provisions of this act on the part of the trustees shall be sufficient grounds for removal from office, and for withholding from the district any share of the public moneys of the state. Any expense incurred by the trustees aforesaid in carrying out the requirements of this act shall be a charge upon the district, when such expense shall have been approved by the school commissioner of the district within which the school district is located; and a tax may be levied therefor without a vote of the district. *Water-closets and division fences to be constructed. Tax for.*

General Acts Relating to Schools.

CHAP. 661, 1893.

VACCINATION OF SCHOOL CHILDREN.

CHAP. 661.

AN ACT in relation to the public health, constituting chapter twenty-five of the general laws.

Approved by the Governor May 9, 1893. Passed, three-fifths being present.

The People of the State of New York, represented in Senate and Assembly, do enact as follows:

CHAPTER XXV OF THE GENERAL LAWS.

THE PUBLIC HEALTH LAW.

Vaccination of school children.

SECTION 200. No child or person not vaccinated shall be admitted or received into any of the public schools of the state, and the trustees or other officers having the charge, management or control of such schools shall cause this provision of law to be enforced. They may adopt a resolution excluding such children and persons not vaccinated from such school until vaccinated, and when any such resolution has been adopted, they shall give at least ten days' notice thereof, by posting copies of the same in at least two public and conspicuous places within the limits of the school government, and shall announce therein that due provision has been made, specifying it, for the vaccination of any child or person of suitable age desiring to attend the school, and whose parents or guardians are unable to procure vaccination for them, or who are, by reason of poverty, exempted from taxation in such district.

Appointment of physician.

§ 201. Such trustees or board may appoint a competent physician and fix his compensation, who shall ascertain the number of children or persons in a school district, or in a subdivision of a city school government, of suitable age to attend the common schools, who have not been vaccinated and furnish such trustees or board a list of their names. Every such physician shall provide himself with good and reliable vaccine virus with which to vaccinate such children or persons as such trustees or board shall direct, and give certificates of vaccination when required, which shall be evidence that the child or person to whom given has been vaccinated. The expenses incurred in carrying into effect the provisions of this and the preceding section shall be deemed a part of the expense of maintaining such school, and shall be levied and collected in in the same manner as other school expenses.

Trustees to report.

The trustees of the several school districts of the state shall include in their annual report the number of vaccinated and unvaccinated children of school age in their respective districts.

DISSOLUTION OF UNION FREE SCHOOL DISTRICTS.

CHAP. 210.

AN ACT to provide for the dissolution of union free school districts in certain cases.

PASSED May 8, 1880.

SECTION 1. In any union free school district established under the laws of this state, it shall be the duty of the board of education, upon the application of fifteen resident taxpayers of such district, to call a special meeting in the manner prescribed by law, for the purpose of determining whether application shall be made in the manner hereinafter provided, for the dissolution of such union free school district, and for its reorganization as a common school district or districts. *(Duty of board of education on application to call meeting to pass upon the question of dissolution of district.)*

* § 2. Whenever, at any such meeting called and held as aforesaid, it shall be determined by a majority vote of the legal voters present and voting, to be ascertained by taking and recording the ayes and noes, not to dissolve such union free school district, no other meeting for a similar purpose shall be held in said district within three years from the time the first meeting was held, and whenever at any such meeting called and held as aforesaid it shall be determined by a two-thirds vote of the legal voters present and voting, to be ascertained by taking and recording the ayes and noes, to dissolve such union free school district, it shall be the duty of the board of education to present to the clerk of the board of supervisors a certified copy of the call, notice and proceedings, and the said clerk shall lay the same before the board of supervisors at their next meeting. If the board of supervisors shall approve of the proceedings of said meeting, the clerk shall certify the same to the board of education. Such approval shall not take effect until the day preceding the first Tuesday of August next succeeding; but after that date such district shall cease to be a union free school district. *(Meetings to vote upon question of dissolution, not to be held oftener than triennially. Proceedings, in case meeting decides for dissolution. Approval by supervisors, when to take effect. Supervisors may direct that the territory of a dissolved district,)*

§ 3. If any union free school district dissolved under the foregoing provisions shall have been established by the consolidation of two or more districts, it shall be lawful for the board of supervisors to direct that its territory be divided in two or more districts to correspond, so *(when such district had been formed from two or more districts be formed into district the same as before consolidated.)*

---

* As amended by sec. 15, chap. 413, Laws of 1883, and by sec. 12, chap. 246, Laws of 1889.

CHAP. 210, 1880.

far as practicable, with the districts theretofore consolidated.

If an academy has been adopted, it shall be transferred to its former trustees.

§ 4. If there shall be, in such dissolved union free school district, an academy which shall have been adopted as the academic department of the union free school, under the provisions of title nine, chapter five hundred and fifty-five of the laws of eighteen hundred and sixty-four, it shall, upon the application of a majority of the surviving resident former trustees or stockholders, be transferred by the board of education to said former trustees or stockholders.

Conditional approval of supervisors.

§ 5. The board of supervisors may make its approval of the proceeding of any such meeting held as aforesaid conditional upon the payment, by the district which has been most greatly benefited by the consolidation in the way of buildings and other improvements to the other district or districts into which the said union free school district is divided, of such sum or sums of money as they may deem equitable.

Moneys on hand to be apportioned.

§ 6. All moneys remaining in the hands of the treasurer of the union free school district when the order of dissolution shall take effect shall be apportioned equitably among the several districts into which such union free school district is divided, and shall be paid over to the collectors of such districts when they shall have been elected and have qualified according to law.

Annual meetings of districts created by dissolution.

*§ 7. The district or districts formed by the dissolution of such union free school district shall hold its or their annual meeting or meetings on the first Tuesday of August, next after the dissolution of such union free school district, and shall elect officers as now required by law.

If proceedings are not approved, no other meeting to be held in three years.

§ 8. If the board of supervisors shall not approve the proceedings of any such meeting, held as aforesaid, for the purpose of dissolving a union free school district, no other meeting shall be held in such district, for a similar purpose, within three years from the time the first meeting was held.

Notice of dissolution to be given superintendent of public instruction.

§ 9. Whenever the proceedings of a meeting, held as aforesaid, for the purpose of dissolving a union free school district, shall have been approved by the board of supervisors and shall have been certified by the clerk of said board to the board of education, it shall be the duty of the board of education of the district affected forthwith

---

* As amended by sec. 16, chap. 413, Laws of 1883, and by sec. 13, chap. 246, Laws of 1889.

to notify the superintendent of public instruction, and to furnish him copies of the call, notice, proceedings of the meeting, and proceedings of the board of supervisors taken thereon.

SCHOOL OFFICERS.

SCHOOL OFFICERS NOT TO BECOME INDIVIDUALLY INTERESTED IN OFFICIAL CONTRACTS.

CHAP. 220.

AN ACT to amend section four hundred and seventy-three of the Penal Code.

BECAME a law without the approval of the Governor, in accordance with the provisions of article four, section nine, of the Constitution, April 29, 1890. Passed, three-fifths being present.

SECTION 1. Section four hundred and seventy-three of the Penal Code is hereby amended, so as to read as follows:

* § 473. A public officer or school officer, who is authorized to sell or lease any property, or to make any contract in his official capacity, or to take part in making any such sale, lease or contract, who voluntarily becomes interested individually in such sale, lease or contract, directly or indirectly, except in cases where such sale, lease or contract, or payment under the same, is subject to audit or approval by the superintendent of public instruction, is guilty of a misdemeanor. *[margin: School officers not to be interested in sales, leases or contracts.]*

§ 2. This act shall take effect immediately.

TAXATION.

RATE BILLS ABOLISHED.

Sections 26 and 27 of chapter 406, Laws of 1867:

Hereafter all moneys, now authorized by any special acts to be collected by rate bill for the payment of teachers' wages, shall be collected by tax, and not by rate bill. *[margin: The rate bills heretofore authorized by special acts abolished.]*

Nothing in this act contained shall be construed to authorize the common council of any city to increase the *[margin: Local tax of city cannot be increased.]*

---

* Members of boards of education not to be personally interested in any contract made by said board. See sec. 15, tit. 9, School Laws, as amended by chap. 485 Laws of 1893.

local city tax for the support of the schools therein, beyond the amounts they are now authorized by law to raise for local school purposes, and such local tax shall be reduced in such city, by an amount equal to the amount it shall receive by the additional tax authorized by this act, for the support of schools in the state generally.

BANKING ACT.

*CHAP. 409.

AN ACT to revise the statutes of this state relating to banks, banking and trust companies.

TITLE XII.

PASSED July 1, 1882.

Stockholders to be taxed on shares where bank is located.

SECTION 312. The stockholders in every bank or banking association organized under the authority of this state, or of the United States, shall be assessed and taxed on the value of their shares of stock therein; said shares shall be included in the valuation of the personal property of such stockholders in the assessment of taxes at the place, city, town or ward where such bank or banking association is located, and not elsewhere, whether the said stockholders reside in said place, city, town or ward or not; but in the assessment of said shares each stockholder shall be allowed all the deductions and exceptions allowed by law in assessing the value of other taxable personal property owned by individual citizens of this state, and the assessment and taxation shall not be at a greater rate than is made or assessed upon other moneyed capital in the hands of individual *Deductions.* citizens of this state. In making such assessment there shall also be deducted from the value of such shares such sum as in the same proportion to such value as is the assessed value of the real estate of the bank or banking association, and in which any portion of their capital is invested, in which said shares are held to the whole amount of the capital stock of said bank or banking association. Nothing herein contained shall be held or construed to exempt the real estate of banks or banking associations from either state, county or municipal taxes, but the same shall be subject to state county, municipal and other taxation to the same extent and rate and in the same manner according to its value as other real estate is taxed. The local authorites charged by law with the assessment of the said shares shall, within ten days after they have com-

---

* As amended by section 2, 3 and 4 of chapter 714 Laws of 1892.

pleted such assessment, give written notice to each bank or banking association of such assessment of the shares of its respective shareholders, and no personal or other notice to such shareholders of such assessment shall be necessary for the purpose of this act.

§ 313. There shall be kept at all times in the office where the business of each bank or banking association organized under the authority of this state, or of the United States, shall be transacted, a full and correct list of the names and residences, and in cities the residences and street number thereof, of all the stockholders therein and of the number of shares held by each; and such list shall be subject to the inspection of the officers authorized to assess taxes during the business hours of each day in which business may be legally transacted, and it shall be the duty of the managing officer or officers of such bank or banking association to furnish to the officers authorized to assess taxes in the town or ward where such bank or banking association is located, when requested to do so by such officers, and, in the city of New York, on or before the first day of December in each year, a list of the names and residences of such shareholders and the number of shares held by each, together with a statement of the nominal capital and the number of shares and par value of shares of such bank or banking association, and the location and assessed value of all real estate owned by such bank or banking association and in which any portion of its capital is invested, such list and statement to be certified under oath by the managing officer or officers of such bank or banking association, and the names of the holders of such shares appearing upon such list shall be deemed the names of the owners of such shares as are set opposite them respectively for the purposes of assessment and taxation, as provided for in this chapter.

§ 314. When the owner of stock in any bank or banking association organized under the laws of this state, or of the United States; shall not reside at the same place where the bank or banking association is located, the collector and county treasurer shall, respectively, have the same powers as to collecting the tax to be assessed by this act as they have by law when the person assessed has removed from the town, ward or county in which the assessment was made, and the county treasurer, receiver of taxes or other officer authorized to receive such tax from the collector may, all or either of them, have an

CHAP. 409, 1882.

A lien upon stock.

action to collect the tax from the avails of the sale of his, her or their shares of stock, and the tax on the share or shares of said stock shall be and remain a lien thereon from the day when the property is by law assessed, till the payment of said tax, and if transferred after such day, the transfer shall be subject to such lien. The county treasurer, receiver of taxes or other officer authorized to receive such tax on default or neglect to pay the same, may by action in any court of record foreclose said constructive and statutory lien, and may also pursue the same remedies as now provided by law for enforcing payment of personal taxes against residents.

Dividends to be retained by bank to pay tax.

§ 315. For the purpose of collecting the taxes to be assessed under the last three preceding sections of this act, and in addition to any other law of this state not in conflict with the Constitution of the United States relative to the imposition of assessment and collection of taxes, it shall be the duty of every such bank or banking association and the managing officer or officers thereof to retain and within thirty days after declaring the same to pay over to the collector, county treasurer or receiver of taxes so much of any dividend or dividends belonging to such stockholder as shall be necessary to pay any taxes assessed in pursuance of the last three preceding sections of this act, unless it shall be made to appear to such officer or officers that such taxes have been paid previously by the shareholders.

Shareholders of state and national banks to be taxed alike.

§ 318. The shareholders of any bank, banking association, or corporation doing a banking business under the general banking law or a special charter of this state shall be assessed and taxed with respect to their shares of stock, only at the same rate and place, to the same extent and in the same manner as shareholders of national banks may be liable at the same time to be assessed and taxed by authority of the state of New York; provided, however, that no debts shall be deducted from any such assessment of any person applying for the benefit of this act, which have been deducted from the assessment of other personal property of such person; and in making application for such deduction, every person making the application shall make oath that he has not applied to have such debts deducted from any other assessment against him and that no such deduction has been made.

Intent of foregoing section.

§ 319. It is hereby declared that the true intent and meaning of the last preceding section of this act is to place and maintain shareholders of banks, associations and corporations aforesaid upon an equality in the particular in this act referred to, with the shareholders of national banks organized under the act of congress, entitled "An act to provide a national currency secured by a pledge of United States bonds, and to provide for the circulation and redemption thereof, approved June third, eighteen hundred and sixty-four;" and all acts and parts of acts inconsistent with the provisions hereof are hereby repealed.

§ 320. Every individual banker doing business under the laws of this state is hereby required to declare upon oath before the assessor the amount of capital invested in such banking business, and each one hundred dollars of such capital for the purpose of this act, and for the purpose of taxation, shall be held and regarded as one individual share in such banking business, and such shares are hereby declared to be personal property. If such banker have partners he shall declare upon oath before the assessor the number of shares held by each of them in such banking business ascertained as above provided; and the shares so held by any partner shall be included in the valuation of his taxable property in the assessment of all taxes levied in the town, school district or ward where such individual banker is located, and not elsewhere; and such individual banker shall pay the same and make the amount so paid a charge in his accounts with such partners; and if such individual banker have no partners, he shall be held to be the owner of all the shares in such business of banking, and the same shall be included in the valuation of his personal property in the assessment of all taxes levied in the town, school district or ward where his bank is located, and not elsewhere.

Tax upon individual bankers.

DELAWARE AND HUDSON CANAL COMPANY.

CHAP. 540.

AN ACT in relation to the valuation of the property of the president, managers and company of the Delaware and Hudson Canal Company in school districts, for the purpose of taxation.

PASSED June 1, 1880.

SECTION 1. It shall be the duty of the town assessors, within fifteen days after the completion of their annual assessment list, to apportion the valuation of the property of the president, managers and company of the Delaware

Assessors to apportion valuation among several school districts.

CHAP. 540, 1880.

and Hudson Canal Company, as appears on such assessment list, among the several school districts in their town in which any portion of said property is situated, giving to each of said districts their proper portion, according to the proportion that the value of said property in each of such districts bears to the value of the whole thereof in said town.

To be in writing.

§ 2. Such apportionment shall be in writing and shall be signed by said assessors, or a majority of them, and shall set forth the number of each district and the amount of the valuation of the property of the president, managers and company of the Delaware and Hudson Canal Company, apportioned to each of said districts; and such apportionment shall be filed with the town clerk by said assessors, or one of them, within five days after being made, and the amount so apportioned to each district shall be the valuation of the property of said Delaware and Hudson Canal Company, on which all taxes against said Delaware and Hudson Canal Company, in and for said districts, shall be levied and assessed until the next annual assessment and apportionment.

Filed with town clerk.

Supervisor to make same in case of neglect by assessors.

§ 3. In case the assessors shall neglect to make such apportionment, it shall be the duty of the supervisor of the town, on the application of the trustees or board of education of any district, or of the said Delaware and Hudson Canal Company, to make such apportionment, in the same manner and with like effect as if made by said assessors.

Certified statement to be furnished trustees.

§ 4. The town clerk shall, whenever requested, furnish to the trustees or board of education of each district a certified statement of the amounts apportioned to such district, and the name of the company to which the same relates.

Certified copy of apportionment to be furnished the company.

§ 5. The town clerk shall, whenever requested, once each year, furnish to the agent of the said Delaware and Hudson Canal Company and to the trustees or board of education of each school district to which any portion of said appropriation belongs, a certified copy of said apportionment.

When alteration is made in school district.

§ 6. In case any alteration shall be made in any school district, affecting the property of the said Delaware and Hudson Canal Company, the officer making such alteration shall at the same time determine what change in the valuation of the said property in such district would be just, on account of the alteration of such district, and the valuation shall be accordingly changed.

§ 7. This act shall take effect immediately.

FOREST PRESERVE.

CHAP. 332.

AN ACT in relation to the forest preserve and Adirondack park, constituting articles 6 and 7 of chapter 43 of the general laws.

APPROVED by the Governor April 7, 1893.

SECTION 100. The forest preserve shall include the lands now owned or hereafter acquired by the state within the counties of Clinton, except the towns of Altona and Dannemora, Delaware, Essex, Franklin, Fulton, Hamilton, Herkimer, Lewis, Oneida, Saratoga, St. Lawrence, Warren, Washington, Greene, Ulster and Sullivan, except {Forest preserve.}

1. Lands within the limits of any village or city, and,

2. Lands, not wild lands, acquired by the state on foreclosure of mortgages made to the commissioners for loaning certain moneys of the United States, usually called the United States deposit fund.

SECTION 106. All wild or forest land within the forest preserve shall be assessed and taxed at a like valuation and rate as similar lands of individuals within the counties where situated. On or before August first in every year the assessors of the town within which the lands so belonging to the state are situated shall file in the office of the comptroller, and of the forest commission, a copy of the assessment-roll of the town which, in addition to the other matter now required by law, shall state and specify which and how much, if any, of the lands assessed are forest lands, and which and how much, if any, are lands belonging to the state; such statements and specifications to be verified by the oaths of a majority of the assessors. The comptroller shall thereupon and before the first day of September following, and after hearing the assessors and the forest commission if they or any of them so desire, correct or reduce any assessment of state land which may be in his judgment an unfair proportion to the remaining assessment of land within the town, and shall in other respects approve the assessment and communicate such approval, to the assessors. No such assessment of state lands shall be valid for any purpose until the amount of assessment is approved by the comptroller, and such approval attached to and deposited with the assessment-roll of the town and therewith delivered by the assessors of the town to the supervisor thereof or other officer authorized to receive the same from the assessors. No {Taxation of forest preserve.} {Assessors to file copy of assessment-roll with comptroller and forest commission.} {What assessment-roll shall state.} {Comptroller may correct assessment.}

tax for the erection of a school-house or opening of a road shall be imposed on the state lands, unless such erection or opening shall have been first approved in writing by the forest commission. Payment of the lawful and just amount of the taxes imposed under this section on lands so belonging to the state shall in every year be made by the treasurer of the state on the certificate of the comptroller by allowing to the treasurer of the county in which such lands are situated a credit of the amount of such taxes due on such lands payable by such county treasurer in such year to the state for state taxes; but no fees shall be allowed by the comptroller to the county treasurers in adjusting their accounts for such portion of the state tax so paid.

RAILROADS.

CHAP. 694.

AN ACT in relation to the valuation of the property of railroad companies in school districts, for the purpose of taxation.

PASSED April 23, 1867.

* SECTION 1. It shall be the duty of the town assessors, within fifteen days after the completion of their annual assessment list, to apportion the valuation of the property of each and every railroad, telegraph, telephone and pipe-line company as appears on such assessment list, among the several school districts in their town, in which any portion of said property is situated, giving to each of said districts their proper portion, according to the proportion that the value of said property in each of such districts bears to the value of the whole thereof in said town.

† § 2. Such apportionment shall be in writing, and shall be signed by said assessors, or a majority of them, and shall set forth the number of each district and the amount of the valuation of the property of each railroad, telegraph, telephone and pipe-line companies apportioned to each of said districts; and such apportionment shall be filed with the town clerk by said assessors, or one of them, within five days after being made; and the amount so apportioned to each district shall be the valuation of the property of each of said companies, on which all taxes against said companies in and for said districts shall

---

* As amended by sec. 1, chap. 414, Laws of 1884.
† As amended by sec. 2, chap. 414, Laws of 1884.

be levied and assessed, until the next annual assessment and apportionment.

*§ 3. In case the assessors shall neglect to make such apportionment it shall be the duty of the supervisor of the town, on the application of the trustees or board of education of any district, or of any railroad, telegraph, telephone or pipe-line company, to make such apportionment in the same manner and with the like effect as if made by said assessors.

§ 4. The town clerk shall, whenever requested, furnish to the trustees or board of education of each district, a certified statement of the amounts apportioned to such district, and the name of the company to which the same relates.

†§ 5. In case any alteration shall be made in any school district affecting the property of any railroad, telegraph, telephone or pipe-line company, the officer making such alteration shall, at the same time, determine what change in the valuation of said property in such district would be just, on account of the alteration of district, and the valuation shall be accordingly changed.

§ 6. This act shall take effect immediately.

RAILROAD COMPANIES.

COLLECTION OF TAXES.

CHAP. 675.

AN ACT to facilitate the payment of school taxes by railroad companies.

PASSED July 25, 1881.

‡ SECTION 1. It shall be the duty of the school collector in each school district in this state, except in the counties of New York, Kings and Cattaraugus, within five days after the receipt by such collector of any and every tax or assessment-roll of his district, to prepare and deliver to the county treasurer of the county in which such district, or the greater part thereof, is situated, a statement showing the name of each railroad company appearing in said roll, the assessment against each of said companies for real and personal property respectively, and the tax against each of said companies. It shall thereupon be the duty of such

---
* As amended by sec. 12, chap. 340, Laws of 1885.
† NOTE.— See following chapter.
‡ As amended by sec. 1, chap. 319, Laws of 1882, and by chap. 533, Laws of 1885.

CHAP. 675, 1881.

county treasurer, immediately after the receipt by him of such statement from such school collector, to notify the ticket agent of any such railroad company assessed for taxes at the station nearest to the office of such county treasurer personally or by mail, of the fact that such statement has been filed with him by such collector, at the same time specifying the amount of tax to be paid by such railroad company.

Railroad company may pay tax with fees to county treasurer.

§ 2. Any railroad company heretofore organized, or which may hereafter be organized, under the laws of this state, may within thirty days after the receipt of such statement by such county treasurer, pay the amount of tax so levied or assessed against it in such district and in such statement mentioned and contained with one per centum fees thereon, to such county treasurer, who is hereby authorized and directed to receive such amount and to give proper receipt therefor.

Collector to collect tax after thirty days.

§ 3. In case any railroad company shall fail to pay such tax within said thirty days, it shall be the duty of such county treasurer to notify the collector of the school district in which such delinquent railroad company is assessed of its failure to pay said tax, and upon receipt of such notice it shall be the duty of such collector to collect such unpaid tax in the manner now provided by law, together with five per centum fees thereon; but no school collector shall collect by distress and sale any tax levied or assessed in his district upon the property of any railroad company until the receipt by him of such notice from the county treasurer.

Amount paid treasurer to be paid over to collector.

§ 4. The several amounts of tax received by any county treasurer in this state, under the provisions of this act, of and from railroad companies, shall be by such county treasurer placed to the credit of the school district for or on account of which the same was levied or assessed, and on demand paid over to the school collector thereof, and the one per centum fees received therewith shall be placed to the credit of, and on demand paid to, the school collector of such school district.

May pay tax to collector.

§ 5. Nothing in this act contained shall be construed to hinder, prevent or prohibit any railroad company from paying its school tax to the school collector direct, as now provided by law.

§ 6. This act shall take effect immediately.

TEXT BOOKS.

CHAP. 413.

AN ACT to prevent frequent changes of text-books in schools.

PASSED June 5, 1877.

* SECTION 1. The boards of education, or such bodies as perform the functions of such boards in the several cities, villages and union free school districts of this state, shall have power and it shall be their duty to adopt and designate text-books to be used in the schools under their charge in their respective districts. In the other school districts in the state the text-books to used in the schools therein shall be designated at the first annual school meeting held after the passage of this act by a two-thirds vote of all the legal voters present and voting at such school meeting.

[margin: Text-books, designation, and use of.]

§ 2. When a text-book shall have been adopted for use in any of the public or common schools in this state, as provided in the first section of this act, it shall not be lawful to supersede the text-book so adopted by any other book within a period of five years from the time of such adoption, except upon a three-fourths vote of the board of education, or of such body as perform the function of such board, where such board has made the designation, or upon a three-fourths vote of the legal voters present and voting at the annual school meeting in any other school district.

[margin: When adopted not to be superseded by others in five years.]

§ 3. Any person or persons violating any of the provisions of this act shall be liable to a penalty of not less than fifty dollars nor more than one hundred dollars for every such violation, to be sued for by any tax payer of the school district, and recovered before any justice of the peace, said fine, when collected, to be paid to the collector or treasurer for the benefit of said school district.

[margin: Penalty for violating act.]

§ 4. This act shall take effect immediately.

---

* As amended by sec. 1, chap. 427, Laws of 1884.

PHYSIOLOGY AND HYGIENE IN PUBLIC SCHOOLS.

CHAP. 30.

AN ACT in relation to the study of physiology and hygiene in the public schools.

PASSED March 10, 1884.

Local authorities to make provision for study of physiology and hygiene.

SECTION 1. Provision shall be made by the proper local school authorities for instructing all pupils in all schools supported by public money, or under state control, in physiology and hygiene, with special reference to the effect of alcoholic drinks, stimulants and narcotics upon the human system.

Candidates for certificates to teach must pass examination in this study.

§ 2. No certificate shall be granted to any person to teach in the public schools of the state of New York after the first day of January, eighteen hundred and eighty-five, who has not passed a satisfactory examination in physiology and hygiene, with special reference to the effects of alcoholic drinks, stimulants and narcotics upon the human system.

WOMEN.

ENTITLED TO VOTE AND HOLD OFFICE.

CHAP. 9.

AN ACT to declare women eligible to serve as school trustees.

PASSED February 12, 1880.

Sex does not disqualify a voter.

SECTION 1. No person shall be deemed to be ineligible to serve as any school officer, or to vote at any school meeting, by reason of sex, who has the other qualifications now required by law.

§ 2. This act shall take effect immediately.

DETERMINING THOSE WHO HAVE A RIGHT TO VOTE FOR SCHOOL COMMISSIONERS.

CHAP. 214.

AN ACT to determine those who have a right to vote for school commissioners.

BECAME a law without the approval of the governor, in accordance with the provisions of article four, section nine of the Constitution, April 7, 1892.

Who entitled to vote.

SECTION 1. All persons, without regard to sex, who are eligible to the office of school commissioner, and have the other qualifications now required by law, shall have the right to vote for school commissioners in the various commissioner districts of the state.

§ 2. All persons so entitled to vote for school commissioner shall be registered, as provided by law for those who vote for county officers; and whenever school commissioners are to be elected at the ensuing election, it shall be the duty of the county clerk to prepare a ballot to be used exclusively by those who, by reason of sex, can only vote for school commissioners. Said ballots shall be substantially in size and appearance like the other ballots provided by law, with the additional indorsement "School Commissioner" and distributed to the several polling places in the same manner.

§ 3. It shall be the duty of inspectors of elections to give to such persons as are only entitled to vote for the office of school commissioner, such ballots as contain the names only of candidates for that office, and to deposit the ballot selected by such persons in the ballot-box wherein other ballots are placed, provided such persons are properly registered, and who shall have selected their ballots in the same manner and form as is required of those who vote for other county or state offices; and no ballot then voted by persons only entitled to vote for school commissioner shall be counted in case it is found to contain, when canvassed, the name of any person for any other office than that of school commissioner. All ballots furnished by the county clerk for the use of those persons who can only vote for school commissioner, shall be separate and distinct from the other ballots, and given only to those who are not privileged to vote for any other officer.

§ 4. In ascertaining the number of those who have a right to vote in any one polling district for the purpose of determining whether such district has more than three hundred voters, it shall not be necessary to count those who, by reason of sex, are denied the right to vote only for the office of school commissioner.

§ 5. This act shall take effect immediately.

CODE.
CUSTODY OF.

CHAP. 672.

AN ACT to provide for the distribution of the Code of Public Instruction to the several school districts of the state, and making appropriation therefor.

PASSED June 24, 1887.

Code of Public Instruction, how to be distributed.

SECTION 1. The state superintendent of public instruction is hereby directed to deliver, or cause to be delivered, one copy of the Code of Public Instruction, the amended and annotated edition of eighteen hundred and eighty-seven, substantially bound in law sheep, to each of the several school districts of the state.

To be the property of the district.

The copies of said Code so distributed shall be the property of the several school districts receiving the same, and there shall be plainly inscribed on the outside of the cover of each book the following words, namely: This Code is the property of school district number   , town of   , county of   ; the blank spaces being filled in by the number of the district and the names of the town and county where said book shall belong.

Trustees custodians of.

§ 2. The trustees of each school district are hereby made the custodians of the Code of Public Instruction belonging to such school district, and shall deliver the same to their successor or successors in office.

In case of loss, how replaced.

And in case such copy of said Code shall have been lost or destroyed through or by means of the fault or negligence of the trustees, the trustees so permitting the same to be lost or destroyed shall, at their own expense, procure a copy of the latest edition of the Code of Public Instruction and deliver the same to their successor or successors in office in lieu of the copy so lost or destroyed.

Penalty for failure of trustees to comply.

§ 3. Every trustee who fails to comply with the provisions of the foregoing section shall forfeit the sum of twenty-five dollars.

Application of moneys received for penalties.

This penalty shall be sued for by the trustees of the district and shall be used in the purchase of books for the district library, but the state superintendent of public instruction may, upon the application in writing of the trustees of the district, indorsed by the school commissioner of that commissioner district, direct that it be applied toward the payment of teachers' wages.

Appropriation for.

§ 4. The sum of eighteen thousand dollars, or so much thereof as may be necessary, is hereby appropriated out of any moneys not otherwise appropriated, to defray the expense of carrying out the provisions of this act, which shall be paid by the treasurer, on the warrant of the comptroller, upon vouchers approved by said superintendent.

§ 5. This act shall take effect immediately.

REPORTS.

*CHAP. 710.

AN ACT to amend chapter five hundred and eighty-eight of the laws of eighteen hundred and eighty six, entitled "An act to provide for and define the public or legislative printing."

PASSED June 25, 1887.

SECTION 1. * * * * * *

§ 2. Section eight of chapter five hundred and eighty-eight of the laws of eighteen hundred and eighty-six, is hereby amended so as to read as follows:

§ 8. In addition to the usual number of regular reports made by the state officers and institutions, there shall be printed as extra copies of legislative documents for the use of the respective departments, institutions and boards; * * * * of the report of the superintendent of public instruction, fifteen thousand copies, all bound in cloth, to be distributed by that officer as follows: Eleven thousand three hundred copies for the school districts of the state, being one copy for each school district; nine hundred copies to school commissioners and city superintendents of schools; two hundred copies to the state normal and training schools; three hundred copies to academies and high schools; one thousand copies to members and officers of the legislature and state officers; one thousand three hundred copies for the use of the state superintendent of public instruction; also three hundred copies, printed on forty-four pound calendered paper and bound in leather, for exchange with superintendents of public instruction of the states and territories, and for distribution among public libraries. * * *

---

* As amended by section 1 of chapter 643 of Laws of 1892.

APPEALS — RULES OF PRACTICE.

STATE OF NEW YORK:
DEPARTMENT OF PUBLIC INSTRUCTION,
ALBANY, N. Y., *July* 1, 1893.

Pursuant to the authority conferred by section 2, title 12, chapter 555, Laws of 1864, the state superintendent has, by an order dated April 25, 1893, established the following amended rules to regulate the practice in appeals:

1. An appeal must be in writing, addressed "to the superintendent of public instruction," stating the grounds upon which it is taken, and signed by the appellant or appellants. The appeal must be verified by the oath of the appellant or appellants. When the appeal is made by the trustees of a district, it must be signed by all the trustees, or a reason must be given for the omission of any, verified by the oath of the appellant, or of some person acquainted with such reason.

2. A copy of the appeal, and of all the statements, maps and papers intended to be presented in support of it, with the affidavit in verification of the same, must be served on the officer or officers whose act or decision is complained of, or some of them; or if it be from the decision or proceeding of a district meeting, upon the district clerk or one of the trustees, whose duty it is to cause information of such appeal to be given to the inhabitants who voted for the decision.

3. Such service must be made by delivering a copy of the appeal to the party to be served personally, or, in case he cannot be found in the commissioner district in which he resides, after due diligence, by delivering and leaving the same at his residence, with some person of suitable age and discretion, between six o'clock in the morning and nine o'clock in the evening.

4. Immediately after the service of such copy the original, together with an affidavit proving the service of a copy thereof and stating the time and manner of the service and the name and official character of the person upon whom such service was made, must be transmitted to the department of public instruction at Albany.

5. Such original appeal and all papers, etc., annexed thereto, with proof of service of copies, as required by rules 3 and 4, must be sent to the department of public instruction within thirty days after the making of the decision or the performance of the act complained of or within that time after the knowledge of the cause of complaint came to the appellant, or some satisfactory excuse

APPEALS — RULES OF PRACTICE. 155

must be rendered in the appeal for the delay. If an answer is received to an appeal which has not been transmitted to the department, such appeal will be dismissed.

6. The party upon whom an appeal shall be served must, within ten days from the time of such service, unless further time be given by the state superintendent, on application, answer the same, either by concurring in a statement of facts with the appellant or by a separate answer, and of all affidavits, papers, maps, etc., in support thereof. Such statement and answer must be signed by all the trustees or other officers whose act, omission or decision is appealed from, or a good reason, on oath, must be given for the omission of the signature of any of them. Such answer must be verified by oath and a copy thereof and of all the statements, maps, papers, etc., intended to be presented in support thereof, served on the appellants or some one of them, in like manner as is provided in rule 3 for the service of a copy of an appeal.

7. Immediately after the service of a copy of such answer and the statements, papers, etc., presented in support thereof, the original answer and papers, etc., together with an affidavit of the service of such copy and stating the time and manner of the service and the name and official character of the person upon whom such service was made, as hereinbefore provided for the service of a copy of an appeal, must be transmitted to the department of public instruction, at Albany.

8. No reply, replication or rejoinder shall be allowed, except by permission of the state superintendent of public instruction; in which case, such reply, replication and rejoinder must be duly verified by oath, and copies thereof served on the opposite party. Immediately after the service of such copy, the original, together with an affidavit of such service, and stating the time and manner of the service and the name and official character of the person upon whom such service was made, must be transmitted to the department of public instruction, at Albany.

9. So far as the parties concur in a statement, no oath will be required to it. But all facts, maps or papers, not agreed upon by them and evidenced by their signature on both sides, must be verified by oath.

10. When any proceeding of a district meeting is appealed from, and when the inhabitants of a district generally are interested in the matter of the appeal, and in all cases where an inhabitant might be an appellant had the decision or proceeding been the opposite of that which was made or had, any one or more of such inhabitants may answer the appeal, with or without the trustees.

11. Where the appeal has relation to the alteration or formation of a school district, it must be accompanied by a map, exhibiting

the site of the school-house, the roads, the old and new lines of districts, the different lots, the particular location and distance from the school-houses of the persons aggrieved, and their relative distance, if there are two or more school-houses in question. Also, a list of all the taxable inhabitants in the district or territory to be affected by the question, showing in separate columns the valuation of their property, taken from the last assessment-roll, and the number of children between five and twenty-one belonging to each person, distinguishing the districts to which they respectively belong.

12. An appeal, of itself, does not stay proceedings. If the party desires such stay he should apply for it by petition, stating the facts why such stay should be made, duly verified. The superintendent will grant a stay, or not, as in his judgment it may be proper, or may subserve the interests of either party or the public; and may direct a copy of the petition to be served on the opposite party, and a hearing of both sides before deciding upon the application.

13. The affidavit of verification, required by these rules to an appeal, answer, reply, replication and rejoinder, must be to the effect, that the same is true to the knowledge of the affiant, except as to the matters therein stated to be alleged on information and belief, and that as to those matters he believes it to be true.

14. All oaths required by these rules may be taken before any person authorized to take affidavits.

15. All appeals and other papers therein must be fairly and legibly written; and if not so written, may, in the discretion of the superintendent, be returned to the parties.

16. When any party, appellant or respondent, is not represented on the appeal by an attorney, the name of such party, with the names of the district, town and county and his post-office address must be indorsed upon each paper of the party so represented, filed in the department on such appeal; and, when represented by an attorney, the name of such attorney, with the name of the district, town and county affected and his post-office address, must be so indorsed upon each paper of the party so represented, filed in the department on such appeal.

17. Submission of appeals may be made upon the papers filed therein, with or without oral argument, or the filing of briefs, as the superintendent, upon application, may determine.

18. The decision of the superintendent in every case will contain the order, or directions, necessary and proper for giving effect to his decisions.

19. A decision upon an appeal will be forwarded by the superintendent to the clerk of the school district in which the appeal arose, or the town clerk of the town, when the appeal relates to the alteration of a district in which the order appealed from is filed, whose duty it will be to file the same in his office as a public record.

PRACTICE ON APPLICATION FOR REMOVAL OF SCHOOL OFFICERS.

UNDER SECTION 18 OF TITLE 1 OF CONSOLIDATED SCHOOL LAW OF 1864, AND AMENDMENTS.

For Willful Violation or Neglect of Duty.

The proceedings are generally termed appeals asking for the removal of the officer against whom the charges are made.

The applicant should prepare a petition addressed, "To the Superintendent of Public Instruction," in which, after distinctly stating the *charge* should proceed with a specification of the facts by which it is established, which must be set forth with such certainty as to time, place, etc., as to furnish the officer with precise information as to what he is expected to meet, and enable him to look for repelling testimony. The charges must not only be distinctly alleged, but they must be specifically *proved*. After being verified, a copy of the petition, and of all affidavits in support thereof, including the affidavits of verification thereto, must be served upon the officer whose removal is sought, together with a notice of the application, which may be substantially in the following words:

SIR.— Take notice that the petition and affidavits, with copies of which you are herewith served, will be presented to the superintendent of public instruction at Albany, and application thereupon made for your removal from the office of   of district No.   of   in   county; and that you are required to transmit your answer to such application, duly verified, to the department of public instruction within ten days after the service hereof, or the charges contained in such affidavits will be deemed to be admitted by you.

A........B..............

Post-office address................................

A copy of this notice, together with an affidavit proving the service thereof, and of the petition and affidavits therein referred to, and the date and manner of such service must be transmitted, with the original petition and affidavits, to the department of public instruction. The officer cannot be prejudiced by any statement which he has not been called upon to answer. The officer must transmit his sworn answer, together with the affidavits of other persons, if he deems them necessary, with proof of service of copies thereof upon the petitioner, to the department within ten days. If, for any reason, as the absence of material witnesses, he is unable to complete his defense in that time, he should, before its expiration, transmit his own answer, duly verified, with a statement, under oath, of the facts which render it necessary that the time to procure further evidence should be extended, and stating the earliest day at which he expects to be able to obtain such evidence. If a probable defense appears from his answer, and the application for further time is reasonable, an order will be made granting it.

If no answer is made by the officer to the petition, etc., the allegations contained in said petition, etc., will be considered admitted as true, and if, as such, a case is established against the officer, the superintendent will at once remove him. If an answer is interposed the question will be decided by the superintendent after an examination of the facts as presented by the papers upon both sides.

For Willfully Disobeying any Decision, Order or Regulation of the Superintendent of Public Instruction.

The practice and procedure in cases of the willful disobedience of any order, decision or regulation of the superintendent should be like that above stated of willful violation or neglect of duty, excepting that upon the filing of the petition, etc., with proof of service of a copy thereof upon the officer, in the department, or upon his own motion, the superintendent will issue an order directing the officer to show cause before him on or before a certain day fixed in the order, why he should not be removed from office. If no answer is made to said order the allegations contained in the moving papers will be deemed to be admitted as true, and if, as such, a case is established against the officer, the superintendent will at once remove him. If an answer is interposed, the question will be decided by the superintendent after an examination of the facts as presented by both sides.

NOTE. — In the papers filed in the department, upon an appeal, the superintendent wants *facts*, not arguments or inferences, much less injurious imputations on the motives of parties.

The facts should be distinctly averred, so that an indictment for perjury would lie if they are willfully misstated. Therefore, they should not be stated by way of recital under a "whereas," or in any similar indirect way. Every material fact should be stated with all practicable particularity as to time, quantities, numbers, etc. Where a statement is ambiguous or doubtful in meaning, that construction is adopted which is most unfavorable to the party making it.

The appellant must establish his appeal by a preponderance of proof, and should make out his own case, so that, if no answer is put in, the superintendent will have, *in the appeal itself*, all the facts to inform him what order ought to be made. No decision can be based upon any facts except those which are stated in the papers in the appeal, and which the opposite party has had the opportunity to controvert, although such facts may have been brought to the knowledge of the superintendent in some other way. The record itself must contain enough to support the decision.

In the bringing and answering of appeals it is recommended that the matters be written upon paper ruled as paper is ruled for legal pleadings. Such paper is kept by all stationers and booksellers, and is known as law paper or *legal cap*. The several sheets should be written, as lawyers write their papers, on both sides, so that the bottom of the first page is the top of the second, and the sheets are fastened or attached at the ends and not at the sides. Manuscript arranged in this fashion is more easily handled, folded and filed. The papers should be smoothly folded and indorsed with the title of the case, briefly stating the substance of the appeal or answer, with the names of the parties or attorneys, and their post-office address and the district, town and county affected.

J. F. Crooker,

State Superintendent of Public Instruction.

INDEX.

[REFERS TO PAGES.]

	PAGE.
ACADEMIES:	
Teachers' training classes in	115, 116
Union Free School Districts may adopt	80
ACADEMICAL DEPARTMENT:	
In Union Free School Districts	76, 80
ACQUISITION OF SCHOOL-HOUSE SITES:	
Proceedings for	122
Trustees may purchase or lease sites	50
ACTIONS BY AND AGAINST SCHOOL OFFICERS:	
Expenses of	40, 87, 88, 89
AFFIDAVITS:	
When State Superintendent may take	11
When School Commissioners may take	16
When district clerks may take	54
AGGREGATE ATTENDANCE:	
How ascertained	26, 27, 84
Public money apportioned on	26, 27, 28
ALBANY:	
Normal School, acts establishing	105, 106
ALCOHOLIC DRINKS:	
Effect of, to be taught	150
ALTERATION OF SCHOOL DISTRICTS. (See School Districts.)	
AMERICAN MUSEUM OF NATURAL HISTORY (New York City):	
State Superintendent authorized to contract with, for instruction of teachers	91, 92, 93
State Superintendent authorized to contract with, for artisans, etc.	92, 93
Instruction to be given in anatomy, physiology, zoölogy, physical geography, etc.	91, 92, 93
ANNUAL REPORTS:	
State Superintendent to Legislature	7, 9, 24
Printing and distribution of Superintendent's Report	153
School Commissioners to State Superintendent	16
Trustees to School Commissioners	55, 56, 57, 81, 137
Supervisors to County Treasurer	29
Trustees at annual district meeting	54
Collector at annual district meeting	65
Boards of Education in Union Free School Districts to School Commissioners	81
Boards of Education of any city or village of 6,000 inhabitants who have contracted to teach children of an adjoining district	133
Joint districts	56
ANNULMENT OF SCHOOL DISTRICTS. (See School Districts.)	
ANNULMENT OF TEACHERS' CERTIFICATES:	
By State Superintendent	10
By School Commissioners	15

11

APPARATUS FOR SCHOOLS: PAGE.
   Trustees may purchase, when.................................... 53
   Inhabitants may vote a tax for................................... 40
   Insurance of.. 40, 50
APPEALS:
   How taken.. 85
   Rules governing... 154
   Testimony may be taken by School Commissioners, when.......... 16
   Superintendents' powers and duties...................... 11, 85, 86
   Decision, effect of... 85, 86
APPORTIONMENT OF SCHOOL MONEYS:
   By State Superintendent.......................... 17, 23, 89, 90
   May be reclaimed.. 21, 22
   By School Commissioners..................................... 25, 29
   Errors in, how corrected.. 27
   Districts entitled to... 27, 28
   Orphan asylum schools.................................... 114, 115
   Indian schools... 19, 103
   Equitable allowance to districts by State Superintendent......... 21
ARBOR DAY:
   Act creating it.. 94
   Duty of school authorities...................................... 94
   Exercises upon.. 94
ASSESSMENTS:
   Of property for school district taxes................... 57–61, 72–76
   Of railroads... 146–149
   Of bank stock... 140–144
   Of banks.. 140–144
   Of telegraph, telephone and pipe lines..................... 146, 147
   Of real estate.. 57–61
   Of personal property.. 57–61
   Of lands in the Forest Preserve............................ 145, 146
   Of property of Delaware and Hudson Canal Company....... 143, 144
   Exemption.. 59
ASSESSORS:
   Duty of, in relation to taxation of corporations............... 140–145
   Duty in relation to forest lands............................... 149
ASYLUMS:
   For blind... 6, 7, 8
      pupils to, appointed by State Superintendent................. 7
   For deaf and dumb....................................... 6, 7, 8
      pupils to, appointed by State Superintendent................. 6
   For idiots.. 6
      State Superintendent as trustee of.......................... 6
   Orphan, schools of, to share in public moneys................. 114
   Orphan, schools of, subject to same regulations as common schools.... 115
BANKING CORPORATIONS:
   Taxable.. 140, 144
BANK STOCK:
   To be assessed... 140, 144
BLIND, INSTITUTIONS FOR:
   Visitation by State Superintendent............................. 6
   State pupils, how admitted.................................... 7
   Admission of State pupils regulated............................ 7

INDEX. 163

BLIND, INSTITUTIONS FOR — (Continued):   PAGE.
   Support of State pupils.. 7,   8
   Term of State pupils..   7
BOARDS OF EDUCATION:
   In Union Free School Districts, powers of......... 75-78, 117, 118, 119, 120
   In cities of less than 30,000 inhabitants, how to acquire building sites.. 122
   May contract for education of children of adjoining district............ 133
   May establish evening schools for instruction in industrial drawing.... 118
   May establish departments for industrial training..................... 117
   To cause drawing to be taught in certain districts..................... 120
   May establish free kindergarten schools........................... 118, 119
   May cause free instruction in vocal music............................. 119
BONDS:
   By supervisors 28
   By collectors... 39, 45, 62, 72
   By treasurers and collectors in Union Free School Districts............ 72
   Collector's bonds to be filed 62
   Fees for, filing 62
   For building school-houses and purchase of sites.............. 43, 74, 75
BOOKS, BLANKS, ETC.:
   Superintendent will furnish.. 10, 11
BOOKS FOR RECORDS:
   Trustees may purchase, when..................................... 53, 54
BOUNDARIES OF SCHOOL DISTRICTS:
   School Commissioners, duty to describe definitely................ 13, 121
   To be filed with town clerks................................... 13, 33, 34
   Alteration of...33, 34, 35
CENSUS, SCHOOL. (See Enumeration.)
CERTIFICATES OF QUALIFICATION TO TEACH:
   Granted by State Superintendent....................................... 9
   List of, to be kept by Superintendent 9
   Granted by School Commissioners..................................... 15
   State Superintendent may annul.................................... 9, 10
   School Commissioner may annul....................................... 15
   Temporary, when granted... 10
CHAIRMAN:
   Of district meetings, how chosen.................................. 38, 39
   Of neighborhood meetings, how chosen........................... 38, 39
   Of meeting to form Union Free School Districts, how chosen......... 70
CHALLENGE:
   Who can offer.. 38, 39, 130, 131
   Proceedings upon.. 38, 39, 120, 121
CHAMBERLAIN OF THE CITY OF NEW YORK:
   State school moneys payable to.. 22
CITIES:
   Apportionment of public moneys to.................................... 19
   Local tax for support of schools.................................. 139, 140
   Boards of education in, may contract with trustees of adjoining school
      districts to educate the children of the district..................... 133
   Common councils of, to report trusts.................................. 23
   Of less than 30,000 inhabitants, how building sites may be acquired... 122
   Certain cities not to be included in Commissioner Districts....... 121, 122
   Evening schools for instruction in drawing...................... 117, 118

CITIES — (Continued):

	PAGE.
Drawing, industrial, in schools of	120
Schools for colored children in	81, 82
Free kindergarten, school in	118, 119
Vocal music may be taught in	119

CLERKS OF BOARDS OF SUPERVISORS:

State School tax, duty regarding... 17

CLERKS IN STATE SUPERINTENDENT'S OFFICE:

Appointment of... 6

CLERKS OF SCHOOL DISTRICTS:

How chosen	39, 46, 71
Qualifications of	44, 71
Term of	44, 46, 71
Salary of, in Union Free School Districts	71
Trustees may appoint, when	46
Vacates his office, when	46
Penalty for refusal to serve, or neglect in office	45, 46, 47, 48
Duties of	35, 36, 37, 130, 131
Resignation of	46, 71
Vacancy, how filled	46
State Superintendent may remove	10

CODE OF PUBLIC INSTRCTION:

Provision for its distribution	152
Custodian of	152

COLLECTOR OF SCHOOL DISTRICT:

How chosen	39, 71, 72
Qualifications necessary	43, 71, 72
Term of	44, 45, 46, 71, 72
Bond of	39, 62, 71, 72
Bond to be filed	63
Fee for filing	63
Vacates, when	45, 72
Resignation of	45, 46
Vacancies, how filled	39, 45, 46, 71, 72, 77
Duties of	60–66
Fees of	64
State Superintendent may remove, when	10
Amount of unpaid taxes payable to	60, 61

COLORED CHILDREN:

Schools for	81
Schools for, in New York city	100

COMPTROLLER:

State school moneys, withheld by... 18

COMMISSIONER. (See School Commissioner.)

COMMON SCHOOL FUND:

What constitutes	17, 18, 19
How apportioned	17–23, 25–29
Error in apportionment may be corrected	21–22
Payable when, and to whom	22

COMMON SCHOOLS. (See Schools.)

COMPULSORY EDUCATION:

Act in relation to ... 95–99

INDEX. 165

CONDEMNATION OF SCHOOL BUILDINGS AND FURNITURE: PAGE.
  Commissioner has power 14, 15
CONTINGENT FUND:
  Apportionment to 19, 20
  Equitable allowance payable from 21
  Supplementary apportionment to be paid from 22
CONTRACTS:
  With teachers 50, 51, 76, 134, 135
  State Superintendent with American Museum of Natural History.... 91–94
  Trustees of district, with boards of education of adjoining city or village, to teach children of the district 133
CORNELL UNIVERSITY:
  State Superintendent a trustee of 6
  State scholarships to, law governing 100, 103
  Duty of School Commissioners, relative to scholarships 101, 102
  Sons of soldiers and sailors to have preference in scholarships 102
  Record of State scholarships to be kept 102
COSTS:
  In actions by or against school officers 87, 88, 89
  District meeting may vote a tax for 41
  Disputed, County Judge to adjust 87, 88, 89
COUNTY CLERK:
  School Commissioner's election or appointment to be certified by 11
  To give notice of a vacancy in the office of School Commissioner 12
  Trustees' reports to be kept by 16
COUNTY JUDGE:
  May appoint School Commissioner to fill vacancy 12
  May appoint persons to receive and disburse public moneys, when.. 28, 29
  To hear and decide appeals concerning school officers' costs and expenses 87, 88, 89
DEAF AND DUMB, INSTITUTIONS FOR:
  Visitations by State Superintendent 6
  State pupils, how admitted 6
  Admission of, regulated 6, 7
  Support of 8
  Terms of instruction 8
  High class in, superintendent may appoint to 7
DECISION OF APPEALS:
  By State Superintendent, when final 85
DELAWARE AND HUDSON CANAL COMPANY:
  Relative to taxation of property of 143, 144
DEPUTY STATE SUPERINTENDENT:
  Appointment of 5
DICTIONARIES:
  District meeting may vote for 40
  Trustees may purchase, when 53
  Library money used for, when 66, 67
DIPLOMAS:
  Of normal schools 10, 48
  How annulled 10, 15
  Record of, in State Superintendent's office 10
DISSOLUTION OF SCHOOL DISTRICTS. (See School Districts.)

DISTRICT ATTORNEYS: PAGE.
    To report to Boards of Supervisors.. 24
    Embezzlement by, a felony.. 25
DISTRICT CLERK. (See Clerks of School Districts.)
DISTRICTS:
    School Commissioner's, what are.. 11
    Common school, how formed.. 13, 33–37
    Neighborhood, how formed.. 36, 37
    Joint districts... 33, 34
    Apportionment of public moneys to............................ 17–23, 25–30
    Alteration of... 11, 33–36
    Consolidation of.. 34, 35
    Annulment of.. 34, 35
    Dissolution of.. 34, 35
DISTURBING SCHOOLS OR MEETINGS:
    Section 448 of Penal Code provides a penalty.
DRAWING:
    To be taught in Normal Schools, Union Schools, school in cities, and in
        Free School Districts incorporated by special act..................... 117
    Industrial drawing, evening schools for.................................. 118
    State Superintendent may excuse the teaching of, in certain Union Free
        Schools... 120
ELECTION OF OFFICERS:
    Of State Superintendent.. 5
    Of School Commissioners... 11
    Of Boards of Education................................... 70, 71, 129, 130
    Of district officers.. 38, 39, 44, 45, 46
    Of district officers in districts having more than 300 children of school
        age.. 129, 130
    In Union Free School Districts....................................... 70, 71
    Superintendent may order... 131
ENUMERATION:
    Of children of school age...................................... 56, 103, 104
EQUALIZATION:
    Of valuations in districts composed of parts of two or more towns.. 58, 59
EXAMINATIONS:
    For teachers' certificates.................................... 9, 15, 115, 116
    For State certificates... 9, 115, 116
    By School Commissioners of schools, etc..................... 15, 115, 116
    Of applicants for admission to Normal Schools..................... 110, 111
    Of applicants for admission to Cornell University.................. 100, 101
FEES:
    For filing collectors' bonds.. 62
    Supervisors'.. 34
    Town clerks'... 32, 34, 62
FENCES:
    On school lots... 135
FINES AND PENALTIES:
    School Commissioner, when liable........................... 13, 86, 139
    Supervisor.. 25, 28, 139
    Trustee............................... 25, 46, 49, 52, 55, 86, 87, 139, 150
    Collector.................................... 25, 46, 65, 66, 139

INDEX.

	PAGE
FINES AND PENALTIES — (Continued):	
Clerk 35, 36, 46, 47, 86,	139
Inhabitant.... .... 36, 39, 46, 67, 68, 86, 97, 131,	149
Other officers or persons.... .... 25, 39, 86, 87, 97, 130, 131,	149
When officer whose duty to sue, neglects.....	86
How paid and apportioned........................	24
FOREST LANDS — FOREST PRESERVE:	
Taxation of... 145,	146
FORMATION AND ALTERATION OF SCHOOL DISTRICTS. (See School Districts.)	
FREE SCHOOL FUND:	
Condition of, to be reported to State Superintendent..................	17
How disbursed..	17
School Commissioners' salaries, to be paid from	120
FUEL, ETC.:	
District meeting to vote tax for.....................................	40
When trustee may provide....................................... 50,	53
FURNITURE:	
School Commissioners may condemn............................	14
GLOBES, ETC.:	
District meeting may vote tax for....................................	40
Trustees may purchase, when...	53
Library money used for, when......... . ... 66, 67,	68
GOSPEL AND SCHOOL LOTS:	
Supervisors, trustees of	29
Report of	23
HEALTH AND DECENCY:	
Act to promote.. ...	135
HOLIDAYS:	
What are...	99
Included in school year; no school in session.......................	20
Falling on Sunday, Monday to be observed.	99
HYGIENE AND PHYSIOLOGY:	
Providing for study of...................	150
IDLE AND TRUANT CHILDREN:	
How persons may be relieved from care of..................... 97, 98,	99
Provisions of "Compulsory Education Act," relative to............	95–100
ILLEGAL VOTING AT SCHOOL DISTRICT MEETINGS:	
How prevented.. 38, 39,	130
Penalty for 39,	131
INDIANS:	
Apportionment of moneys for............................... 19, 103,	104
State Superintendent has charge of........................... 6, 103,	104
Education of 48, 103,	104
Appointment of, to Normal Schools................. 113,	114
INDUSTRIAL DRAWING:	
Evening schools for instruction in..................................	118
INDUSTRIAL TRAINING:	
Public schools to give instruction in	117

INHABITANTS: PAGE.
  Who are taxable.. 59
  Who are voters at school meetings. 38

INSTITUTES. (See Teachers' Institutes.)

INSURANCE:
  Of district school buildings, etc............................. 40, 50
  Of apparatus... 50
  Of district libraries.. 50
  Of Normal School buildings.. 113

INSTALLMENTS:
  When tax may be collected by................................. 42, 43
  When in Union Free School district.................... 72, 73, 74, 75

JOINT DISTRICTS:
  How to be formed... 33, 34, 35
  Alteration or dissolution of............................... 33, 34, 35
  How to be numbered... 33
  Reports from... 56
  Penalties imposed in... 25

JUSTICES OF THE PEACE:
  Jurisdiction of, under compulsory education act................... 99

KINDERGARTEN SCHOOLS:
  Free Kindergarten Schools may be established in cities and villages.. 118, 119

LANDS FOR SCHOOL SITES. (See Sites.)

LEGISLATURE:
  State Superintendent chosen by...................................... 5
  To regulate trusts for benefit of schools.......................... 23
  May alter or modify School Commissioner districts.................. 11

LIBRARIAN:
  How chosen.. 39, 46
  Qualification of... 44
  Term of... 44, 46
  Duty of... 47, 66, 67
  Resignation of... 46
  Vacancies, how filled.. 46

LIBRARIES. (See, also, libraries under heading "State Superintendent of Public Instruction"):
  State Superintendent has supervision over................. 66, 67, 68
  Public moneys for... 19, 66, 67
  School Commissioners to examine.................................... 14
  School Commissioners to apportion money's for................. 25, 26
  Trustees have custody of and to appoint teacher librarian.......... 67
  District meetings may vote a tax for.......................... 40, 67
  Regulations of.. 66, 67, 68
  When moneys apportioned for, may be used for teachers' wages...... 52
  Trustees may insure, when.. 50
  Book case for.. 40
  Free public libraries.. 67, 68
  Public not to use school libraries................................. 68

LICENSE TO TEACH:
  By State Superintendent....................................... 9, 10
  By School Commissioners.. 15
  Annulment of.. 9, 10, 15

MAPS, ETC.:
  Trustees may purchase, when. 53
  District meeting may vote tax for............................... 40
MEETINGS, ANNUAL:
  In school districts... 37, 38
    Powers of............................. 39, 40, 41, 42, 43, 67
  In neighborhoods.. 36, 37
    Powers of.. 39
  In Union Free School districts................................... 78
    Powers of....................... 71, 72, 73, 74, 75, 78, 79
  Board of Education in Union Free School districts.................. 72
    Powers of.. 70-80
MEETINGS, SPECIAL:
  Trustees to call, when................................ 14, 15, 36, 37
  Notice to be given................................. 35, 36, 37, 47
  School Commissioners may call, when 36
  Form of notice 36, 37
  Neighborhoods 36, 37
  Trustees to call 36, 37
  Notice to be given.. 36, 37
  Union Free School districts 68, 69, 72, 73, 74, 75
  In dissolved districts 35, 137, 138, 139
MISDEMEANORS:
  School Commissioner acting as agent for publisher, etc............. 13
  Embezzlement by supervisor or other officer....................... 25
  Refusal by supervisor to give security............................ 28
  False declaration by person offering to vote........... 38, 39, 130, 131
  Trustees paying unqualified teacher's wages....................... 49
  Trustees signing false report.................................... 25
MUSIC, VOCAL:
  May be taught 119
NARCOTICS:
  Effects of, to be taught 150
NAUTICAL SCHOOL (New York city):
  Act relative to 104, 105
NEIGHBORHOODS:
  Apportionment of public moneys to............................. 21, 27
  Formation and alteration of................................... 33, 34
  Annual meetings... 32
  Special meetings.. 37
  Power of voters at meetings................................... 38, 39
  Clerk of....................... 38, 39, 43, 44, 45, 46, - 47
  Report to School Commissioners................................... 57
  Penalty for signing false report................................. 25
NON-RESIDENTS:
  Lands of, how assessed.. 58
  Bank stock of, how assessed...................... 140, 141, 142, 143
  Children may attend school on terms........................... 48, 76
  Taxes paid by, to be deducted from charge for tuition...... 48, 76, 134
NON-RESIDENTS, LANDS OF:
  Taxable.. 58
NORMAL SCHOOLS:
  Power of State Superintendent over....................... 6, 106, 111
  Local boards in.. 109, 111

INDEX.

NORMAL SCHOOLS — (Continued): PAGE.
   Pupils, how admitted... 110
   Diplomas of, constitute holder a qualified teacher............ 48, 110, 111
   Diplomas may be annulled....................................... 10, 15, 111
   List kept in State Superintendent's office of holders of diplomas........ 10
   Protection of property of.. 112
   Albany, act for its establishment.. 105
   Albany, act for its permanent establishment............................... 107
   Other acts providing for.. 108–115
   Insurance of buildings... 113
   Industrial drawing to be taught in... 120
   Industrial training in... 117
   Indians may be appointed to.. 113, 114
   Tuition moneys, how to be used.. 114
   Teachers in, number of and wages.. 110
   Physiology and hygiene to be taught in.................................. 150
   Vocal music may be taught in... 119

NUISANCES:
   School Commissioners may direct trustees to abate..................... 14
   Trustees to abate, when.. 53

OATH:
   State Superintendent may administer..................................... 11
   School Commissioner may administer, when........................... 16
   On challenge at school district meeting.............. 38, 39, 130, 131
   Teacher's, to school record.. 54

OFFICERS. (See Election of.)

ORDERS:
   For teachers' wages.. 30, 31, 51, 52, 53

ORPHAN ASYLUMS. (See Asylums.)

OUTBUILDINGS:
   Trustees must erect, when.. 53, 135
   Expenses of, how paid... 53, 135
   School Commissioners may direct repair of............................. 14
   Separated by fence, and kept clean...................................... 135

PARENTS:
   When entitled to vote... 38

PHYSIOLOGY AND HYGIENE:
   Providing for study of... 150

PLANS FOR SCHOOL BUILDINGS:
   Superintendent to furnish.. 132

POLICE JUSTICES. (See Justices of the Peace.)

POPULATION:
   Public moneys apportioned according to............................ 18–23

PRIVIES:
   Trustees must construct and maintain, as provided by law........ 53, 135

PROPERTY:
   Of districts, held by trustees as a corporation............................ 49
   Of consolidated districts... 34
   Of annulled and dissolved districts.................................... 34, 35
   What is taxable.. 56, 57–61, 140

PROPERTY — (Continued): PAGE.
Railroad property... 146, 147, 148
Telegraph, telephone and pipe line companies................... 146, 147
Delaware and Hudson Canal Company............................. 143, 144
Held in trust 22, 23, 49

PUBLIC MONEYS:
For State Superintendent's salary.................................... 5
For compensation of clerks in State Superintendent's office........... 6
For support of State pupils in asylums................................ 8
For salaries of School Commissioners............................. 12, 120
For support of Common Schools.................................... 17, 18
For Teacher's Institutes.. 82–84
For Orphan Asylum Schools.................................... 114, 115
For Indian Schools... 89, 90, 103, 104
For teachers' training classes..................................... 115

PUPILS:
Who are eligible to common schools.................................. 48
Indian 48, 103
Non-resident, when may be... 48, 76
Deaf and dumb... 6
Blind... 7
Trustees to report number of....................................... 56
Trustees to enumerate 56
Vaccination of... 136

QUALIFICATIONS OF:
Voters... 38
District officers... 44, 71
Teachers 48, 150
Pupils... 48
Pupils in asylums... 6, 7

RAILROAD COMPANIES:
Property of, how apportioned...................................... 146
Notice to be given to................................... 63, 145, 147, 148
Taxes against, how collected...................................... 148
Delaware and Hudson Canal Company's property, apportionment of... 143

RATE BILLS:
Abolished 139, 140

RECORDS, TEACHER'S:
Of scholars.. 49, 53, 54
Verification of... 54

RELATIONSHIP:
Employment of teachers affected by............................. 50, 51

REMOVALS FROM OFFICE:
By State Superintendent.. 10, 81
By Boards of Education in Union Free School Districts............... 77

REPAIRS:
District meetings may order....................................... 40
School Commissioners may direct................................... 14
Trustees may make, when.. 50, 53, 125

REPORTS:
By State Superintendent...................................... 7, 9, 24
Distribution of Annual Reports................................... 153
By School Commissioners....................................... 16, 84

REPORTS — (Continued):

	PAGE.
By trustees to district meetings...	54, 55
By trustees to School Commissioners ... 55, 56, 57,	83
Of joint districts...	56
By collectors...	65
By Boards of Education of Union Free School Districts......... 78, 79,	81
Of libraries, by trustees...	66, 67
False, penalty for...	25, 55
School districts whose officers neglect to report, effect on...	21, 22
Supervisors... 23, 24,	29
By local boards of Normal Schools...	109, 110
County treasurer to report fines, etc...	24
District attorney...	24
Of trust funds...	24

RESIDENCE:

Of district officers...	44, 71

RESIGNATION:

Of School Commissioners...	12
Of district officers...	46, 77

ROOMS:

Trustees may provide temporary, for schools...	53

RULES OF PRACTICE:

On appeals...	154–159

SALARY:

Of State Superintendent...	5
Of Deputy State Superintendent...	5
Of clerks in State Superintendent's office...	6
Of School Commissioners...	12, 120
Of Superintendent of Schools...	77
Of clerks of Boards of Education...	71

SCHOOL COMMISSIONERS:

Election of, term of, and qualification by...	11, 12
Salary of...	12
Salary payable from Free School Fund...	120
Salary may be withheld, when...	13
Removal of...	10
Expenses of, audit by...	12
Duties and powers of.... 11, 17, 21, 25–29, 33–37, 42, 43, 44, 45, 46, 53, 70, 77, 82–85, 94, 101, 102, 116, 121, 135, 139,	150
Reports by...	16, 84
Resignation of...	12
Vacates his office, when...	12
Vacancies, how filled...	12
Term of appointee...	12

SCHOOL COMMISSIONER DISTRICTS:

What are...	11
How altered...	11, 121, 122
Commissioners of, how chosen...	11
When boards of supervisors may form...	121, 122
Division of...	11, 122
Erection of new districts...	11, 122
Cities not included in...	121

SCHOOL DISTRICTS WITH MORE THAN THREE HUNDRED CHILDREN OF SCHOOL AGE:

Elections in...	129, 130, 131

INDEX. 173

SCHOOL DISTRICTS: PAGE.
Formation of.. 33, 34, 35
Alteration of.. 33, 34, 35
Consolidation of districts....................................... 33, 34, 35
Annulment of... 34
Dissolution of... 34, 35
Joint districts.. 34
Dissolved, exist in law for certain purposes....................... 35

SCHOOL-HOUSES:
Care and custody of... 49, 50
Use of, other than for schools..................................... 54
When taxable inhabitant exempt from tax for building............... 59
How condemned.. 14, 15
Building of..................................... 15, 40, 41, 42, 50, 72, 73, 74, 75
Furniture of, may be condemned..................................... 14
Plans and specifications for..................................... 132
Plan of, to be approved.. 42
Sale of.. 43
Insurance of... 40, 50, 113
Sites for................................... 40, 41, 42, 72, 73, 74, 75, 122
Repairs of.................................... 14, 50, 53, 72, 73, 74, 75
Fuel, etc., for... 40, 50, 51
Nuisance about, how abated.................................... 14, 53
Outhouses for............................... 52, 53, 72, 73, 74, 75, 135
Tax for building, may be collected by installments.... 42, 43, 72, 73, 74, 75
Money for building may be borrowed.............. 42, 43, 72, 73, 74, 75
Lease or purchase of.. 40, 53, 54

SCHOOLS, COMMON:
Visitation of, by State Superintendent.............................. 7
State Superintendent may appoint visitors to....................... 9
State Superintendent's report of................................... 9
Who may attend as pupils.. 48
Non-resident pupils in, law concerning................... 48, 76, 134
Temporary rooms for, and branch schools........................... 53
For colored children... 81, 82
State moneys for the support of................................ 17–23
Trusts for the benefit of...................................... 22, 23
Teachers of, when qualified................................... 48, 150
Teachers, record of... 49, 54
Closed without loss of time, when................................. 83
Industrial training, instruction in........................... 117, 118

SCHOOL, NAUTICAL (New York City):
Act relative to.. 104

SCHOOL OFFICERS:
Removal of.. 10, 77, 81
Actions by and against....................................... 87, 88
Not to be interested in official contracts................... 78, 139
Duties of. (See Respective Titles,)

SCHOOL TAX. (See Tax.)

SCHOOL YEAR:
What constitutes.. 20

SCHOOL VISITOR:
Appointment of.. 9
Duties of... 9
How designated... 40, 42, 43, 72, 73, 74, 75
Title to, how acquired................................ 40, 50, 122, 127, 129

174 INDEX.

SITES: PAGE.
  Tax for purchase of 40, 73, 74, 75, 126
  Change of 43
  Sale of 43
SOLE TRUSTEE. (See Trustee.)
SOLDIERS AND SAILORS:
  Sons of, to have preference in Cornell scholarships 102
SPECIAL MEETINGS. (See Meetings.)
STATE CERTIFICATES:
  Issuance of 9
  Annulment of 9, 10, 15
STATE SCHOOL MONEYS:
  Consist of 17-23
  Appportionment of, by State Superintendent 18-23, 89, 90
  When payable 22
  Apportionment by School Commissioner 25-29
  Disbursement of, to Supervisors 29, 30
  Unqualified teachers cannot be paid 48, 49
  Apportionment by trustee 52
  Supervisor to report to County Treasurer concerning 29
  In apportioning, Union Free School districts regarded as a school district, 75
  School closed during institute, no loss of 84
  Loss of, by school officers 86
STATE SUPERINTENDENT OF PUBLIC INSTRUCTION:
  Election of, term, salary 5, 6
  Deputy, appointment of, and duties 5
  Clerks of, appointment 6
  Seal of, effect of 6
  Vacancy, how filled 5
  Regent of the University 6
  Trustee of Cornell University 6
  Trustee of New York Asylum for Idiots 6
  Powers and duties of:
    American Museum of Natural History, authorized to contract
      with 91, 92, 93
    Appeals to, when may be taken 85
      To regulate practice on 154
      May grant stay pending 85
      May decline to entertain or dismiss 85
      May direct School Commissioner to take evidence in 16
      To file and arrange all proceedings on 85, 86
      To decide 85, 86
    Arbor Day:
      To prescribe exercises 94
    Blind, institutions for 6, 7
      All incorporated, subject to his visitations 6
      Appointment of State pupils to 8, 9
      May extend term of instruction 8, 9
      To regulate admission to 8, 9
    Code, to distribute to districts 152
    College Graduates:
      May issue teacher's certificates to 9, 10
    Cornell University:
      Appointment of State pupils to 100, 101, 102
      Examination of applicants conducted by 101, 102
      Record of appointments to be kept by 102, 103

STATE SUPERINTENDENT OF PUBLIC INSTRUCTION:
Powers and duties of — (Continued):

	PAGE.
Deaf and dumb, institutions for 6, 7,	8
Incorporated, subject to his visitation...................	6
Appointment of State pupils to........................ 7,	8
High class in.......................................	7
To regulate admission to.......................... 7,	8
Drawing, instruction in, may excuse, in certain Union Free School Districts...	120
Elections in certain districts may be ordered by..................	131
Fines and penalties apportioned by..........................	24
Indian children:	
To provide for their education.......... 48, 103,	104
To cause annual enumeration of, to be made........... 103,	104
Apportionment for their schools............ 19, 103,	104
May appoint to normal schools................ 113,	114
May be admitted to district school by.....................	48
Industrial training, may prescribe extent of instruction in, in normal and training schools................................ 117,	118
Inhabitant, may be directed to give notice of meeting......... 38,	68
Teachers' institutes, may provide instruction in vocal music in....	119
Joint districts, to prescribe form of reports for.................	56
Libraries:	
Shall apportion school library money.......................	66
No district to share unless equal amount be raised and used...	66
No part of school library money to be expended except for books approved by Superintendent.....................	66
School libraries to consist of reference books for use in the school room, etc....................................	66
School library part of school equipment and kept in school building, etc..	66
School library not to be used as a circulating library, except, etc.	66
Teacher appointed by trustees as librarian...................	67
Trustees and teacher responsible for safety and proper care of books...	67
To report concerning library as and when required by Superintendent...	67
School districts to raise money by tax for libraries as other school moneys are raised, etc..........................	67
Districts may give books and other library property for free public libraries, etc...................................	67
Public not entitled to use libraries in custody of school authorities, but may appoint trustees, etc..................	68
Superintendent may withhold share of public school moneys, when...	68
Rules for, may alter and amend...........................	66
Neighborhoods, special reports may be required from.............	57
Normal Schools:	
To have general supervision.............................	106
To appoint local boards.................................	109
To report to Legislature annually relative to......... 106,	110
Course of study to be approved by.......................	110
Teachers, number of, and wages	110
Pupils, number of, to be admitted................... 110,	114
Non-residents, tuition fees to be prescribed................	110
Examination of applicants, he to prescribe..................	110
Indians, appointment of, to	114
Diplomas to be granted and may be annulled......... 110,	111
Tuition money, to direct expenditure	114
Industrial training, to prescribe course of study in........ 117,	118

STATE SUPERINTENDENT OF PUBLIC INSTRUCTION:
Powers and duties of — Continued) : PAGE.
  Industrial drawing to be taught 120
  Vocal music may be taught.......................... 118, 119
  Outbuildings, may order erection of....................... 53
  Penalty, may direct its application for teachers' wages........ 152
  Plans for School Buildings :
    To cause to be prepared for use of districts 132
  Registers, blanks, etc., to prepare and furnish.................... 10
  Reports :
    Annual report of.. 9
    When to be presented..................................... 9
    What to contain.. 7, 9, 24
  School to visit as far as possible.............................. 9
  School Commissioners :
    When appointed by... 12
    Salary payable on certificate of.............................. 12
    May withhold salary for cause.......................... 12, 13
    May require duties to be performed in adjoining district...... 13
    May require testimony to be taken by, on appeals......... 15, 16
    May require reports at any time............................. 16
    Subject to rules and regulations of 16
    School officer, may remove for cause. 10
  State School moneys:
    To draw drafts on.................................... 17, 18
    With State Treasurer, to borrow money when necessary........ 18
    To apportion and divide............................ 18, 19, 20, 21, 22
    To make supplemental apportionment................... 21, 22
    To reclaim excess in apportioning 21
    To certify result of apportionment........................... 22
    Supervisors' accounts, may require town clerks to furnish copies, 32
  Tax lists:
    May authorize trustees to amend and correct................ 64
  Teachers' certificates :
    To grant State certificates, and may revoke................ 9, 10
    May annul certificates of School Commissioners or diplomas
      of Normal Schools...................................... 9, 10
    Record of State certificates to be kept in his office............ 10
    Record of Normal diplomas to be kept....................... 10
  Teachers' Institutes:
    To advise with School Commissioners relative to.............. 82
    To employ suitable conductors........................... 82, 83
    To visit as many as possible................................ 83
    To establish basis for appropriations for..................... 83
    To regulate the issuing of certificates of qualifications......... 83
    To direct trustees to include district complying with law in
      apportionment of public money......................... 83
    Expenses of, to be paid on his certificate................. 83, 84
    May require particular report of............................ 84
  Teachers' Training Classes:
    Under his supervision................................ 116, 117
  Trusts:
    May be grantee or devisee of property for use of schools.... 22, 23
    To advise and supervise the trustees of such trusts......... 23, 24
    May require reports as to trusts............................ 24
    To report condition of 24
  Trustees:
    May require special reports from time to time............... 57

INDEX. 177

STATE SUPERINTENDENT OF PUBLIC INSTRUCTION:
Powers and duties of — (Continued). PAGE.
  Union Free Schools Districts:
    May direct inhabitant to call meeting to consider the formation of, 68
    To determine what are contingent expenses................... 79
    Subject to his visitation...................................... 81
    May require special reports from............................. 81
    May remove from office members of boards for cause.......... 81
  Visitors:
    To schools, may appoint...................................... 9

STATE TAX:
  Authority for... 17

STIMULANTS:
  Effect of, to be taught... 150

STOCKHOLDERS IN BANKS:
  Taxation of... 140–144

STUDIES:
  School Commissioner to recommend............................. 13
  Industrial and free hand-drawing to be taught in certain districts.. 118, 120
  Industrial training may be given................................ 117, 118
  Physiology and hygiene must be taught.......................... 150
  Vocal music may be taught 119

SUPERINTENDENT OF SCHOOLS:
  In certain villages and Union Free School Districts 77
  Appointment of... 77
  Salary of... 77

SUPERVISORS:
  Powers and duties of, in relation to State school moneys.. 27, 28, 29, 30, 31
  Reports of, in school matters.................. 23, 24, 29, 30, 31
  To give bonds, when 28, 29
  Liable for neglect, etc................................. 25, 28, 29
  Duty of, in altering, etc., school districts 34
  Fees of... 34
  Sale of property by, in annulled districts.................... 34, 35
  To sue for moneys belonging to dissolved districts........... 30, 35
  Duties of.............................. 29, 30, 31, 32, 33, 34, 35
  To sue for penalties.. 31
  Cannot be a trustee.. 44
  When assessors neglect to apportion valuation of railroad companies,
    duty of.. 147
  To equalize valuations in certain districts.................... 58, 59

SUPERVISORS, BOARDS OF:
  Salary and expenses of School Commissioners.................... 12
  To levy amount of school district taxes returned unpaid....... 60, 61
  Power to divide School Commissioner districts, in certain cases.... 121, 122
  Power to create School Commissioner districts, in certain cases.... 121, 122

TAX:
  State, for the support of common schools, how raised.............. 17
  For school-house sites, etc......................... 40, 42, 72, 76, 126
  For teachers' wages................... 40, 41, 51, 52, 75, 77, 79
  May be levied by installments, when................... 42, 43, 72–76
  List and warrant to collect................................. 50, 57, 62
  Any legal expense may be raised by.............................. 53
  When to be assessed.. 57
  Warrant for collection.. 62
  Upon towns for School Commissioner's expenses.................. 12
  Notice of, to be given....................................... 63, 64

178   INDEX.

TAX — (Continued);   PAGE.
  For building school-houses...................... 14, 15, 40, 42, 43, 72–76
  For expenses of vaccination 136, 137
  For school library........ 67
  Unpaid, procedure........................... 60–66
  When trustees may sue to recover 64
  In Union Free School Districts.................. 69, 72, 73, 74, 75, 76, 79
TAX LIST:
  Trustees to make out......... .... 50, 51, 57, 74, 75
  When to make.. 57–74
  Directions for making........................ .... 57, 58, 59
  Errors in, how corrected... 64
  Warrant to....................... .... 57, 62
  Returned, to be filed... 65
TAXABLE INHABITANTS:
  Who are....................................... 59
  Powers of....................... 66
TAXABLE PROPERTY:
  What is................... ....57, 58, 59, 60
  Valuation of... 58
TEACHERS:
  Who are qualified... .... 48, 150
  Shall keep record of scholars.... ... . 49, 54
  Employment of... 50, 51, 76
  When required to assist in library. 67
  Certificates to, how annulled.... .... 9, 10, 15
  Examinations of..... .... 9, 15
  Candidates for, must pass examination in physiology and hygiene...... 150
  Institutes......'................. 82–85
  Wages of........ .... 40, 41, 48, 49, 50, 51, 52, 53, 134, 135
  Term of employment by trustees limited......................... 50, 51
  Instruction of, in academies and academical departments of Union
    Schools 115, 116, 117
  Contracts with............................. .... 50, 51, 76, 134, 135
  Of neighborhood schools, when deemed qualified..................... 30
TEACHERS' INSTITUTES:
  When to be held.. .... 32, 82
  Apportionment for........................... 83
  Regulations for.. 82–85
  Schools shall be closed during..................................... 83, 84
  Teacher's absence from school attending, excused................. 83, 84
  Reports of 83, 84
TEACHERS' TRAINING CLASSES:
  In academies and Union Free Schools........................... 115–117
  State Superintendent to supervise 116, 117
  Subject to visitation by School Commissioners.. 116
TELEGRAPH, TELEPHONE AND PIPE LINE COMPANIES:
  Assessment of.. 146, 147
TENANTS:
  May be taxed.............................. .... 57, 58, 59
  May charge owner with amount of tax paid, when.................... 59
TERMS OF OFFICE:
  Of State Superintendent.... 5
  Of School Commissioner..... ....11, 12
  Of trustees........................... .... 44, 45
  Of district officers 43, 45, 46
  In Union Free School Districts 70, 71, 72

INDEX.   179

TEXT BOOKS: PAGE.
  To prevent frequent changes of.................................... 149
  For poor children 40, 97
  Boards of education in cities, villages and Union Free School Districts
    to designate 149
  Annual meeting to designate in common school districts.............. 149
  How changed... 146, 149

TOWN CLERK:
  Duties of.. 31, 32, 33, 62, 63, 64
  Fees, expenses and disbursements of.......................... 32, 34, 62
  To furnish certain statement....................................... 144, 147
  To file returned tax-lists, etc.. 65

TREASURER (STATE):
  Powers and duties of, in relation to school moneys.......... 6, 17, 18, 146

TREASURER (COUNTY):
  State school moneys payable to................................... 22
  Uncollected taxes, duty regarding............................... 61, 62

TRUANT CHILDREN:
  How persons may be relieved from care of....................... 97, 98
  Provisions of "Compulsory Education Act," relative to............. 95–99

TRUSTEES:
  How chosen 39, 70, 129–132
  Qualification of 44, 151
  Term of 44, 45, 70, 71
  Number of, how determined..................................... 44, 45, 70, 71
  Powers and duties of.. 14, 15, 23, 25, 33, 34, 36, 37, 40, 41, 42, 43, 44, 45,
    46, 47, 48, 49, 50, 51, 52, 53, 54, 55, 56, 57, 58, 59, 60, 61, 62, 63, 64, 65, 66,
    67, 68, 69, 70, 71, 72, 73, 74, 75, 76, 77, 78, 79, 80, 81, 82, 83, 84, 85, 86, 87,
    88, 89, 94, 95, 116, 117, 118, 119, 120, 122, 128, 129, 130, 131, 132, 133, 134,
    135, 136, 137, 138, 139, 140, 141, 142, 143, 144, 145, 146, 147, 148, 149, 150, 152
  Control of district property 49, 152
  Reports, annual... 53, 54, 55, 56
  Reports of..................... 54, 55, 56, 57, 67, 80, 83, 84, 133, 137
  False reports, penalty for... 25
  Removal of... 10, 77, 81
  Vacates office, when.. 46
  To indorse approval on collector's bonds........................ 62, 72
  To file collector's bonds.. 62
  Teachers' institutes, duty regarding............................ 83, 84
  Vacancies, how filled 39, 45, 46, 77
  Expenses of, actions for and against........................ 40, 87, 88, 89
  May sue to recover tax, when....................................... 64
  Powers and duties of, in relation to vaccination...................... 136
  Powers and duties of, in relation to compulsory education act. 95
  May contract with adjoining city or village in certain cases............. 133

TRUSTS FOR BENEFIT OF COMMON SCHOOLS:
  By and to whom made.. 22, 23
  Legislature regulates.. 23
  Reports concerning... 23, 24

UNION FREE SCHOOL DISTRICTS:
  Formation of.. 68, 69, 70
  Officers of, how chosen.............................. 70, 71, 72–76, 129
  Board of Education in.............................. 70, 71, 72, 73, 74, 75
  Board of Education, powers and duties of........ 71, 72, 73, 74, 75, 76,
                                                                                 77, 78, 79, 80, 81
  Board of Education, annual meeting of................................. 74

UNION FREE SCHOOL DISTRICTS — (Continued): PAGE.
   Inhabitants, meetings of 70, 71, 72, 73, 78
   Inhabitants, annual meetings of 78
   Report to 78, 79
   Teachers, how employed 76, 134, 135
   Academical department in 76, 80, 81
   Teachers' training classes in 115, 116
   Superintendent of Schools in 77, 78
   Colored children in 82
   Dissolution of 137
   Sites for, how acquired 122
   Industrial training, instruction in 117, 118
   Evening schools for instruction in drawing authorized .. 118
   Drawing, industrial 120
   Free Kindergarten Schools, may be established .. 118, 119
   Vocal music may be taught in 119

UNITED STATES DEPOSIT FUND:
   Apportionment of 18, 19, 20, 21

UNIVERSITY OF THE STATE OF NEW YORK:
   State Superintendent a Regent of 6

VACANCIES, HOW FILLED:
   Office of State Superintendent 5
   In office of School Commissioner 12
   In district offices 45, 46
   In offices of Union Free School Districts 71, 72, 77

VALUATION OF PROPERTY:
   How determined 58, 140
   Provisions relating to 57, 58, 59, 60, 140-144, 145, 146, 147

VILLAGES INCORPORATED:
   When Board of Education may appoint Superintendent of Schools .. 77, 78

VISITORS:
   State Superintendent may appoint 9

VOTERS:
   Qualifications of 38
   Challenge of 38, 39, 130, 131
   Declaration by 38, 39, 130, 131

VACCINATION:
   Of school children 136
   Expenses of, how raised 136, 137

WATER-CLOSETS:
   Law concerning 135

WARRANT:
   Form of 62
   Who issues 62
   Execution of 62, 63, 64
   Renewals of 64, 65
   Returned, to be filed 65

WOMEN:
   Eligible to hold office 151
   Eligible to vote at school meetings, when 38, 39, 151
   Determining who have a right to vote for School Commissioner .. 150, 151

YEAR:
   For term of officials 44
   For schools 20
   Holidays, included in; no school in session on a legal holiday 20

www.ingramcontent.com/pod-product-compliance
Lightning Source LLC
Chambersburg PA
CBHW031445160426
43195CB00010BB/857